MW00778237

For Lawmakers —
with best wishes

STAR-SPANGLED

SAILORS

Cary Roberts

1-20-12
Leesburg VA

ABOUT THE AUTHOR

Carey Roberts was born in North Carolina, attended Agnes Scott College in Georgia and received an MA in Psychology from Marymount University in Virginia. Her family roots go deep in the South along with her interest in American history, particularly regarding the capital city, Washington, DC, and Virginia's colonial and early years. She served as Executive Director of the Montgomery County, Maryland Bicentennial Commission during the 1976 national and county celebration. Carey has spoken on historical subjects and travel and mystery writing to numerous women's organizations and Rotary Clubs, at the Smithsonian Institution and at school programs. She was honored to be chosen by the seniors of a local Washington D.C. high school to be their graduation speaker.

Carey's articles and essays have appeared in national newspapers and magazines. Her previous historical novel is *Tidewater Dynasty: A Biographical Novel of the Lees of Stratford Hall* (co-authored with Rebecca Seely). Her two other books are DC-based mysteries: *Touch a Cold Door* and *Pray God to Die*. Her film script, Chesapeake Morning, is based on the story of the *Star-Spangled Sailors*, and won the 1996 WorldFest International Film Grand Award for Best Screen Play.

She lives in Leesburg, Virginia and Charleston, South Carolina.
You can email the author at CareyCRoberts@aol.com.

ISBN: 0615435610
ISBN-13: 9780615435619
LCCN: 2011900265

Illustration by Tara Schultz BA (Hons),
Oxfordshire school of Art and Design, Banbury, UK.
Contact fazbee@aol.com.

Cover faces by Carey Roberts.

Star-Spangled SAILORS

A NOVEL OF THE BRAVE WATERMEN
DEFENDERS OF CHESAPEAKE BAY IN
THE WAR OF 1812

CAREY ROBERTS

For

Trey, Will, Brent, Liam, Chase and Lucas,
the brave boys in my life,

Bob, who taught me to treasure Chesapeake Bay,

and

Jack, who journeyed with me from
St. Leonard's Creek to Fort McHenry.

Our unknown young American men in the ranks about whom there is no record or fame, no fuss about their dying so unknown, but I find in them the real precious & royal ones.

WALT WHITMAN

Between me and the world
You are a bay, a sail
The faithful ends of a rope
You are a fountain, a wind
A shrill childhood cry

BEI DAO
(*translated by B. S. McDougall*)

Maryland

Baltimore

Washington Bladensburg Annapolis

Alexandria • Navy Yard

Upper
Marlborough

Pigs Point

Chesapeake Bay

Benedict

Virginia

Potomac River

Chesapeake Bay

1814

TABLE OF CONTENTS

ST. Leonard's Creek

Patuxent River

Escape

CHAPTER ONE

ESCAPE

Dawn, June 26, 1814

Summer nights are black as pitch in Chesapeake country. The first sign of morning comes from the Atlantic with a shading to silver in the eastern sky. Sometimes there's a coolness in the dawn. But sometimes not.

All day, they'd been on the water, at oar or poling the barges through the mud as the gunboat flotilla made its way down Maryland's St. Leonard's Creek toward the inlet and the open waters of the Patuxent River. Nearing midnight, they'd anchored here in the inky shadows of the oaks and poplars sheltering the bank near to the inlet.

Five hundred men and boys waited for dawn. The younger watermen kept their eyes fastened on the horizon, like hawks eager to snatch their morning prey. It was mostly nerves that drove them. The older seamen, long accustomed to nights on dark waters, mostly gave themselves to the creak of the boards and the rustle of chains for that was the music that soothed their fears. Some thought of their women in the small shore towns of the Chesapeake, who at this hour were already stirring up flap-jacks and pouring out coffee.

Few of this flotilla crew had slept as they were pressed upright - shoulder against shoulder - on the hard wooden benches of these American gunboats, "if a man can call a flat-ass barge that tips like a teacup so fancy a name as *a gunboat*," Sailing Master Tom Warner had once been heard to mutter.

Even now, heat lay heavy in the reeds and tall grasses along the creek bank. The weight of the heat choked the throats of the men and boys waiting for daybreak, waiting for the chance to round the last bend in St. Leonard's Creek and reach the river and open water. This time, there'd be no turning back.

✯ ✯ ✯

Twice in the past three weeks, the Chesapeake Flotilla—for that was the name of this squadron of vessels—had traveled from the safety of a cove upstream, intent upon escape. Both times, the American barges had met the belching of cannonballs from the long guns of British frigates standing watch just off the inlet in the Patuxent River.

Even more terrible were the Congreve rockets. Shot from the enemy vessels out on the river, the snake-like spears had streaked across the low sky.

"Devil's eyes...dragon tails," the flotilla men whispered among themselves as they fought back their fear of such strange, unknown things.

In fact, the rockets were aimless in flight, being only iron tubes, the heads packed with gunpowder and bits of iron. There was a lighted fuse attached. Still, more than a few rockets had exploded overhead and rained hot iron bits into the barges. In the second escape attempt, an oarsman on barge 127 was hit directly in the chest and screamed as he'd leaped in the water and drowned, which caused the flotilla men in barge 127 to cover their heads and turn their bows and row as if fleeing from a nightmare.

✯ ✯ ✯

For the most part, the crew of this flotilla was made up of young fisherman, crabbers and oysterman from Maryland's Eastern Shore. But, for sure, there were farm boys among the enlistees. Even a number of free black men and boys had signed on as crew before the Chesapeake Flotilla set sail down the Bay in mid-April. Nearing three months on the barges, the flotilla men still scoffed to hear themselves called 'warriors' for few had aimed a musket except into an autumn sky of wild geese, or plunged a knife into human flesh, just that of fish or deer or rabbit or wild turkey.

✯ ✯ ✯

It was Commodore Joshua Barney's challenge that brought them to this creek and to this dawn.

Come all ye lads that know no fear. Those were the words on banners hung about in the taverns of Baltimore in the winter past. The seamen and the watermen, stranded land-side because of the trade embargo holding their merchant ships captive, stared over their tankards and muttered to their mates, "Joshua Barney, he's an old salt now, but a hero he was…a blasted hero in the first war with England. Ready to sail again, is he?"

Barney's challenge moved like the winter wind from the Baltimore docks along the rivers—the Potomac, Susquehanna, Patuxent, and Patapsco, along the tidal creeks, and across the corn rows and the tobacco fields of Maryland and Virginia.

Then, an ad appeared in the pages of Baltimore's *Federal Gazette*: "*Where an honorable and comfortable situation offers to men out of employ during the Embargo; where Seamen and Landsmen will receive two months pay advanced for aged parents, and widows, for helpless children, the same manner; with the advantage of being near their families and not to be drafted into the militia, or turnd-over to any other service. Apply to the recruiting officer, or JOSHUA BARNEY, Com'dt of the U.S. Flotilla.*"

Barney's call made the blood run hot, especially in young men, most offering their own version of the same refrain: "Two months' pay up front and sailors' garb to be issued at enlistment, black derbies and crimson sashes, aye! It's God's own adventure, and only the brave need apply." That last part brought a pause. "Damn right, we'll fight! We'll show 'em what we're made of… the shit-green limeys."

✫ ✫ ✫

Once aboard the barges, the farm boys were not so steady on their feet. But they took to the guns, especially *the smashers,* the swiveling carronades that were lashed to the rails of the barges. They kept their eyes on the sailing masters who commanded the barges so they'd know what to do.

As for the watermen, they'd lived with a thin board between their feet and the deep water all their lives and their hands were blistered hard from pulling in nets and throwing out lines. They shouted and sang as the flotilla swept down the bay and talked of tides and oyster beds while they handled the sheets on the single mast that centered each barge.

The Chesapeake Flotilla was just beginning to mold into a fighting unit – their maiden cruise being marked by brief encounters and skirmishes with the British on the bay's choppy waters - when on the first morning in June, Commodore Barney was forced to save his barges from a confrontation with a British "ship of the line" mounting seventy-four guns. Reluctant but prudent, the commodore led his barges into the Patuxent River and up St. Leonard's Creek, where the deeper-hulled enemy vessel couldn't follow.

✠ ✠ ✠

Now, dawn was nearing on this day of testing—the testing of their courage— and the gunners stretched their legs among the picks and rammers and yawned and poked each other hard in the ribs. They didn't admit to fear, at least not out loud.

Sailing Master James Sellers was the captain of the third barge from the lead. He pictured the line of barges stretching up the creek like a dark, sleeping snake. Soon the snake would lash its tail and the fight would begin. His hands trembled at the thought.

Sailing Master Tom Warner waited in the stern of the last barge, number 320. He was thinking of a woman he met in Baltimore in the winter past—only a tavern girl with a hard laugh, but whose skin was soft to the touch.

✠ ✠ ✠

Last night, while still in the cove, Commodore Barney stood among the sailing masters and said with a certain bitterness, "They think us cowards, a squadron of gutless jellyfish fishermen. I know the British devils. I can read them from experience." He'd paused, for he knew that his officers were well aware of his history, his victories at sea, and his three imprisonments behind British iron bars.

"They doubt our nerve." That being said, Barney had hooked a thumb in his leather belt and straightened his shoulders as if to offer the young captains new confidence. "But"—he spat out—"in their arrogance, the British devils will lose the edge. We'll reach the Patuxent River by stealth and take them by surprise at first point of light. If we can hold the crew steady through the rockets, there will come a moment, a chance."

He did not need to say it was the last chance.

✭ ✭ ✭

The men and boys of the flotilla were in uniform and ready for battle. Their white trousers were mostly stained and ripped now, after some three months on the water, their blue jackets smelled of sweat. A few of the younger boys had pushed back their stiff black hats to ease their brows; others held the round hats in their hands, creasing them just slightly with their fingers. The watermen sat easier now with the farm boys and the two backwoodsmen, who wore their hair long and greased with bear fat. With more than a few curses and slaps to their necks, they suffered together the mosquitoes—"gallinippers," the drummer boy called 'em - and also the gadflies that sucked blood but were easier to swat.

A dozen muskets, wrapped in canvas, lay under the benches in the lead vessels, and every man in the flotilla had a cutlass that was freshly sharpened. The commodore's order was to clean the personal weapons and the small guns and big cannons not once but twice, and then once again. Before coming aboard, every man and boy had been issued a double ration of rum by the commodore's orders.

When the moon was up, Barney had walked among them and called out in his strong voice, "Every man jack aboard this flotilla will do me proud. I say it, and I know it. Damn, but we'll escape the British beggars this time, or my name's not Joshua Barney! What say you, my tars?"

They'd cheered him, for they loved him. When Sailing Master John Kiddall broke out with "*When the Stormy Winds Blow*" and "*Lovely Nancy,*" they joined in roaring out the old chanteys with their strong, husky voices—as if they had no fear in their hearts for the morning.

✧ ✧ ✧

Sailing Master Jack Webster could see a slash of crimson now marked the horizon to the east. "Soon now, sir, we'll stand the bastards down," he said aloud, as if it were a fact, not an assumption.

"Your confidence is admirable, Mr. Webster, but worthless."

Webster flinched at the retort. He was the captain of barge 112, the lead barge in the flotilla, but the man standing beside him at starboard was his superior, the fleet's master commandant, the man he most admired in the world.

"There's no standing down this enemy, Mr. Webster. To escape this blasted creek will be victory enough."

It wasn't a rebuke, only nerves on edge from this confounded wait for sunrise and the battle that would surely follow. Webster allowed himself a glance at Barney's profile—the strong mouth, the gold-tasseled epaulet on the older man's right shoulder. He'd studied the commodore's ways and knew Barney's jabs were most often aimed at the men in his command from whom he expected the most.

What's more, Webster shared the scorn the commodore carried for the British. In Barney's case, it was a scorn close to hatred, as it originated three decades earlier when he was the youngest man to captain a frigate in the War for Independence. Barney was now fifty-six years old but he was still a warrior gutsy enough to lead this barge flotilla against a vastly superior fleet of enemy vessels. The Chesapeake Flotilla was America's only naval defense in the bay.

Webster rocked on his heels and felt the vessel surge just slightly against the anchor. He'd not forgotten their last attempt to escape this creek. What had rankled most was not those damnable Congreve rockets, but the arrogance of the enemy—fiddles thumping out lively songs, as if accompanying a tea dance, on the decks of the British frigates.

"Chickenhearts, I say, sir. Or worse, dandies. I've respect for their swords and cannon fire. But, I must say, they haven't our grit. For the most part, I mean."

"Only the flick of a knife's blade."

"I don't get your meaning, sir."

"Grit's not the issue, Mr. Webster. This war is nothing to the British, not after Napoleon and the war with France. Who the devil were we to challenge British power? An upstart nation with a blue-water navy of seven frigates, rash enough to declare war against a nation with a thousand ships! They see us as riffraff, the scum of their empire. Aye, we won our war of revolution. Now we fight for our honor, our independence, a place among nations. To us, it's everything."

Jack Webster offered a sigh that was mostly a groan. He couldn't think that far or that deeply. Not now. Today would bring a battle for the flotilla's survival, challenge enough to live through. He wiped the sweat from his forehead, tasting the brine that rolled down into his mouth. An hour ago, he'd shaved with creek water, using the last cut of French soap given to him two years past by a Newport girl with hazel eyes. He'd saved it for such an occasion as this morning's battle.

The soap was wrapped in a piece of the girl's lace shift, and when he'd untied the lace, he'd caught the scent of summer flowers. Clara was her name. She'd pulled a wooden tub in front of a fire, and she'd bathed, and he'd watched. And then they'd made love.

Webster's throat was tight and he coughed into his palm.

The commodore had turned as if to see the last of the stars still visible over the Atlantic. "So, we cast off with Mars behind us. The god of warriors…the god of battle, Mars."

"Appropriate for the day, I would say, sir." Webster drew in a ragged breath, but his throat wouldn't loosen. His full name was John Adams Webster, fairly given, as his mother claimed to be a distant cousin of the second president. Since running off from his Maryland home at the age of fourteen to join the merchant marines, he'd preferred to be called "Jack," that name being short and strong, befitting a man of the sea. He glanced over at the commodore. "Shall we shake shield and spear and pray, 'Watch over us, oh Mars'?"

Barney chuckled. The old myth was one of his favorites—how no self-respecting Roman general went off to war without first visiting the temple of Mars to swing the sacred shield and spear and to offer that prayer. He was filled with sudden affection for Webster, a sailing master by rank, who reminded him of himself when he was a twenty-eight-year-old firebrand, ambitious to prove his worth.

The younger man was strong in his legs and broad of shoulder. Too thin in the chest, Barney had more than once noted. But the long bones served him well. Webster's eyes were slate blue, intelligent enough, and quick to show humor, which was a good thing in a man. What's more, he carried himself with the uncommon grace that some men have by nature. Barney had heard that said of General Washington, and he'd noted it for himself on a visit to Mount Vernon shortly after the war.

To be noted, Captain Webster showed a confidence that might be taken as swagger. Even in this dawn hour, as the flotilla of gunboats prepared for a desperate venture downstream, toward what could be a bloody death, Webster stood beside Barney with his feet apart, hands loosely gripped behind him, shoulders squared, as if prepared for any eventuality.

Still, Jack Webster had yet to prove himself in battle.

"Courage is not easily come by," Barney offered and frowned, uncertain where the thought came from.

"A coward's the worst thing man can be called," Webster said.

"It might be courage is only chance and endurance, but I swear it calls for something pithy in the soul."

"I say…in the gut." Webster laughed to ease the moment.

In silence, the two officers watched a pair of gulls swoop low over the creek, their cries breaking the quiet. An old seaman once told Webster that the cries of herring gulls were like the cries of women left on shore when their men were fighting at sea. He thought of the girl in Newport, with her teasing way and white arms and her warm breath on his face. Would she cry to hear the news, if he were killed in the battle today?

A half-dozen American cannons waited on a slight rise of land near to the meeting of creek and river. When Joshua Barney notified President Madison that the flotilla would make this third attempt to escape St. Leonard's Creek, the president ordered a militia artillery unit to be posted on that stretch of higher ground called Malvern Hill. Colonel Wadsworth and a company of D.C. militia had brought down two eighteen-pounders. Captain Sam Miller and a company of marines had rolled some smaller cannons up the hillside as well.

The American guns would provide the artillery cover for the flotilla's escape—that was the plan. At dawn, the roar of those guns would deliver the signal for the Chesapeake Flotilla to race toward the inlet and freedom.

✻ ✻ ✻

Now, the sun broke like a flaming ball over the trees to port and threw a shimmer of thin gold down St. Leonard's Creek. As if in concert, the American gunners on Malvern Hill let loose the two eighteen-pounders. The roar of the big guns was like a roll of thunder.

The watermen scrambled to their feet and called out to each other in the soft dialect of the bay: "It's tam now to go dane this blasted creek!" "They be waiting for us sure, them yellow-bellied johnnies." "'Deed we'll show the bastards what we're made of this day!"

✻ ✻ ✻

Captain Jack Webster touched the ruffle of gold lace at his neck and reached for his leather belt and the sheath that held his cut-and-thrust sword. He handed over a heavier sword, red-tasseled and dented from past battles, and watched as Barney strapped the sword to his left side.

The echo of the eighteen-pounders was joined now by the roar from the three-pound cannons manned by the marines stationed a few yard south of the militia unit. Webster turned to the commodore. "Like music to our ears. What say you, sir?"

A smile touched Barney's lips. "I say we join the chorus. Downstream, Captain Webster. All haste."

✯ ✯ ✯

Joshua Barney once said there's a kind of inland man that makes the sea his country. Webster watched the creek bank slide past, the tall marsh grass, the tangled vines and branches and overhanging tree trunks. He breathed in the scent of field-ripening tobacco. Tobacco was in his blood. He had that in common with the commodore, and the thought pleased him.

The commodore came from a prominent family in Baltimore County, inland people. But, he'd told Webster he'd always carried a passion for adventure: "the kind of life a man can't find in law or farming."

Jack Webster had known a great stirring of happiness, as Barney's words matched the feelings in his own heart. He, too, was born inland and had spent his boyhood wheezing and coughing in the tobacco fields of his father's farm in Harford County some miles northeast of Baltimore. Granted, The Mount was a fine spread of land, 114 acres to be exact, owned and farmed by the Webster family for more than a hundred years. As a boy, he'd learned how to train a horse to saddle and how to fill a tobacco barn for the curing. He was not above the work, but his heart was never in it.

In the still of country nights, he'd lost himself by candlelight in the pages of the *Iliad*, the best book he'd discovered in his father's library. When he could stand farm life no longer, he defied his father and entered the merchant marines. Like Barney, he was looking for adventure. He found it in the summer of 1812 aboard a privateer out of Baltimore bearing letters of marque and a fervent mission to sink or capture British merchant ships.

The *Rossie* was captained by Commodore Barney, who'd come out of retirement on his Maryland farm to offer his services in the newly declared war with England. The *Rossie* mounted only fourteen cannons. Yet in that one brilliant summer, the little clipper sank or captured eighteen enemy vessels bearing almost four thousand tons of produce and merchandise.

When fired with brandy, Webster could reel off the names of those British vessels: the *Princess Royal*, the *Kitty*, the *Fame*, the *Devonshire*; the schooner *Squid*; the brigs *Henry* and *Two Brothers*; the *William*, captured with a cargo of coal and butter; the *Rebecca*; and the twelve-gunned *Jenny*, her hold filled with salt. He liked most to boast of the *Princess Amelia*, an English packet who'd not struck her colors until her masts went down, with the captain and first officer lying dead and both decks turned to bloody shambles.

To his regret, he'd not boarded the *Amelia*, being ordered by Barney to remain at the *Rossie's* helm. Still, it was one of Jack Webster's keenest pleasures to play that battle over in his mind, and he'd relate the taking of the *Princess Amelia* to anyone who'd listen.

Last fall, at Barney's recommendation, Jack Webster had received a warrant to serve as a sailing master on the Chesapeake Flotilla. He'd watched barge 112 take shape in the Baltimore boatyard and was the first to step aboard her newly laid planks in April.

✳ ✳ ✳

With the ease of a man who'd spent months living on water, Webster made his way aft. His boots crunched in the gritty layer of sand around the truck carriage of 112's long cannon. Just past the single mast pole, he put a hand on the shoulder of Midshipman Asquith, a pudgy, flushed-faced boy who'd just recently joined the flotilla.

"Keep a steady heart, lad," Webster whispered for the boy was wide-eyed and holding hard to the cables.

When he reached the stern, Webster stood beside the coxswain. Although he could see the foremost crewmen in the barge directly in 112's wake, he knew only a few of the non-commissioned flotilla men by name, even those on his own barge. It was difficult—he'd struggled with this—to draw the proper line between officers and crew in such small vessels. A proper distance is vital to command and requires a certain stance, a coolness of manner.

"Mr. Kiddall is pressing hard, sir," reported the coxswain whose name was Jesse Stewart.

"Hold to your course, cox'sun." Webster couldn't resist a mocking grin at Kiddall, who was raising a fist in challenge from the bow of his barge. The third vessel with Tom Sellers in command was gliding hard to midstream. Kiddall and Sellers, along with Tom Warner, were his mates, the sailing masters against whom Webster measured himself in the struggle for the commodore's favor. It was the sport of the barge captains to test one another. Even now, as the flotilla raced downstream to face the enemy cannons, each sailing master was pushing for advantage.

Webster motioned to the drummer boy. "Are you sleeping, lad? Give us a hard beat."

"Aye, sir, as you'll have it." Caleb was a small-boned boy nearing twelve years, or so he claimed, wearing leather pants and worn black boots. Thrusting out his elbows, he began a well-paced beat to guide the men at oar. The sound of the boy's drum moved down the waterway like the reassuring echo of a heartbeat.

✲ ✲ ✲

As the creek widened at the bend, the second barge pulled alongside barge 112. Kiddall's eyes were shining as he shouted across the water, "Ahoy, you slugs. We'll be waiting for ye at the inlet."

"Like hell you will! We'll be in the thick of battle long afore ye!" Webster grabbed the port rail to steady himself as the foremost barges swept down-stream into the current that would, God willing, carry the Chesapeake Flotilla across the inlet into the Patuxent River.

Already, he could see the squadron of British vessels commanding the river some four hundred yards beyond the inlet. They appeared like painted boats on the sun-glinted water.

Deadly, beneath that beauty. A deadly force. He stared at the impressive gold and black hulls of His Majesty's frigates, *Loire* and *Narcissus*. He could see some brigs and a few schooners and a sloop of war with the name *Jasseur* on her hull. A fair number of rocket boats were hovering around the larger vessels.

"'Tis a wall to be climbed, sir," the coxswain gasped behind Webster.

"Aye, and we'll climb it, Mr. Stewart," Webster responded coolly, although he could feel his heart pounding inside his chest.

The gun deck of the HMS *Loire* showed a broadside line of eighteen pounders. He could clearly make out the snouts of the long guns.

For a brief moment, Jack Webster let himself consider how the American barges must look to the seamen who were watching from behind those imposing guns. Pathetic, no doubt. The flotilla vessels must resemble a flock of squat brown ducks with their soaring feathered wings ruffling out on the water. He felt himself flush as if with shame. The barges measured a scant fourteen feet at beam and forty feet fore and aft, with close-set sweeps extending twenty feet on either side. Insignificant, even laughable, to men in the British frigates, who with any skill or any luck, could demolish the lead barges with a few well-placed broadsides.

At the thought of such a dismissive death, Jack Webster held his breath, then sighed with relief as he heard again the roar of cannon fire—a volley from one of the American eighteen-pounders stationed on Malvern Hill. He stared at the *Loire*, hoping for an eruption of side timber. At the least, a shattering of mast and beams.

"Misjudged, I say, sir. A full cable length short." Jesse Stewart groaned, for both captain and coxswain could see the frigate *Narcissus* had come awake, and she was now bearing to starboard and showing the arc of her guns.

✫ ✫ ✫

Webster swiveled in search for the commodore. Joshua Barney had moved to mid-ship and stood with braced legs, his saber in his hand. Although Barney carried the aura of a large and powerful man, he was only of middling height, his weight resting in his waist and strong legs. He wore the long blue jacket of the French navy. His official rank was that of captain in the U.S. Navy, but the long coat was an affectation Barney favored, a reminder of the years after the Revolution when he briefly served in the French navy as a commodore. The cut of the jacket favored his shoulders and hid the softening belly. This day, the commodore was without his wig, for he rarely wore it on the water, his hat being sufficient to conceal his close-cropped hair.

When Barney smiled, it was Webster's belief that his true character broke through and spoke to his belief in fair justice and to the generosity inherent in the man. For certain, his smile, which appeared like an occasional sunrise on his weathered face, bonded his seamen to him.

At this moment, Barney's face was flinty, his dark eyes narrowed in concentration. "Stand by to fire as you bear! On the up-roll, my men," he roared.

The crew might be new to war, but they'd had hours of practice and understood the command. As barge 112 tipped and swayed in the inlet waters, a sizzling cannonball was pulled with tongs from the brick hearth below the afterdeck and gingerly carried forward to the gun platform. The touchhole at the cannon's breech was then flipped open, and the powder cartridge pricked.

Instinctively the gunners tumbled back for safety as the length of smoldering rope, the "slow match," rose on a forked stick—ready at the commodore's command to press to the touchhole.

The the little barge rose again on the swell. The commodore lifted his sword and brought it down in a sweeping arc: "Fire!"

✧ ✧ ✧

What a glory war can be when it goes well, thought Jack Webster.

Bright ribs of flame were climbing the square-rigged masts of an enemy brig. He could see the British seamen leaping from the riggings.

Around him, the flotilla men roared at the sight—but, too soon.

The British cannons had begun to fire at the flotilla barges as they attempted to cross the mouth of the creek.

A cannonball skimmed the creek waters and thudded into Tom Sellers' barge. The bow cannon was knocked askew, its iron muzzle landing hard on a gunner's legs just as two of Sellers' oarsmen, jolted from their benches, disappeared over the side of the barge.

"Help...for God's sake, help me!" one of the floundering oarsmen cried, his blood already darkening the water. But the crew of 112 offered no help for the recoil of their own bow cannon had set their barge at a thunderous tilt. Barney grasped the oarsman, Mingo Jones, by the arm. "Steady, my man," he commanded, as if ordering his own body to resist the pitch and tumble. "Steady on."

✳ ✳ ✳

Mingo Jones was a man of uncertain age who studied the world through skeptical dark eyes. Settling again on the wooden bench, the gunner waited as Captain Webster passed out cartridges of gunpowder to the few crewmen who'd been issued one of the rare muskets.

Mingo Jones caught two cartridges and tore open one of the paper packets with his teeth. When he was a boy growing up at Snowden, a plantation in Virginia, he'd often followed his master into the woods on the hunt for quail and deer. As a slave, he'd not been allowed to shoot, only to retrieve game from the brush and thickets. But he'd watched and learned how it was done. When he'd shot a wild turkey in the brush at the cove a week ago, the commodore judged him worthy to carry one of the flotilla's muskets.

Mingo braced the gun against his left knee. Adding a little gunpowder to the priming pan, he poured the rest of the powder and a load of shot down the barrel and rammed in the cartridge paper. Bringing the musket chest high, he pulled the doghead to ready and turned the musket's barrel toward a British rocket boat gliding toward the inlet.

"As she settles. Hold for the count, I say." Captain Webster had pulled off his hat and was waving it over his head like a flag. The feather rippled in the breeze.

"Aye, say you, buckra," Mingo murmured under his breath. "Me, I hold for the commodore's command." Captain Webster had an air about him that brought to Mingo's mind the master's son at Snowden, who walked about as if he owned not just the land and its people, but also the birds in the trees and the sky itself. The memory brought bile to his throat.

"Ready…aim…fire!" Joshua Barney shouted when the enemy rocket boat was within a hundred yards. The stubby carronades on the port rail let loose their iron balls. At the same moment, the muskets in the hands of a dozen flotilla men let go with a barrage of grapeshot as barge 112 skidded across the surface of the creek's mouth.

Mingo jammed the musket between his knees and grabbed hard to his bench. The rocket boat had taken a hit. She was sinking at the bow, and the British swabs that manned her were already flailing about in the water. Mingo Jones was not a man to smile, but he allowed himself a grimace of pleasure.

✲ ✲ ✲

Mingo's sole intention was to survive this hour on the water. The British rocket boats and barges were closing on the inlet and raining grape and canister shot on the American barges. He could smell burnt flesh, for young Asquith had taken a shot clean through his chest. The boy lay groaning and blood was dripping near to Mingo's knee.

"Water and toweling for Asquith! For God's sake, move, lads," Captain Webster yelled. Sweat streaked the faces of the oarsmen manning the sweeps. Still, the wall of British ships had not given way.

✲ ✲ ✲

The commodore's eyes were fastened on Malvern Hill. He watched the rise of smoke above the cannons. "Blast it. They've positioned the guns short."

Jack Webster had no time to answer, for a round shot whizzed past his head and buried itself in the planking of 112's afterdeck. The barge keeled with the impact, and the gunner's boy, a young kid with skin the color of light chocolate, tumbled over the rail of the boat. Mingo watched the boy disappear beneath the frothy water, then rise and flail about with his skinny arms.

"Overboard to starboard!" In Captain Webster's tone was a clear order to Mingo Jones to leap overboard and rescue the boy.

"Go after him, Mr. Jones," urged the commodore from the afterdeck.

Mingo put both hands on the rail. "Little pisser," he whispered.

Jason Hayes was his name. Something about the gunner's boy infuriated Mingo. Maybe it was Jason's long-lashed, black eyes. They reminded Mingo of a lamb's eyes before the slaughter. By all rights, the boy should be home in his momma's skirts. Still, Mingo hesitated.

At this moment, barge 112 surged, and Captain Webster reached into the swirling water and grasped Jason's outstretched arm. "I have him," he shouted and dragged the boy into the barge. Wearing a broad grin of triumph, Webster pulled off his blue jacket and threw it to Jason, who was trembling and gasping for breath.

"I could've grabbed the lil' thumbsucker," Mingo muttered. "I could have grabbed him easy on the wave." He stared at Captain Webster, whose linen shirt was drenched with creek water. In the sailing master's eyes was a flicker of contempt.

Mingo turned away and spit over the side of the barge.

✲ ✲ ✲

Joshua Barney had turned his attention elsewhere. All his senses were alert to the sounds and the movement of the British vessels. He knew the music of war, and he'd noted a pause in the enemy cannon fire. He couldn't think why the *Narcissus* and the *Loire* might withdraw, as the British vessels had the advantage.

He put his spyglass to his eye and drew in a breath.

The sweeps on the enemy frigates were in motion, maneuvering the great ships out into the river and away from the creek's mouth. Were they reconnoitering? A conference between captains? It was probable the British feared the American army on the bluff had reset the guns and the next shots would cause serious damage to their vessels. The reason for the frigates' retreat mattered not. Barney had staked everything on the belief that this battle would offer one chance for his flotilla's escape.

And now, by the grace of God, that chance had come. He motioned to Webster, who'd scrambled after him to the bow. "If we fly with the speed of gulls, we'll have passage from the creek. Alert all barges to follow. No, leave the two disabled barges. All men to oars and poles, sweeps to the ready! Now, Mr. Webster, now!"

☆ ☆ ☆

Jack Webster shouted Barney's orders to the boatswain. He could see Kiddall's and Sellers's barges were listing badly, the oarsmen shouting and bailing frantically. Gritting his teeth against panic, Webster ordered the gunners in 112 to grab up the long poles and prepare to maneuver the lead vessel through the inlet's shallow water.

Webster heard the commodore shout out in his loud, hoarse voice the same stirring quote of the Bard's that he'd called out on the *Rossie* as she closed on the *Princess Amelia*: "...'Tis true that we are in great danger; the greater, therefore, should our courage be."

For a moment, there was stillness on the barges—like a drawn-in breath.

Then, in an agonized thrust, the oarsmen bent to the sweeps, and the gunners thrust out with the poles. The barges began to form a ragged line behind the lead barge. Webster threw a canvas over young Asquith's body. Then he cried out, "Drum, boy! Drum for all you're worth."

Caleb stood with his back to the mast. The watermen, the farm boys and the lads of Baltimore—their faces and arms streaked with smoke, sweat, and blood—gave themselves to the steady beat and bent to their oars. The British frigates kept their distance, and the barges of the Chesapeake Flotilla slipped from the confines of St. Leonard's Creek.

From the bow of the second barge, Captain Kiddall's strong baritone rose on the wind, "*A hundred years is a very long time, ho, yes, ho.*"

As the flotilla began to beat its way slowly out into the Patuxent River, the young watermen joined in, belting out the old chantey. "*Ho, yes, ho, they used to think that pigs could fly…ho, yes, ho…*"

✡ ✡ ✡

Two months later

Joshua Barney said it right, a truth granted. This was not a very important war to the British. The aim of Great Britain was to control, punish, and embarrass, but not to conquer the United States. Still, the declaration of war by the American Congress in June of 1812 remained an insult to the Crown. The insult must be dealt with.

It was Canada that mattered to Whitehall, the audacious American invasion of that vital holding of the Crown. Now, the long war with France was over and Napoleon was in exile. England, flush with victory, could turn her resources—her superb navy and her crack army—to settling the dispute with the United States. The goal of the Chesapeake campaign was clear to those in command. They were to freeze and facilitate the invasion of upstate New York, to isolate and cut off American trade with the Continent. Already, a blockade extended from New England down to the southern states. Chesapeake Bay was now securely under British control—an action easily accomplished. Despite the fact that the enemy fleet was in control of American waters so close to the young nation's capital city, there'd been no defensive action by the Americans except for Joshua Barney, that old renegade, and his ragtag crew on the Chesapeake Flotilla.

✡ ✡ ✡

Dinner was over on this August night—the main course being terrapin freshly caught—and two British commanders sat with their coffee and brandy in Rear Admiral George Cockburn's paneled stateroom aboard his flagship, the frigate *Albion*.

"See here, Ross, the bastard's run out of river."

"Barney?"

"Aye." George Cockburn pointed to a hand-drawn map of Maryland and the empty space where the Patuxent River disappeared from the map. He offered his thin, arrogant face in a triumphant smile. "We had him buggered up St. Leonard's Creek some weeks ago, but he escaped. His crew's a scrappy lot, and they've caused no end of trouble. A mosquito fleet, I say, but with a scorpion's sting. But I've got him now. He's caught upriver in the marsh at the river's mouth, his scum flotilla and his crew, eh?"

Major General Robert Ross listened, but he made no reply. He was only a few days arrived in Chesapeake Bay and was not yet accustomed to the oppressive humidity, and to this war—this small, unimportant war. He leaned forward so that his shoulders barely touched the chair back and spoke in his cultured English accent that was tinged with a flavor of Ireland, "I say, Co'burn, a desolate place, this great bay. I've not seen its likes before. Empty, except for the gulls, and so blasted hot, more humid than the Barbados. Is it always so?"

"Actually, I rather relish the heat."

Ross tried to read the naval officer's glittering eyes. George Cockburn was a strange, fierce fellow. Forty-three years old, five years younger than Ross himself. It was said that Cockburn had spent his entire life since boyhood aboard one ship or another. A good grounding, if not necessarily the education of a gentleman. His men admired him, and for certain, he had a sterling record in His Majesty's Royal Navy.

Cockburn's signet ring glistened in the candle's glow as he leaned over the map and put his forefinger on a circle he'd marked midway up the Patuxent River. "You'll disembark your troops here at the port town of Benedict, a small village, undistinguished, as they all are, without a single painted house anywhere to be seen. There's a fair dock, a fisherman's pier at best, but better than most in this godforsaken countryside."

"Will my troops be safe from ambush during the disembarkation?"

Once again, Cockburn flashed a mocking smile. "My good fellow, there's only Barney and his fleet of scows and barges. As I've told you, those wretched vessels are now mired in the swamp above Benedict. I'll personally go after Barney and his barges, and take his seamen as my prisoners and his cannons for our use. It shall be my pleasure, a sweet pleasure, to rid us of that old salt and his crew...a parcel of black men among them. Aye, blacks. We'll capture them all, what say you? Deliver them to the admiral. Cochrane will be pleased with that, eh?"

The navy man's gloating energy lingered in the humid air.

It was true. Sir Alexander Cochrane, the supreme commander of His Majesty's naval forces along the Atlantic and the Gulf coasts, claimed he wished to rouse the slaves and the runaway blacks of the Chesapeake and have them join with the British forces. Thus far, the plan had not been particularly successful.

"As you will, Co'burn," Ross responded curtly. He'd had enough of George Cockburn's obsession with the American barge squadron known as the Chesapeake Flotilla. More than that, he was sweating badly, for as the occasion demanded, he wore full dress, the scarlet-and-black wool uniform of a British major general.

Robert Ross toyed with his brandy glass as he assessed the situation.

Cockburn was a renegade admiral with a renegade crew that had terrorized this American countryside since February a year ago. He'd heard the talk of pillage and villages burnt and the rumors of rape of local women by Cockburn's seamen. He couldn't resist blurting out a challenge. "You've lived off the land, have you not?"

Cockburn chuckled as if delighted at this thrust against his reputation. "Don't speak to me of protocol, my friend. I'd not let my men eat rancid cheese and dried jerky on our vessels when they could hear the cackle of chickens and smell hot bread baking in farmhouses along the shore. The natives asked for this war."

"So they did. And are the worse for it."

Cockburn poured fresh coffee from a silver server into delicate china cups. "You'll find the locals interesting, Ross, if primitive. When my men go ashore, even in search of fresh water, the farmers shoot from behind trees like savages."

Ross waved away the coffee cup and stared at the map.

He had no particular quarrel with the Americans. His initial orders were to effect a diversion on the lower coast of the United States in order to divert American arms and militia units from the war in Canada. He'd hoped for a short campaign, hoped to go home within a few months, home to his wife and his manor house on the Irish Sea near Dublin—his house, his horses, his violin sorely missed—and to his children, whom he'd not seen in almost seven years.

Closing his eyes, the British general allowed his head to fill with remembered music. Beethoven, the German, his music. *Sonata 5 in F Major.* Intoxicatingly beautiful. For the past few days, he'd caught himself fingering the notes as if the violin were in his hands. For the first time in his notable career, Robert Ross was homesick. He longed for his wife, Elizabeth Catherine. He always thought of her as "Ly," a name used only in private between them. On a gold chain around his neck, he wore a miniature, which did not do Ly justice but showed her fair hair, blue eyes, and English smile.

Ly was more than just a wife. He thought of her as his dearest friend. When he was wounded while fighting the French at Orthes earlier this year, she'd traveled over the snowy mountains of the Pyrenees to tend his wounds and, more importantly, his spirits. On the voyage to America, he sent a note back to her from the Azores that read: "My Ly must look to the prospect of our speedy meeting with glee and cheerfulness."

There was, however, no glee in Ross' heart this night as he sat at dinner aboard Admiral George Cockburn's command ship. Only a profound weariness. He finally spoke. "My men are three months aboard ship and sickly. I say we—"

Cockburn interrupted with a dismissive wave of his hand. "I doubt more than a few militia units will stand in our way as we strike for the capital. I understand Washington City is only a country village, a sheep's walk. Together we shall wipe it off the map, eh?"

Ross looked away. He had a fresh face, surprisingly unmarked by his years at war, coal-black hair, and startling blue eyes that reflected his Anglo-Irish heritage.

He also had the tendency to stare into space when he was thinking through a situation, as he was now.

What was this talk of striking at the American capital? Was it necessary to destroy Washington? He believed not. But then, this entire American venture had an uncertainty about it. Upon his arrival in Maryland, he received fresh orders from Admiral Alexander Cochrane, new orders that suggested the ultimate goal of the British force might be the capture of Washington City to exact retribution for American assaults that the British judged as excessively brutal on Port Dover, York, and the Niagara frontier.

Ambiguity there, Ross decided. Although he served under Admiral Cochrane, a Scotsman of favored birth who carried an imposing record of naval service to the Crown, he himself was an army man and retained the right to decide when and where to use his troops. He would fight to keep that right of decision. Whether or not to allow his troops to attack Washington was a question he must carefully consider.

Cockburn drained his coffee cup. "We'll show these farmers they can't burn Canada's capital city and not pay the price. Washington will be set afire in reparation for the Yankees' burning of York? Fitting, eh? A tooth for a tooth?" Cockburn laughed, but there was no humor in it. He stared hard at Ross and narrowed his eyes as if a challenge hung in the air.

On Ross' breast were pinned three medals for valor. This past spring, he'd been commended by Wellington for the example of courage he'd set for his troops in the six years he'd led his soldiers against the French on the continent. To hell with Cockburn and his assumptions.

Ross stood and bowed slightly. He would follow Admiral Cochrane's orders and take his transport ships and landing barges up the Patuxent River. At Benedict, his soldiers would disembark into unknown and, as yet, un-scouted territory. It must be done. More than that, he would not yet agree to.

"On the morrow, I will prepare my staff officers," he replied.

George Cockburn twisted his signet ring and smiled companionably as if to say they'd reached common ground. Above their heads, on the *Albion*'s deck, the boatswain sang out the midnight hour.

✡ ✡ ✡

Morning, August 22

Jason Hayes watched a snake slither off a rock into the pale Patuxent water. A water snake, most likely, although it could be a moccasin. Once he'd seen moccasins swimming in the river. He'd watched the two heads, like tiny flint-carved stones, moving fast above the current on one side of the barge. He'd reasoned them to be turtles until Mingo set him right.

Mingo claimed he saw a man die once from a water moccasin bite.

"His foot swole up and then he died." Mingo's mouth turned hard when he said it, like it was the man's fault he died. "Them snakes is easy to rile. They quick to turn on you. The thing is to keep your eyes open when you going about barefoot on the bank."

Jason wiggled his bare toes, and his eyes followed a stream of sunlight that had made its way to the splintered boards near his knees. All morning he'd been sitting here in the stern of barge 112. He'd chewed on some cold, roasted corn ears, there being no fried pork left and no bacon, neither, because Cookee—that being Mr. Soames—said he hadn't the "gol dern time" to fry it.

The boy had peed a few times over the side, but for the most part, he'd been just sitting here with his feet dangling above the water. A long time, maybe hours, dozing some. But now that he'd seen the snake, he hunched his shoulders, pulled his feet up close, and wrapped his arms around his knees.

✡ ✡ ✡

Mingo Jones stared over the port rail of barge 320 at black tree trunks rising in the inky pools of water. So the Patuxent River had ended at its beginning—a place called Pig Point in the upper reaches of the river.

Mingo allowed himself a spit over the rail. He wasn't sorry to be done with seagoing. It was only because of the commodore he'd joined the flotilla.

That being a curious thing he liked sometimes to think on.

✫ ✫ ✫

On a dark night in the winter just past, he'd come upon a Baltimore tavern. He'd stared through the door and noted with amazement and some suspicion that white and black men were mingled inside. He was a runaway. For five nights, Mingo had been traveling on ice-rutted roads in the back of a wagon loaded with fresh-cut timber from the mountains of Virginia.

Even now he remembered how he had been trembling from the cold and even more from hunger. He'd pushed through the swinging doors and entered a tavern that smelled of whiskey and sweat. He'd stood close in the shadows with his back to a wall.

Men and boys made a straggly line across the tavern. Mingo didn't like to call attention to himself. Still, he'd edged closer to the table that faced the line and observed two black youths just reaching for manhood standing before a white man whose dark hair was threaded thick with silver. For a moment, his stomach tightened, and then it struck him that the black lads were standing straight-backed and looking the white man straight in the eye. It was something he'd never seen before, and the sight amazed him.

The white man was a sea captain. Mingo was certain of that, and it came to him this was an enlistment of some sort.

The captain's words sounded in Mingo's ears, and he saw the black youths nod. The white man continued, and the timbre of his voice carried a message that was more stirring to the men in the tavern than his words. "Joshua Barney is my name, and I carry through on my word. Seamen of experience are needed, but courage is the only requirement."

The two lads held out their hands, and Barney laid coins on their palms. He didn't pour the coins out on the table, but with his own hand, he put them in the black boys' hands. Mingo saw that and it made him feel hopeful. It was only an edging of hope. He'd spent all the years of his life—he could not say how many—on a tobacco plantation, and he'd never set foot in a boat of any kind.

But if this white man was looking for courage, he might stand a chance. Mingo took his place at the end of the line. When he reached the table, he said nothing of his past, but only faced Joshua Barney and allowed that his name was Mingo Jones and that he was able and strong and could do what he was bid to do. They'd stood eye to eye, which was a strange and terrible thing to do with a white man. Barney only nodded his head in a thoughtful way and studied Mingo's long, strong arms that were marked by scars.

"Have you your freedom papers?" Barney asked.

Mingo answered slowly, "Had 'em. Lost 'em."

It wasn't true. Barney knew it, and Mingo could tell that he knew it.

"I own the courage," Mingo said in a harsh, strangled voice. It was the first time he had ever said that word, but he knew its meaning. He knew it had taken courage to do what he had done, to leave the plantation and become a hunted man with a price on his head.

A flicker of understanding came into the sea captain's eyes. Then he said, "You'll need new papers. I'll see to that."

He'd given Mingo four copper coins and a fold of paper marked with a wax seal that allowed him to sleep and eat in a seamen's boardinghouse near to the docks. Within a week, the freedom papers were done. Just how it was managed, Mingo didn't know. He knew only that Commodore Joshua Barney procured the papers and, because of those papers, he could fill his belly and close his eyes and sleep at night.

For two months, Mingo carried the papers in an oilskin packet around his neck while he worked in the boatyard. He'd given thought to taking off for Pennsylvania. But he breathed easiest when he was around the commodore. When the barges were ready to be launched, his freedom papers had gone for safekeeping into Barney's sea chest with all the other important documents pertaining to the flotilla.

✭ ✭ ✭

Mingo shook his head against the memories and stared around him at the deck of barge 320—empty excepting an old rope hammock and two wooden barrels brimming with gunpowder. The crew was gone, leaving only himself and the drummer boy waiting like a couple of fools in the bow and two sailing masters standing together at mid-ship.

Mingo could make out their shoulders, the feathers on their tall black hats. Captain Warner was a decent sort. It was said among the gunners on this barge that Mr. Warner had a sure hand for the eighteen-pounder and was decent and fair with his crew. But the presence of the other man set Mingo's teeth on edge. Of all the officers on the Chesapeake Flotilla, he had the least liking for Captain Webster.

The boy beside him swatted at a swarm of gnats. "Well, I think—"

"Don't pay you to think, drummer boy." Mingo stiffened and turned his head downstream, aware of a tremor in the soles of his feet.

"You hear something, Mr. Jones? What you hear?"

Mingo waved Caleb into silence. He could hear the sailing masters' jesting voices. To his ears they sounded like fool boys. They were longtime mates. Captain Webster and Captain Warner sailed together on the *Rossie* in the first year of the war and were likely to brag on it. The officers didn't look up at his approach, as they were reminiscing about a dark-eyed woman they knew in Newport when the *Rossie* was docked there two years ago.

"The British, they be coming now," Mingo offered in his hard, flat voice.

"What say you?" Captain Tom Warner wheeled around. "I don't hear anything. Do you hear anything, Jack?"

Webster shook his head and squinted as he looked down the line of close-linked barges. At the far end was his vessel, barge 112, with her mud-spattered bow pointed downstream as if ready to flee. His crew was gone, gone ashore—all except for the gunner's boy, Jason Hayes.

✭ ✭ ✭

An hour ago, Webster had left the deck of 112, his heart full of gloom, thinking that some time with Tom Warner would ease his distress. The bad news had come from two of Barney's own seamen. Disguised as farmers, they'd studied the enemy transport ships out in the Bay. Three days ago, they brought the commodore a disturbing report: British gunboats had entered the Patuxent escorting some of the smaller transport vessels loaded with enemy soldiers. Their destination appeared to be the port at Benedict.

"Troops coming ashore in Maryland means only trouble for Washington. Or Annapolis. Or Baltimore." Barney had expressed his opinion to his officers. "But I'm more concerned about that devil Cockburn. He too was seen moving upriver in a convoy of small-armed vessels. He's after us. And he won't rest until he's got me…my cannon and my men."

The commodore had taken swift action, dispatching his second officer, Lieutenant Solomon Rutter, to Baltimore to take command of the naval barges and seamen still in the home port. As for Barney's beloved flotilla, the barges must be destroyed.

"A man can't be sentimental in times of war," he'd announced. But his face betrayed him and showed his anguish. He'd ordered the flotilla men to prepare themselves to go ashore with him. And the cannons, ropes, and tackles. "We'll take our guns with us. Even if we have to push and pull those damn cannons through a hundred miles of forest," Barney had declared. "For sure, we'll not let Cockburn have them."

✻ ✻ ✻

Webster narrowed his eyes as he stared at Mingo Jones. He struggled to keep his tone civil. "The commodore's positive orders were that we take action ONLY if the enemy appears in full force. I see nothing. I hear nothing but the cry of gulls. Why do you say this, Mr. Jones?"

"They be coming now," Mingo muttered. "It's time for me to go."

A quick rage rose in Jack Webster's chest. "Mr. Warner captains this barge. He'll give the orders."

A pause, as if a reckoning on the black gunner's part, then in the same flat voice, Mingo said, "The commodore done give me my orders already."

Before the officers could respond, Mingo stepped to the rail and leaped with ease from barge 320 into the stern of the next closest barge. Without hesitation, he moved down the line of barges.

What Captain Webster said was true. Before Joshua Barney went ashore, he'd visited each barge. He'd paused in front of Mingo and spoken words meant for him alone. "I've confidence you will see it through, Mr. Jones. You have the courage for it." And with that, the commodore went down the plank and disappeared into the woods with the main body of flotilla men who were already grunting and swearing as they prepared to pull the wooden carriages of the big cannons into the woods.

Leaping with ease from bow to stern, Mingo moved along the line of close linked barges. Startled faces, some white and some brown, turned in surprise as he passed. He saw the bandy-legged Cookee with his shaved head and drooping mustache, and the petty officer, Mr. Daniel Frazier, who slammed shut his Bible and rose quickly from the bench when Mingo went past.

Soft-footed as a cat, Mingo landed in barge 112's stern. Always the flotilla's lead vessel, Barney had reversed the flotilla when they reached the marsh so that 112 could lead the barges downstream—if the chance came. But that chance never came.

There was now only this last order of the commodore's to carry out.

The gunner's boy was sitting in the bow, his head on a bow bench, his eyes closed. Mingo put his hand hard on Jason's shoulder. "You paying heed?"

The boy roused. "Sure I am. "

"You sitting there dreaming about your pa?"

Jason looked up, seeing in a sort of blur Mingo's face and the wool cap and old leather vest he always wore. He could see the faint, sand-colored scars that showed on both of the black man's shoulders. "Why you say that to me?"

"They be coming soon," he said curtly. "You remember what I tole' you."

Jason scrambled to his feet. He too could hear a faint rustle downriver that was like the rush of wind in trees. He knew it to be the dip and pull of oars. In the glare of midmorning sun, he could make out a British brig sloop just making the turn of the river at Pig Point, with a flock of gulls dipping and rising above its bow. Close behind the sloop, he could see a long tail of shallow-draft boats with mounted guns.

The boy was stilled by the sight, but Mingo turned away. He leaped onto 112's afterdeck and faced the line of American barges stretched upriver. He held up both hands and gave a sharp clap. On each barge, a man repeated the gesture, and the clapping moved like a wave up the flotilla to the last barge, number 320.

☆ ☆ ☆

For a long moment, Tom Warner simply waited. His eyes moved over the vessel he had commanded since the flotilla came down the Bay from Baltimore in April. What a damn pity! He searched out the drummer boy, half hidden in the ropes by the mast.

"Over the side now, Caleb. Move quickly!"

When the boy had cleared the boat and was splashing toward the bank, Warner grasped the slow match from its bucket and blew the smoldering rope into a flame. Then he pressed the flame to a trail of gunpowder that led like rat droppings across the deck to the gunpowder-packed barrels.

A line of fire began to make its way across the deck of the barge. Warner turned to Jack Webster and held out his hand. "We'll meet when we meet…on shore. Godspeed."

After a hand clasp between friends, the two sailing masters pulled off their blue jackets and black half-boots and followed the drummer boy over the side of barge 320.

☆ ☆ ☆

Explosions filled the air like thunder, like ragged fireworks, as one barge after another flew apart in a fling of flying timber and riggings.

When he'd put the flame to the line of gunpowder on barge 112, Mingo Jones gave Jason a boost to the rail and then scrambled after him. The water reached only up to Mingo's shoulders. Still, it was a test of will. Using his strong arms to thrust himself forward, he waded gingerly toward shore.

As his fingers clutched at the reedy grass of the bank, more explosions rocked the water behind him. Mingo pulled himself from the water, wiped the droplets from his face and knelt on the bank. Already he could feel the heat from the burning barges and smell the bitter scent of scorched timber, blazing hemp, and burning tar.

✫ ✫ ✫

A man's voice rose above the crackle of the flames. "Put ashore. I want prisoners!"

Mingo could see the brig-sloop was flying the bloody red square of a British ship engaged in battle. Also, the white ensign of an admiral. A few yards downstream, British gunboats were bumping against the riverbank, and the enemy swabs were scrambling ashore.

He eased to his feet and stared at the shards of sunlight filtering through the thickly packed trees inland. He could see the indentation of a path. Commodore Barney's last command was clear: "Follow our trail. We'll find a place to stand. We have the cannons."

The words meant little to Mingo. What mattered was getting away from the lime-juicers who were creeping through the brush along the shoreline. He could hear their shouts and the echo of a musket shot. He had no wish to be any man's prisoner.

For a brief second, he surveyed the water's edge for a sign of the gunner's boy. It might be Jason had drowned. He remembered the tears in the boy's eyes when he blurted out the reason he was on the flotilla. It was late at night, and the boy had crept close and told his story in a tumble of whispered words, as if it were important that Mingo understand.

"It's nothin' to me. That boy is nothin' to me," Mingo muttered out loud and moved on his hard, bare feet into the safety of the woods.

CHAPTER TWO

RETREAT

As if he were a small water duck, Jason Hayes pressed himself deep in the marsh grass. He felt for the knife he wore in a sheath on his belt. The knife once belonged to his pa, and was now Jason's only possession.

It came to him that Mr. Mingo Jones wore a knife strapped to his chest under his leather vest. Only moments ago, Jason had seen Mingo standing on the creek bank, the water droplets beading his cap. Then he'd glided into the woods—moving fast like he was easy on the land. More than once it had come to Jason that the black oarsman looked something like his own pa. It wasn't just the shadow Mingo cast and the brown of him that was darker than some others on the flotilla. The likeness was something more.

When he heard the clink of metal as a bayonet struck a rock close by, Jason closed his eyes. He lay almost breathless until the noises slowly faded. Then he crept to his knees. Smoke darkened the sky above the burning vessels like a long black cloud over the river.

He ran into the woods with a boy's quickness. He leaped over rocks and old tree branches, no matter that vines slapped his face or that pinecones cut the soles of his feet. He ran until he was almost out of breath. Then, suddenly, without warning, the ground gave way, and he felt himself stumbling and falling forward as if he were flying. When he came to himself, he could see he'd fallen directly into a ravine thick with stones and fallen pine branches.

There was a bad rock cut on his shoulder. It was terrible to see, and he thought of his mother, who'd say, "Oh my, oh my," if she could see him lying here all alone with blood on him. He let the tears run down his cheeks and loud sobs rise in his throat, as there was no man or boy anywhere around to see or hear.

Sleep overcame him. When the boy woke, the woods seemed strangely quiet and still. A black-winged hawk was circling overhead. After he'd climbed from the ravine, he stood, confused, then limped through the scrubby brush, moving slowly for fear that snakes might be about.

☆ ☆ ☆

The tree line ended in a cornfield with an old gray shed stuck in the middle. Jason limped toward it, and when he'd pushed open its slatted door, he saw there were bunches of old stalks, brown and crumbly, in the corners. Swallowing a sob, he stretched out in the dirt and tried not to think about the blood caked on his arm and the throb in his ankle. He thought instead about his pa.

"Ben Hayes." He liked to say his father's name aloud. It was like saying something important and safe. Saying Ben's name made everything easier to make do with, like being lost and hungry and scared of snakes.

Jason could still see his pa clear in his head, standing in the door of the little house in Norfolk, his old pack slung over his shoulders, with oranges in his pockets and sweet sugarcane in his pack. Ben always smelled of salt and rum and something harsh like gunpowder. He'd show up at home without warning, toss his pack in the corner, and jingle a pile of coins into Ma's apron. He would wrestle with Jason and his little brothers and call them "scamps and no-good young'uns." He'd hold them against his chest hard, like he'd missed them sorely.

When he heard a rustle outside the shed, Jason felt for his knife. Before he could close his fingers on it, something heavy, like a sack of potatoes, flew through the door and landed full on his stomach. A bony elbow smacked into Jason's face.

"Get offen' me," Jason cried out. "Leave me be!"

"By dondy, I was thinking you wuz a British johnny. Did I hurt you now?"

Jason stared into the face of the drummer boy from the flotilla. For sure, he knew this white boy, who walked with his elbows out, and his too-big black boots and the sound of his drum. He turned his face away from Caleb's eyes and put his hand over his eyes to hide his tears. "A bear was chasing me, tha's all. My ankle…"

"A bear, was it now?" Hard fingers pressed Jason's ankle. "I was loblolly boy for a ship's surgeon once't. I've felt of many a broke leg. Hold still, I say. This here leg of your'n, it just be a sprain." The drummer boy went back on his heels, ripped a strip from his own ragged shirt, and deftly bound Jason's ankle.

"Ain't no call to tear your shirt," Jason mumbled, "but thank ye kindly."

Caleb pulled two peaches from the wide top of one of his boots. He thrust one at Jason and took a bite from the other. He wiped the juice on his sleeve and stared at Jason with a curious expression. "Sure, and I seen you a hundred times on the flotilla. You're Jason Hayes, gunner's boy on Capt'n Webster's barge. I'm thinking you be a slave boy what's run away to sea. Am I right?"

"You're no way right. I be free. Born free."

Caleb raised a skeptical eyebrow. "Your pa…he be a free man, too?"

"Aye. He born free, too, and as brave as any man, black or white, I say. All his life my pa was a seaman, shipping out of Norfolk. My pa was a mast man on the *Constitution* when she burned the *Guerriere*."

Caleb threw his peach pit hard against the wall. "Me, now, I never needed no ma or pa. Had no use for 'em."

Jason pulled his treasured knife from its sheath and laid it flat on his palm. "See…this here's my pa's knife, give to me now."

"Well, I swan…" Caleb stuck out a dirty finger and touched the knife. "How come he give it to you? Where your pa be now?"

"I ain't saying." Jason slid the blade back into its sheath and pulled his blue jumper down hard over the knife.

A flush reddened Caleb's face and he leaped onto Jason, straddling him with both legs. For a while, they wrestled like puppies in the crisp rustle of the cornstalks.

Finally, Jason rolled Caleb away. "Get off me, I say."

"I was just foolin' with ye, sure enough." Caleb's voice broke into a whine. "It ain't fair now, is it? There's gonna be a battle somewhere inland with horses and muskets and cannons firing. The commodore can't start this war without me! I want to kill me some redcoats!"

Jason said nothing, only watched Caleb picking at a scab on his elbow. He couldn't say he liked the drummer boy much. Still, Caleb had ripped his own shirt to bind up his ankle. He struggled to make sense of that. Now Caleb looked close to tears.

What for? As for himself, Jason couldn't see it being any use to cry over missing some horses and some fighting. Finally, he said in a voice that sounded in his own ears like Ben's voice, "Rest yo'self now. We be staying in this old shed for a while, I'm guessing, 'less you want to be tromping off through the woods with bears and snakes about."

Caleb lifted his head and grinned. "I'm willing to stay here some hours with ye, Jason boy, 'cause you're ailing. But I aim to be with the flotilla men when the shooting starts. If that's agreeable with ye."

"I'll set off with you soon as I'm able," Jason said slowly. "An' we'll find the flotilla men, sure enough. Me, I got my own reasons."

✥ ✥ ✥

Late day

In the twilight of this August evening, Jack Webster rode into the flotilla men's camp on a horse named Shoe Tail. The very fact that he'd found the campsite gave him satisfaction. The way to this meeting spot, some six miles inland from the Patuxent, had been roughly sketched in damp sand on the riverbank by the commodore early this morning before he marched away with the main body of flotilla men.

After the burning of the barges, Webster had climbed ashore. He was soaking wet and his rucksack lost. He'd steeled himself to carry out the commodore's last order—hiding at the edge of the woods until he could see the barges "in full conflagration."

Barney would want a full accounting and the assurance that the British had gained nothing of value.

That task accomplished, he'd done something impetuous. Sighting a farmer with a wagon heading north into Anne Arundel County, Webster hitched himself a ride. His destination was a tobacco farm called Sugar Valley, belonging to the Baltimore merchant James Biays, a longtime friend of the Webster family.

Twice in recent weeks, Biays had appeared on the banks of the Patuxent—the first time with a rack of wild turkeys for the crew, the second time bearing jugs of hard-cider whiskey, baskets of eggs, a dozen loaves of fresh-baked bread, and a crock of churned butter. Not trusting the locals—most of whom were Federalists, their emotions concerning this war questionable—he'd come to feed the flotilla men whose barges were caught in the marsh.

✯ ✯ ✯

It had seemed right to head to Sugar Valley. He wasn't running away. No man could accuse Jack Webster of that. He was sodden and filthy and hoping for some dry clothes, perhaps a solid meal, and a chance to see the Biays family, of whom he was quite fond.

The loss of the barges was like a pain in his heart, and he wanted to tell James Biays and his wife about the burning of the Chesapeake Flotilla. They'd greeted him wet and muddy as he was with open arms, and he'd sat down in their handsome country house to a Sunday dinner of fresh-caught crabs and biscuits and a bowl of hot buttered grits. James Biays lent him a pair of trousers and a fine-pressed white cotton shirt to wear while his own garb dried, and Biays's good lady mended his blue coat as best she could, considering two of the brass buttons were gone and the jacket was ripped badly at the shoulder.

Over dinner, he had told them about the events of the past hours and said how sick to the gut it made the flotilla men to burn their barges. But how damnably worse it would have been if the cannons had fallen into enemy hands. They grieved with him. "Barney's seamen aren't done with fighting the British, not by a long shot. It's a matter of honor," Webster finished, closing his fingers into a fist on the table.

James Biays's eyes had darkened as he listened to Jack's account. He'd let out his indignation in an angry cry, "Despicable redcoats! Do they think we're still subjects of their king? This is our country, earned by hard labor and blood. Our kin cleared and measured and worked this land for two hundred years now. We fought to claim it as our own, didn't we...fought and won, didn't we?"

Jack Webster had stared at the slice of buttermilk pie before him and struggled to explain his thoughts. "We've brave fellows fighting in this war as well. There's Perry's victory on Lake Erie, and Commodore Decatur and the taking of the HMS *Macedonian*... outmaneuvered her and shot her to pieces. I heard it told she lost her top masts and the whole of the mizzen mast. It was a great victory. He paused before adding, "I've wished I was there."

He heard a choke of regret in his own voice, and cleared his throat. "But now, of course, Commodore Decatur is cooped up in New York. I'd rather be in the Chesapeake, where there's some fighting still to do."

For a moment, there had been silence at the table. "For damn sure, there'll be a land battle," James Biays said to his wife, "and Jack ought to have a horse."

That thought had already come into Webster's mind but he wasn't about to bring it up unless Biays himself suggested it. He hadn't been able to resist a jolt of delight when they'd walked out to the stable, and a familiar, long-legged chestnut with a faint star on his forehead was led from his stall.

"Yours, Jack," Biays had announced. "For as long as you might need him."

Shoe Tail was the very horse Jack had been hoping for. He offered to pay for the horse, explaining there was prize money from the *Rossie*. Only that money was stashed with his papers, and his papers were with the commodore. Money for Shoe Tail would have to be delivered to the Biays farm later. He had explained this ruefully.

"No need for payment," Biays had quickly replied. It was a patriot's duty to support the American defense against the thieving British. He himself was a colonel in the First Baltimore Hussars. "If Baltimore's threatened, if horsemen are needed to defend the port city…" Biays's voice had dropped off at the very thought of such a possibility.

Shoe Tail had been watered and saddled. The high-spirited horse danced about as Jack mounted, but settled when he felt the rider's firm hand. Aware that the young officer's rucksack was lost, James Biays had brought out a linen sack in which he'd put a comb, an ivory-handled shaving knife, and a new shaving brush. Madame Biays had added a slice of freshly made soap and some foodstuffs wrapped in cloth. The sack was handed up, and the farm gate was opened.

Just as Webster had been about to trot Shoe Tail onto the dirt road, Biays's youngest daughter appeared from the orchard. He rose in his stirrups when he heard her call out, and watched her run toward him.

✫ ✫ ✫

Two years. No, three, at least, had passed since he'd seen Rachel Biays. It struck him that she must be all of seventeen now. He remembered her as a tangle-haired, obstinate child, ever devoted to her dogs and horses, something of a pest.

He could see she'd grown tall and slender. Her hair was a dark plait hanging almost to her waist. When she grew closer, he smiled, for there was still something boyish and challenging about the girl. He could see a tear in her skirt and a disconcerting flash in her eyes, and naturally there were dogs at her heels.

"Where are you going on my horse?" Rachel had cried out.

Another memory flooded into his mind: this girl, a fence, and this horse. And, with the memory came an awareness that Shoe Tail was Rachel's horse. Despite his need to be on his way, he had dismounted and held out his hand. As a young girl, she'd slept in the stall when Shoe Tail was a colt and ailing. Even now, Shoe Tail turned his head at the sound of Rachel's voice and tossed his mane.

Rachel kept her eyes fastened on the horse until James Biays stepped forward and put his arm around his daughter's shoulders. He leaned his head against hers and whispered, "Jack is going to battle, and he needs a good mount."

She had frowned at that whisper from her father, but she took Webster's hand and stared at him hard. She said with just a touch of a challenge in her voice, "I thought you were a seaman, Jackaroe, a master of the waves. We got your letter from Newport two summers ago when you were on the *Rossie,* and thank you for it. And then we heard in Bal'imore that you'd a warrant to sail with Commodore Barney."

"Aye," he had responded, "all that's true." Rachel's hand was slender but surprisingly strong. He had tightened his fingers and started to say more, but she had pulled away abruptly.

"What do you need a horse for anyway, Jack Webster?"

"We've lost our barges, Rache, that's the hell of it. The red-coats are coming a'shore at Benedict, and the militias called out. There's a battle brewing. Somewhere. I can't say just where or when. I need to be there."

Tears had risen in her eyes. "I hate this. Shoe Tail is *my* horse."

"You must do your duty, girl," Biays had admonished in a gentle tone. Once again, he put his arm around the girl's shoulders. "Will you let Shoe Tail go?"

For a long moment, she didn't answer. The dogs were yelping around her skirts. She had reached down to pet the bitch and then looked up and rubbed her eyes, leaving a streak of dirt across her cheek. She had said with reluctance, "If it's to save Chesapeake country and for battle, then it's fitt'en. He'll do you proud, Shoe Tail will. Only let me fetch his favorite feed bag."

Her pain and her grace in giving up her beloved horse had touched Jack Webster. He walked beside her as she led her horse into the shadowy stable, and then said in a consoling voice, "Ah, little Rache…"

"Don't call me that. I'm not little Rache anymore. Just look at me."

Jack blushed as his eyes quickly took her, keenly aware now of the dark beauty of the young woman.

"Forgive me … Rachel," he'd stammered. "I remember you with your petticoats tucked up, taking him over the fence. You trained him well. He's got spirit, this fellow."

She had smiled then and stepped closer to him. "Take care of him. He's not an ordinary horse. I lend him to you for the fierce battle that lies ahead. But, only to you … could I lend my Shoe Tail."

He suddenly felt his heart racing and stepped away to stare out into the trees beyond the stable. He saw the sunlight dappling gold on the great oaks in front of the house. He thought of Barney and the flotilla men somewhere south in the forest. He felt more composed and came back to her where she stood rubbing her horse's neck.

He whispered, "I'll bring him back to you, I promise. Only, I can't say when it will be. I don't know what the future holds, Rachel, but we'll take our stand against the British. The commodore says—"

"Oh!" Her eyes had grown huge and dark, and she had pulled her arms from around her horse's neck and thrown herself hard into his chest, hugging him as tightly as she could. "You must come back, Jack … Shoe Tail and you," she whispered into his ear. She then looked into his eyes, and said more urgently, "Come back!"

Her passion had astounded him. It struck him that Rachel was not like any girl he'd known before. Just as quickly, they pulled back from each other and the awkwardness of the moment and Jack took the feed bag from her. After remounting Shoe Tail, he had trotted the spirited horse through the open gate without looking back.

He had followed the sun across the fields and into the tangled woodlands until he came to a meandering creek the commodore had drawn as a crooked line in the sand. Just as the sky darkened to the blue of twilight, the woods had opened onto the flotilla men's campsite.

✳ ✳ ✳

Several hundred men were milling about under the pines with their packs and blankets spread about. In a rough center clearing, the flotilla cooks had started the fires, and the scent of pine knots burning was sharp in the air. Jack Webster spotted

Soames throwing a chunk of bloody meat of some sort into his pot, and he groaned.

Soames was a miserable cook, given mostly to boiling salt junk, dried pork pickled in brine. In fact, the Englishman was no cook at all, but a deserter from one of Cockburn's frigates, picked up by Barney's flotilla on the Poole's Island pier. Soames was quick to say he despised the British navy, hated the Maryland countryside, and resented cooking for a crew of louts and grimy tars. He'd accepted the mess-man spot on the Chesapeake Flotilla solely for the pay, a fact he admitted freely.

Avoiding Cookee, who'd likely throw out a scoffing remark considering his tardiness in reaching camp, Webster heeled Shoe Tail around the edges of the clearing in search of the commodore. An oarsman from barge 112 was sprawled with his back against a fallen log, mouthing his harmonica as if this were any night on the flotilla.

Only, it came off different on land. This was a low, mournful tune, somehow fitting to the day and the burning of the barges.

With a surge of relief, he spotted Tom Warner. Considering the boldness and usual luck of barge 320's captain, Webster hadn't doubted he'd find his friend had reached the campsite safely. As well, he caught sight of Sellers squatting beside one of the fires while binding up a midshipman's wrist. It might be the boy had burnt himself or sprained his arm in the scramble over the side when the powder trail was set afire this morning. Sellers had a hand for tending to cuts and sprains and he was quick to make up a salve of chickweed for rashes and rope burns. Jim Sellers was two years older than Jack Webster, but he'd received his commission only a few weeks before the flotilla came down the bay.

Webster didn't allot his affection to his fellow officers by their seniority on the flotilla, but it was a recognized truth—one he was secretly proud of it—that he'd been the first among them to receive his commission. That was last September, nearly a year ago. Warner had signed on a week later, and Kiddall, in October. He could see both sailing masters standing together now on the far side of the clearing with tin mugs—grog, most likely—cupped in their hands. There was no sign of Commodore Barney.

✮ ✮ ✮

Webster kneed Shoe Tail into a trot. As they circled the camp-site, he came upon Sailing Master Jesse Huffington squatting beside a rail fence. He was down on one knee scraping the mud from a cannon's carriage wheel.

Webster's mouth tightened just slightly. It was not a sailing master's job to care for a damaged carriage wheel. Every officer knew that. Trust Jesse Huffington to dirty his knees like a common sailor. Reining in Shoe Tail, he called down, "How is it you're fixing the wheel, Mr. Huffington? Aren't there tars about to tend to it?"

Huffington was a round-bellied young man with a ruff of ginger-colored hair and always a hint of whiskers, a scruffy sort of fellow, in Webster's opinion. As usual, he had a chew of tobacco tucked in his right cheek. He spit the brown gout in the grass and grinned as if Webster had said something amusing.

"I had the tame to do it," he responded in his soft accent. "See this here cracked spoke. I rounded it with my scarf, but it ain't tight enough by a fahr piece. Can ye give me a hand with it, Jacky?"

Reluctantly, Webster dismounted. Huffington was an odd sort, a former ferry captain, an oyster-man who called himself an "*ayester-man.*" He was known on the flotilla to be as stubborn as a mule.

"See thar," Huffington said, "She's done splintered bad, ain't she?" The cannon's carriage wheels were meant for duty aboard a ship, and the day's trek through the woods had caused the wheel to crack.

Reluctantly, Webster pulled off his scarf and handed it over. "Bind it tight, Jesse, so it don't give."

"Thanky." Huffington spit a second wad of tobacco into the grass and accepted Webster's scarf with a dirty hand. "I say, you're looking for the commodore, I reckon? He's fahr off… and night's coming on. He done took off to look for the militia what's come out of Bal'imore."

"Is he traveling alone?"

"Can't say."

Picturing the commodore traveling alone through the woods with the British on land was disconcerting. Webster turned away and leaned his elbows on the split-rail fence. In the fast darkening sky, he could see the bright star he recognized as Venus, with Mercury above it, a beacon in the dark blue western sky.

✳ ✳ ✳

Commodore Barney had taught Jack Webster to follow the stars. "Heaven being unimaginable and possibly nonexistent," Barney had said as if it were a joke, but there was a meaning in his words. "We, men of the sea, can always look to the stars for guidance. We know for goddamn sure they're there! I sometimes think that whatever rightness and goodness a man can find in his heart comes from the stars."

Webster wouldn't say yea or no to that belief, but for certain, the stars were beacons that had always safely guided men on land and at sea. As he stared skyward, an odd sensation broke his thoughts. A tightening of his senses—like cold water on the back of his neck—caused him to jerk his head. He glimpsed a man standing under the nearby trees watching him.

Those shoulders, that hat pulled low, could belong only to Mingo Jones. Leaving Huffington and his cracked truck wheel, Webster strode across the grass to the trees and said shortly, "I see you found this camp all right, Mr. Jones."

"Aye, sir. Found it right easy enough."

Webster shifted back on his heels. Something cool and hard lay between him and this black man. It was not color that stood between them. One in five flotilla men was black or brown-skinned, which was not unexpected. Freed slaves had long worked the rafts and fishing vessels and barges that, for more than a hundred years, had beat up the Bay hauling sea catch, corn, tobacco, and wheat into Baltimore. A man was judged here not so much by his color as by his skill with poles and nets and knowing when to drop the dredges, and by how a man handled himself in a hard blow.

Chesapeake born and bred, Jack Webster had worked with free blacks all his life. Aboard ships, rank set the tone. He searched to say what was in his head, but in words that would keep the appropriate distance between the gunner and himself. "The barges blew well enough, sunk to the river bottom in the face of the British. It grieved me to think on 112 splintering apart. It was better I was with Captain Warner on his barge. You and the gunner's boy, you did it right. I'll say that much."

Mingo only nodded and studied the mud-splattered horse at the fence. He wondered where the sailing master came across such a fine mount. Folding his arms over his chest, he called out, "Yours?"

"Aye. Shoe Tail's his name. He's sorely in need of a brushing and a rubdown." Webster pulled off the horse's saddle and removed a curry brush from the saddlebag.

For a long moment, the two men eyed each other.

"Is that an order, sir?"

Webster choked down a retort. Before he could respond, Mingo picked up the brush and began to clean the horse's shoulders and flanks. He was surprisingly competent, calming Shoe Tail with a sure hand to his nose and ears.

If Sailing Master Huffington annoyed Webster, Mingo Jones caused a stronger emotion—a combination of dislike and disdain. The gunner had showed himself to be a coward during the escape from St. Leonard's Creek in June. It was a strong thing to say. Jones would've left the gunner's boy to drown, for God's sake!

"Where's the lad, Jason Hayes?" Webster asked in a gruff voice. "Might be he came in with you?"

"He ain't come with me. I'm no nursery maid for kidlings."

The words were muttered under Mingo Jones's breath, and Webster retorted, with a flash of anger, "I won't have impudence. A lashing might serve you well, my man."

"I dare you try it."

There was no time for Webster to reply. A commotion near the main campfire caused both men to wheel about, alert to danger. The oarsman from barge 112 had abruptly thrown down his harmonica. In the smoke and shadows by the fire, the flotilla men were on their feet, all staring in the same direction.

Webster could hear the crackling of branches and the thundering of hooves on packed dirt. A figure on horseback broke from the woods. All thoughts of Mingo Jones were forgotten. He ran toward the seamen gathered around the campfire, where, in their midst, a mud-spattered Joshua Barney was swinging down from his roan.

☆ ☆ ☆

The trials of this long, difficult day showed in the mount's lathered coat and the sweat circles under the rider's arms. Joshua Barney dismounted and drank his fill from the bucket, then looked up and wiped the water from his face with the back of his hand. "We're moving camp, my men, putting to the wind. Aye, this very night, on the double! Where are my officers?"

Jack Webster pushed his way in among the seamen. "Here, sir."

Tom Warner stepped forward, his peaked hat in his hands. Webster could see the brass buttons on Warner's blue coat flash in the firelight as he cried out, "On the move, you say, sir? Where are we headed?"

"Battalion Old Fields, an encampment some four miles west, to join with the Washington and Baltimore militia."

There followed a moment of stunned silence.

"By the president's orders," Barney continued. "We'll be there before midnight if we step lively." He spoke loudly so all could hear.

The murmurs began then, like the rising of a slow, angry wave. Pig sounds filled the air. A young oarsman from Webster's barge pushed forward. Topps was his name. His voice carried something of a stutter, but his passion was evident. He addressed the commodore. "We're seamen, sir, signed on to the flotilla. We d-don't aim to fight on land with no city-boy m-m-militias! Not me. I ain't about to join up with some militia d-d-dandies."

Webster swiveled to face the oarsman. "Don't matter what you aim or don't aim to do. If the commodore says you're going, then, damn it, man, you're going."

The heat in Captain Webster's voice caused Topps to lower his head, but he kept his fists clenched at his side. The Baltimore boys and the watermen stamped their feet and muttered among themselves. A rough voice rose from the crowd. "We ain't break-ing our backs pulling them cannons farther. We're seamen. We ain't pack mules."

Jack Webster grasped their mood just as surely as he could always sense a storm brewing at sea. The escape from St. Leonard's Creek some weeks past had sobered this young crew, muted their spirits—ten men killed or wounded that day, includ-ing young Asquith. And then, the burning of their beloved barges this morning. Humiliation cut to the bone. It was their loyalty to Chesapeake country and their promise to the commodore hold-ing them here this night. He watched Barney remount his roan, grasp a torch from a seaman's hand, and trot, straight-backed, through the campsite, pausing before each clump of seamen so they could see him clearly.

Joshua Barney held the torch high so that the glow added a density to his face. "My lads," he called out in a strong and poetic voice, "I went to sea when I was young and uncertain of my courage. I've sailed in stormy waters when I could not see the land nor make out the stars. I was sure afraid when the night was black and the waves high, but I had my captain to believe in, and I gave him my trust. I ask you for that trust now. Are you brave enough? Are ye strong enough to fight with me, my lads?"

The officers rallied first—the young barge captains, Webster, Sellers, Kiddall, and Warner—with the rest of the sailing mas-ters quickly joining in. The cheers of the barge captains were strengthened by just a few of the bay watermen. Then, more voices rose in shouts, and there was the hard stamping of feet.

The commodore had turned the tide of their emotions. They would follow him—"follow anywhere," they called out, the oys-termen and the farm boys and the three backwoodsmen, the black seamen and the Baltimore town fellows—all proud to be called "Barney's boys." They didn't much like the idea of fighting alongside the militia, but they'd die for their commodore. They didn't say those words, but that pledge was evident in their faces and in their shouts of "Huzzah!"

Barney beamed a smile. The officers were already barking out orders, and the seamen seemed to have put their weariness behind them. They hustled to prepare for another march, as if that were, all along, what they'd wished to do.

✧ ✧ ✧

From where he'd lingered in the shadows of the trees, Mingo Jones could hear the flotilla gunners cursing aloud, but without rancor, as they began to push and drag the cannon carriages across the ragged grass. He watched as they attached the ropes they'd use to pull the heavy guns.

He saw Captain Webster throw an arm around Captain Warner's shoulders, their faces ruddy in the firelight. He listened as Mr. Webster turned again to the white boy called Topps. He heard Webster say in a jocular voice, "You're coming, too, my man. I need you at my side in battle, even if you aren't worth a handful of hardtack."

Mingo edged away in disgust. He'd forgotten himself when asked to tend the horse called Shoe Tail. For sure, there was no need to rile the hot-blooded young officer, although he'd not have minded a knockdown fistfight. He'd have won the fight. In his life, he'd weathered more blows and given more in return than ever Captain Jack Webster. Of that, Mingo was certain. But what would it have gained him?

As the flotilla men gathered their packs and meager belongings and stumbled into marching formations, Mingo remained in the shadows. He'd long had an instinct for passing unnoticed, and he used it to his advantage.

The commodore's sea chest was nearby, ready to be loaded onto one of the wagons they'd acquired from a friendly farm during the day's retreat from the Patuxent River.

When Joshua Barney caught sight of Mingo, he motioned him forward.

"Mr. Jones, I hear tell the burning went as I ordered. Had you a problem with it?" He studied Mingo as if trying to make out the man's face in the darkness. "What might be on your mind?"

Mingo waited before he spoke. When he did so, his voice was cool, as if he were entirely detached from all the excitement. "I'm thinking I done my bit, sir. The barges is burned right enough.

I'm thinking now I might set out for the north; find me a place there. Only thing is I need my papers."

Thumps, thuds, and shouts filled the space between them. Someone called out in a boy's fresh voice, "We're going after them British johns! We'll chase 'em into the river and turn 'em into shark bait, right enough!"

"I never figured you'd be one to run from a fight." Barney said softly.

"It ain't the fighting I fear. I can handle myself on the land well enough." Mingo gave a short laugh. "It's the other thing. This here is tobacco land. You know what I'm thinking."

Barney studied Mingo Jones, his muscles coiled, legs apart, steady on his feet. Then he replied, "I understand your concern, but we're miles from Virginia. And you have your papers, Mr. Jones, there in my trunk." He inclined his head toward the sea chest.

"No matter, sir, I smell it in the air, smell the man, smell the tobacco. I know that sweet stink. I ain't easy here. I'm feeling like I done my time with you, and I wants to move on. It's in my nature."

Barney bent, unfastened the latch on his chest, and took out the oilskin-wrapped parcel that held Mingo's freedom papers. He delivered the papers into Mingo's hands, and then he went on in a voice that carried a certain urgency.

"You must hear me out before you leave. I gave my word, Mr. Jones. I said to the president that my seamen and I, we'd stay the time and fight the good fight. Damn it all, man! This is the revolution come again. We've got to prove to that oily sea-snake, George Cockburn, that we—"

Mingo was not one to interrupt a white man, but he did so now. "What you call a revolution?"

"The revolution was the war that made us a nation," Barney responded hotly. "It means saying no man can insult you. Saying what's mine is mine. We can't lose our self-respect now."

Mingo considered Barney's words, holding the packet of freedom papers against his chest. "I had me a little calf onc't. A little brown calf what I believed was mine. I carried that little fella around in my arms, and at night the little critter slept in the straw beside me. Then it grow'd, and I saw it butchered. Couldn't stop that, but my head came close to bursting with my cryin'. Saw my pa carried off…felt the whip on my shoulders when I tried to go after him. I don't know nothing about what you say 'what's mine is mine.' Don't care nothing about it, either. All I know is I got to take care of myself."

Joshua Barney let out a long sigh. His shoulders ached as if he'd been carrying a mast on his shoulders. His flotilla burnt, his seamen nervy, and on the march to God knows where to meet with an army as yet unfathomed. Yet, he understood the pain in the other man's voice, respected the vulnerability that this black man had shared with him.

In a voice gruff with emotion, he made Mingo a promise. "You have your freedom papers, Mr. Jones. You've done right by me on the flotilla, and you are free to leave. Only I say this to you, man to man, as long as you stay with me and fight with me, you have a place by my side. I ask that you consider this as a pledge. I ask that it be enough for you."

✠ ✠ ✠

Just after midnight

A thin crescent moon cast its light through the window onto the narrow bed in which Major General Robert Ross was struggling to push away his restless thoughts. He lay flat on his back with his head resting on his crossed wrists—an army man's pillow. He generally slept well. It was so in Spain. His wife had been with him on the Iberian Peninsula, her soft body curled close to his on their cot. But Ly was not here with him now in this Chesapeake country.

Yesterday, he'd watched his solders—forty-five hundred of His Majesty's finest infantrymen—disembark from their transport barges onto the rickety dock in the small Maryland town of Benedict. Descending into hell, he might say, a sleepy, godforsaken land that contained neither history nor charm nor value, none that he could see. Only the heat of Hades.

This morning he'd observed George Cockburn's brig sloop glide by on the Patuxent, moving upstream toward the river's headwaters with a squadron of gunboats. Cockburn had been standing at the prow of the sloop and hardly looked his way, so intent was he on the capture of the American commodore, Joshua Barney, and his flotilla of barges, known to be stuck in the marsh upstream.

Ross smiled to himself in the darkness. Cockburn had returned to Benedict with a handful of sullen prisoners, not an officer among them, and no cannons; a great loss not capturing those guns. Cannons would be an advantage for the battle ahead.

The thought of battle caused Ross to sit up on the cot. He pulled on his high boots and jacket and tied his sash. He wasn't a man to walk about disordered in his dress, even at midnight. He moved quietly past his dozing orderly and his two highest-ranking officers and stepped outside.

A breeze greeted him. It was a faint breeze, but cooling, and for that he was grateful. He'd bivouacked for the night in the home of a local doctor named Beanes in this Maryland village called Upper Marlboro. The house sat at the edge of a meadow, and he could see the campfires of his soldiers in the meadow. They trusted him, these good men. They had fought with him in France and Spain, and now he was leading them in this quiet land of North America.

His orderly came up behind him, holding Ross' red silk cape. "You should've waked me, sir," the young man said reproach-fully. He rubbed his eyes and stared out at the campfires.

"I judge we are twenty miles inland from the fleet," Ross said, "with no cavalry and uncertain intelligence. I've marched my army forty miles in the past two days, first inland, then a reverse, and back upon ourselves. Confound it. We've met not the slightest resistance. Where's the American army, I ask you? The uncertainty makes me sleepless."

The jingle of swords and spurs in the darkness caught their attention.

A small party of horsemen reined up sharply before the farm-house. When the lead rider caught sight of Ross and his orderly standing in the darkness, he slid from his mount's back and walked toward them. They could see their visitor was Admiral George Cockburn.

"What's this, Ross? Beset with before-battle jitters, are you?"

Ross pulled his cape around his shoulders as if to show his disdain for the question. He responded coldly, "I've led my troops against the finest of Napoleon's army and never had a fear. But, this assault on Washington City, Co'burn, I question the reason for it."

The moonlight showed Cockburn's frown. "Would you have us retreat? What would they think of us in London if we did so?"

Ross shook his head in despair. He'd heard it said that a private citizen in America was offering a thousand dollars for Cockburn's head on a platter, or was it five hundred for each of his ears? That anger was understandable; the fellow was a ruthless bugger.

"This is not a major campaign, Co'burn," he said patiently. "It's my understanding Admiral Cochrane intends to make a major assault on New Orleans next year. I must shepherd my soldiers' health and morale for such an undertaking. It's my opinion a drubbing of Washington City without cavalry or artillery is unnecessary, a risky undertaking. Indeed, I sincerely question our success in an assault on Washington."

"Pray, do not question," Cockburn replied in a voice hoarse with resolve. He stood face-to-face with Ross. "I pledge everything dear to me as an officer that we shall succeed. If we turn back now, without striking a blow to their capital, it will bring a stain upon our arms. We shall meet little resistance in this endeavor, Ross. I swear it! Their militia, however great the numbers, will not—indeed, they cannot—stand against your trained and disciplined troops."

Cockburn could wear a man down by his passion. He was convincing in his certainty, a vigor that emanated from him even in the darkness.

Ross put his hand to his forehead. "Well, be it so. We shall proceed."

The naval officer's laugh lightened the moment. He turned to his aides, who were now standing at his side. "A jolly prize, what? Queen Dolley…when we deliver her to St James's Palace. Set the Court on his ear, think you?"

Thrusting his arm hard around Ross' shoulder, Cockburn eyed the candlelit farmhouse. "Have you some brandy, my good man? What say we have a glass or two before we bed, eh? My scouts have been out in the countryside. I've a plan to put before you concerning our advance."

✱ ✱ ✱

August 23

A haze lay over the Maryland countryside in the early morning, but it had faded into the glare of the noon sun. A militiaman wearing a yellow scarf stepped from behind a tree and waved his musket in their direction as two ragged young boys appeared from the dense forest. "Halt," he cried in a thundering voice. "Where you lads think you're going to?"

"We be flotilla men, rejoining Commodore Barney," Caleb shouted in reply.

The militiaman offered a derisive smile; one sorry-looking white lad and a black boy leaning on a peeled stick. He laughed. "Ye didn't run into no redcoats, did ya?"

"Not no more'n we could handle," Caleb retorted.

"Make yourselves to home then, if'n you're able."

Beyond the rim of trees, the boys could see that Battalion Old Field was only a round field and mostly dirt. "Like to a race-track," Caleb said to Jason as they scrambled over a low fence, leaving grass and clumps of yellow flowers behind as they landed on the hard-packed dirt.

Gathered in careless formations and scuffing their boots as if annoyed with standing about in the sun were more white men than Jason had ever seen in one place. Militiamen for sure, he considered, eyeing their spiffy yellow jackets and shiny boots, and some with tall hats with feathers. They reminded him of bright-colored birds or a swarm of bees.

Holding the center of the field was a squadron of marines, tight-packed around five cannons, two of them being eighteen-pounders. Black and white men were standing together, the marines marked by their leatherneck stocks. Jason caught sight of some muddy-booted farmers wandering about the edge of the field, carrying pitchforks and axes over their shoulders. Their hounds were barking, fit to kill, and chasing one another between the legs of mules and skittering behind the farmers' wagon wheels.

Jason felt himself small and without any bearings to set course by.

Caleb nudged him in the ribs. "Looky there. Mr. Mingo Jones is sitting under that there tree."

"Well, I swan," Jason grinned. "So he be."

Mingo sat upright in the shade of an old oak tree. He was cleaning his musket. Dan Frazier was sprawled close by, along-side Topps, who was carving on a stick. Lying on his back in the grass was the black gunner, Charles Ball. It wasn't just the familiar faces, but the smell of victuals cooking that made the boys smile. Soames had spread a canvas on the ground and was passing around chicken legs, hard cheese, and biscuits to the crew of flotilla men.

The Baltimore boys were joking, like always, and calling out that Cookee's biscuits tasted like "rocks what's been in the sun a week." It made Jason's heart swell near to busting, and he limped after Caleb toward the seamen.

No one welcomed them. No one called Jason's name. He had no quarrel with that. He and Caleb were not of any importance. They were only like lost ropes of the flotilla floating close to the boat again.

✲ ✲ ✲

Mingo finally looked up from under his hat brim. "Li'l thumb-suckers," he murmured half aloud. "What good they gonna be to the commodore, I don't know. More trouble than they worth."

The boys threw themselves down, and Caleb pulled off his boots.

"Found us, did ye?" Topps opened his eyes and said with a grin.

"It were a wearying walk, shore nuff," Caleb groaned. "We done followed the trail them cannon wheels made in the woods. I'm plumb wore out."

"Good thing you wasn't around earlier. We got here near to m-midnight, and we hardly rested an hour. Not yet two b-bells, and the drums was sounding reveille. This General Winder kept us in f-formation half the night thinking them r-redcoats was about to come down on us. T'weren't so, God be praised!"

"This here General Winder don't know his ass from his forehead," Mingo said, breaking in, his voice harsh with disgust. "You should've seed the commodore in his dress uniform saluting the president as we went marching past on parade this morning. The rest is sorry enough. Half the militia was marching out of step. Not all even got muskets."

Jason felt a ripple go down his back. It wasn't like Mr. Mingo Jones to speak up. He tried to catch the black man's eye, but Mingo was intent upon his musket, staring down the barrel like it was a spyglass. A feeling of great weariness came over the boy. But his hunger was worse. He crawled to his feet and staggered over to Soames and the spread of canvas. "I needs some cornbread or somethin', please, Cookee," Jason whispered.

"We're out of cornbread. Out of chicken, too, black boy. All you get is what's left of the cheese."

Soames turned his back, and Jason stared at the small hunks of dry, curled cheese spread in hunks like rats' turds on the canvas. For a moment, he studied the green-tinged clots and then threw himself again on the ground.

"Here you go, young fella." Petty Officer Frazier shook Jason's shoulder and handed him a dipper of cool well water and then a biscuit with molasses smeared on it. "Eat this now. You looking all tuckered out."

The boy chewed down the biscuit and took a long swallow of water, and then another and another. He tried to pass the dipper to Caleb, but the drummer boy was lying flat on his back in the red-brown dirt, fast asleep.

Jason put down the dipper and edged closer to Mingo's legs.

"How come you left me, Mr. Mingo Jones?" he whispered. "I was thinking you'd be looking for me after we done blow'd the barge. I was thinking you'd be worrying some."

"'Bout you?" Mingo scoffed." I figured you'd make it safe enough. And here you is, ain't you?"

Jason nodded. "I wuz thinkin' I got to catch up and find the commodore and the resta' the flotilla men. You know why. You know what it is I'm planning to do. I tole you about it."

"I don't want to hear about your dreamin' and you planning what you gonna do. This here war is about to start. And you in the midst of it, like you is thinking you safe at home on your momma's knee. Well, you ain't. You and that white boy are li'l bait hooks; that's all you is."

It was said harshly. The words cut like pebbles thrown in Jason's face. He turned away, curled into a ball with his back to Mingo, and closed his eyes.

"You're damn rough on the boy," Dan Frazier murmured. "He riles you some. How is that so?"

Scorn came easy to Mingo's lips. He couldn't say why, except that the words had bubbled out of the anger in his heart, the anger that had no trust for softness or for anything but survival. "Black boys got to be hard, their minds sharp, their hearts like stones. Can't spend time in planning deeds that won't do 'em a spit of good, won't do nothing to save their skins. He gonna be shark bait if he's not thinking sharp."

Dan Frazier reached for a piece of long grass and chewed on it. "I know a man what knew the boy's pa. This feller said he sailed with Hayes in the old days out of Norfolk. He said Ben Hayes was a good man for the high ropes, a man you could trust in a storm. He was killed, I heard tell. Killed in a brawl in Philadelphia."

The boy stirred slightly in the grass. His eyelashes were long and dark on his cheek.

Mingo allowed himself a glance at Jason then turned his head away. "I ain't gonna let myself bother about some ragtag boy hanging on my shirttail. There ain't nothing in it for me to do that"

Still, he found himself looking back at the sleeping boy.

⋆ ⋆ ⋆

Late that day

The orders from Washington called for a quick march tonight. The War Secretary, John Armstrong, wanted the militiamen and the seamen who were presently gathered under the command of General Winder at Battalion Long Field to make the eight-mile trek into Washington City at all possible speed.

"A damnable retreat," Webster muttered. Although in truth, a man could hardly call a march to the capital city "a retreat," since the majority of militiamen in the field didn't come from Washington in the first place.

Barney offered speculation that General William Winder feared a surprise attack by British troops at Battalion Long Field. He feared his untrained army would be overwhelmed by soldiers with bayonets at the ready.

The commodore wasn't overly impressed with the American commander. In the first year of this war, Winder had led a detachment of Maryland militia to Canada. "Captured by the British, paroled, and returned, a blasted hero in Maryland," Barney pointed out in amused scorn, but then admitted the Baltimore lawyer was "bloody well let down" by the powers above him as he attempted to set up the defense of Washington.

"Humiliated by the damn war secretary" is how Barney put it.

Webster was accustomed to a commander who commanded and demanded respect. And he was accustomed to men on ships who moved quickly and efficiently. As word of the "retreat" into Washington's Navy Yard spread from campfire to campfire, there was disorder, even panic, throughout the campsite. Some of the militiamen set out at a run for Washington, leaving their dinner fires smoldering and blankets and canteens strewn about. Shoes, muskets, barrels of flour—even whiskey kegs—were abandoned at the campsites.

This disorganization was disgraceful, a reflection on General Winder. It was Jack Webster's habit to judge himself against other men. Achilles was the first hero to fire his heart when he read of the Greek's long siege to rescue the beautiful Helen.

In his boyhood, he'd also studied a volume of Greek mythology and touched on Shakespeare and Cervantes. He felt he knew what a hero was supposed to be: honorable, dominant, courageous. A naval hero like Captain John Paul Jones or Commodore Stephen Decatur, who was Maryland-born like himself and only a few years older. Commodore Joshua Barney, of course. One needed only the opportunity to be a hero.

Now, on Shoe Tail's back, he found himself galloping at Barney's side through the night toward Washington. He was the only sailing master to be mounted, and his horse was sure-footed. When the British were defeated, he'd go again to Sugar Valley. He'd deliver Shoe Tail home with rosettes in his mane and tell the Biays family of his adventures. That stormy-eyed girl would listen to his stories. He thought again of Rachel and her dark beauty and how she threw herself against him and seemed so desperate for his safety.

She confounded him, that girl; no, that young woman, being a world different from the bar girls in the Baltimore taverns, those saucy gals who laughed too loudly and showed their elbows and were ever ready to down a tankard before bedding. To be certain, he'd known some hours of true pleasure with those girls. He'd liked them well enough, but excepting the red-haired one in Newport, there was not a single one among them who had stayed long in his mind.

☆ ☆ ☆

Night

Torches cut the darkness above the wooden gates of the Navy Yard. To reach the gates, one crossed the river, and that barrier of water would make the difference. This eastern branch of the Potomac was the barrier the British army must cross to reach the capital city and the Yard. Therefore, the decision to regroup the American defensive force on the western side of the river was not without merit. As Shoe Tail clattered across the bridge, Webster admitted to the wisdom of this "retreat."

The commodore and his officers drew up their horses and waited for the last of the seamen to enter the open gates and stream down the parade ground. On either side of the open field were wooden barracks, their windows flickering with candles. A small stone house appeared to be a command center, noted Webster, judging by the press of militia officers on the front porch. Close on the river he could see the sheds for carpenters, rope-makers and bricklayers. And beyond were visible the shadows of towering masts, as several vessels appeared to be anchored at the dock in various stages of construction and repair.

The flotilla men stumbled wearily down the parade ground, the cannons rolling with them. Barney rose in his stirrups and called out, "Rum and grub in the marine barracks, my tars. Bunk wherever you can find yourself a resting place."

Barney looked over his shoulder at Webster. "This may prove a hard night if the British troops are truly on our heels. You, Jack, rest while you can."

"I await your orders, sir," Webster replied.

"My orders will depend on the blowing of the wind."

Joshua Barney didn't have to explain to Jack Webster that he was now without authority, in a line of command that he must follow. One of Sam Miller's marines rushed up to breathlessly inform Barney he was invited to sleep in the quarters of Commodore Tingey, commandant of the Navy Yard. The invitation didn't surprise Webster. He watched Barney canter off toward a large house at the top of the Yard, and then he trotted Shoe Tail toward the stable. He asked the stable boy to give the chestnut extra hay and a pail of cool well water. Before he left the stable, he kissed the horse's velvety nose and slid his hand down Shoe Tail's neck in an affectionate stroke.

A pot of coffee, hot, and with sugar, was waiting in the marine barracks. He drank three cups and stoked his hunger with chunks of cold ham, some bread, and quince jelly. And then he looked about with some unease, uncertain what he should do or where he should go.

There weren't enough bunks for all the men crowded into the low building. The flotilla men were mostly bedding down on the wooden floor. He heard one of the Baltimore militia, a young fellow with a shiny hat and red cheeks, sounding off hotly to Jesse Stewart about the British, "Slimy bastards! I heard it told on the Eastern Shore, they like to gut and roast American babies!"

Tom Warner seemed deep in a game of dice with four marines. He waved the beaker in Jack Webster's direction. Webster considered joining in the game, but he was restless, too restless for dice.

With his linen bag slung over his shoulder, he went out into the dark Yard and walked past the campfires of the militiamen along the riverbank. He could see the white bodies of men in the water. He took off his boots and dusty trousers, placed his shirt and his blue jacket neatly on top of them, and slid into the river.

For more than an hour, he lolled about, floating on his back, thinking some about Rachel Biays, remembering how she'd pressed against him. He'd felt the heat of her breasts through her thin summer dress. He wondered how it would be to have a woman pressed against him in the water, how good it might be to stand and face a woman in the water.

☆ ☆ ☆

When he'd dried himself with his linen shirt and slicked down his hair, he walked back to the barracks. The wooden building had cooled some and was not as noisy as before. Most of the men were sleeping now or playing cards.

John Kiddall was slouched in a cane chair near the open door, with some of the younger flotilla men around him. One of the lads had a mouth harp and was accompanying Kiddall in an old favorite ballad. Kiddall sang in a soft voice as if telling a bedtime story: "*There was a silk merchant, in London, he did dwell. He had only one daughter...*"

In the near darkness, Webster all but stumbled over the flotilla gunners and oarsmen stretched out on the plank floor. Sailing Master Jesse Huffington was sleeping among them. His round head rested on his folded coat, and his dirty boots were still on his feet.

☆ ☆ ☆

"Jack...over here." Warner motioned from beside the open door. "I've a bottle of rum, won it off some marines. Let's head outdoors and finish it off."

In a matter of minutes, the two young officers had spread a blanket on a patch of grass just beyond the barrack's porch.

Warner sang out to his friend in the darkness surrounding them: "*The young lady she was courted by men of high degree. There was none but Jack the sailor would ever do for she...*"

The rum was sweet in Jack Webster's throat. He stared up at the stars, and it came into his mind to ask his mate a question, "I'm thinking, you ever been in love, Tom?"

"'Bout a hundred times," answered Warner with a laugh.

"Not just wooing and bedding. I mean, you think you'll ever settle down...maybe when the fighting's done...and get married?"

"Too restless, mate."

"Yeah, and too ugly, I'd say."

"I ain't half as ugly as you. I wager I've had more gals sighing for my kisses than you can even dream of."

That might be true, Jack thought. Tom had a kind of laughter in his face that women were drawn to. He'd seen Tom Warner with the girls in the taverns in Baltimore, and been jealous. Still, he retorted, "What sweet-smelling gal is gonna want the likes of you, is what I'm asking."

"I don't care about the sweet-smelling part. Me, I like 'em to have handy curves and be willing, you know what I mean."

Jack yawned, which gave him time to consider that remark. Rachel Baiys was not the kind of girl Tom would call "willing." He sighed in his confusion and then remembered the bag of foodstuff Madam Biays had fixed for him at Sugar Valley yesterday. A hunk of pound cake remained. He opened the linen bag and, with his knife, sliced the cake in half. "What if she's a high-spirited one, got a mind of her own?"

"You ain't thinking to get married, are you, Jackaroe?"

"No...hell, no! I'm asking about you."

"Mebbe one day, but not yet. Like I say, I'm restless." Tom threw his head back for a last swallow of rum. "Remember us on the *Rossie*...that little clipper running before the wind, her sails set, and the spray flying, and the pennants whipping out ahead. You remember those days?"

For a long moment, there was a peaceful silence between them. Then Warner continued. "I ain't much for land fighting, Jack. I'm not a man for facing a line of soldiers across a field with their damn muskets at the ready. And me with no way to draw canvas or skim or glide or close on the bastards."

What was it about the sea that held a man's heart so, Jack wondered. He felt so damned alive on the water…the fine order of ship's life, the danger, the beauty. It hurt even to think about it.

"Damn shame having to scuttle the barges…"

"You drinking all that bottle?"

Tom Warner made a few pig noises and handed over the rum. "God, I'd rather drown at sea than fall in a briar patch or die in my bed like an old man what's given up living. What about you, mate? You scared of facing those redcoats tomorrow?"

The stars were whirling over his head. Jack could hear the high thin sound of the mouth harp and Kiddall singing: "*Poor Jack has gone to sea with troubles on his mind. A'leaving of his country and darling girl behind.*"

"Can't tell if I'm scared or not."

"*The war being over, she hunted all around…among the dead and wounded, her darlin' boy she found.*"

He closed his eyes and thought how clean and content he felt after his dip in the river. His belly was full of cake and rum. And, there was Rachel, a shadow in the back of his mind like a question to be answered. Tomorrow there might well be a battle. There was nothing to fear, he told himself. If there was a battle, he'd be on Shoe Tail's back, fighting the British alongside the commodore, who'd be swinging his red-tasseled saber.

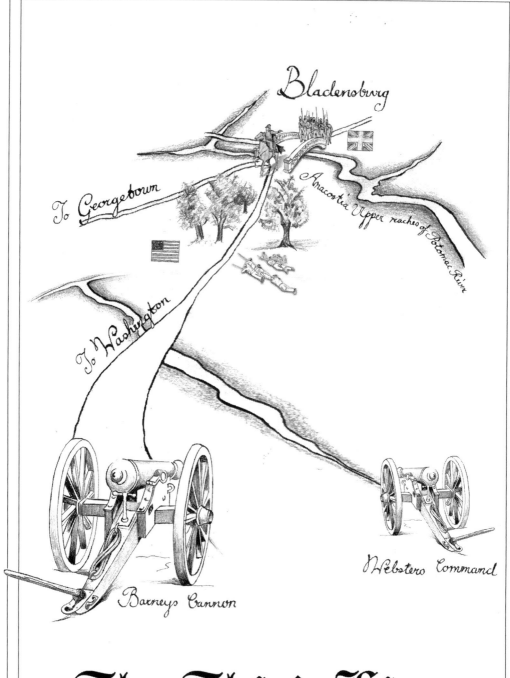

Bladensburg

To Georgetown

Anacostia Upper reaches of Potomac River

To Washington

Barneys Cannon

Websters Command

The Third Line

CHAPTER THREE

THE THIRD LINE

Early morning, August 24

The day dawned sunny and clear. The unlikely American army of militiamen, marines, farmers and flotilla men waited on the grassy slope of the Navy Yard, although for what purpose, they knew not.

"I hear tell them r-redcoats got bayonets a yard l-long," claimed Topps. The boy was homesick and sorely missing his fishing boat and his girlfriend, whose name was Julie Riley. He'd carved her name on the dirk stuck now in his belt. He stared down at his bare feet, blackened with tar from his months on the flotilla.

No one offered a rebuttal.

"I swan…" Jason murmured finally, scratched a mosquito bite on his ankle, and squinted into the sun.

The hours passed. At midmorning, four militiamen clattered into the Yard, reined in before the brick house, slid from their saddles, and raced up the steps. Before any man or boy could make sense of this, someone shouted, "The president! Here he comes!"

James Madison and War Secretary John Armstrong were cantering down the drill field. Madison's face was set, unreadable. Respectfully, men and boys stumbled aside to offer a clear path and watched as the two men dismounted and climbed the wooden steps of the little brick house. The flotilla men crowded in behind a company of Baltimore militia at the foot of the steps.

Jason heard Captain Sellers mutter, "The war secretary claims them redcoats are marching on Annapolis. Some say it's to be Bal'amore. Me, I say Washington."

Jason could barely breathe in the press of knees and bellies. He ducked under Captain Sellers's arm and climbed onto a nearby rock, where he could see what was happening. Captain Sellers claimed a stubble of reddish beard. His blue jacket was wrinkled, hanging by a finger over his shoulder. Captain Webster's brown hair was clubbed at the back of his neck, showing neat beneath his cocked hat. It was curious and pleasing to the boy to see how fine Captain Webster carried himself, with his head held so straight and his shoulders back, like he was certain of how things should be.

Jason himself was not certain of anything, except the commodore had gone off somewhere and there was more waiting to do. One good thing was that Barney's crew was all together now on land. Jason knew he had a fair chance to find the white man that he'd been looking for in secret.

He told himself he'd knife the murdering bastard straight in the chest and watch the blood run down his belly. Jake Simpson was the man's rightful name. Jason heard he was mostly called Sharkey, 'cause of the tattoo of a shark on his shoulder. He'd heard tell in Bal'imore that Jake Simpson was signed onto the Chesapeake Flotilla. So he'd slipped away from his momma's house, and he'd signed on as well.

Only it weren't so easy to find this man called Sharkey.

Even now, when the boy looked out at all the flotilla crewmen who were crowded in behind the sailing masters, he could hardly tell one white seaman from another. Beneath the round brims of their black glazed hats, their noses were all burnt red by the sun, and their side whiskers looked the color of squirrel's tails. The boy drew in upon himself, gave up looking, and squatted on the rock.

"Steady, men," Captain Webster called out. "Wait for the commodore."

The door of the brick house banged open, and the president walked out on the porch, followed by Secretary Armstrong and the four militiamen. Madison was the smallest man of the six, and he stood to the side as a militiaman waved his arms to quiet the restless crowd. The man's voice was high-pitched, and his words were indistinct to the flotilla men.

The Baltimore militia unit, having surged close up at the foot of the steps, could hear the men on the porch clearly. They responded with shouts and began to race across the ragged grass toward their regiment colors.

One of the older men shouted back to the seamen, "The redcoats are said to be marching on Bladensburg! It's the God's truth! The militia's been ordered to move out...Lavel's cavalry and Scott's regulars. And Scull's riflemen. Only they ain't got no rifles. We're all going, just the same."

Angry shouts rose among the flotilla men. "What about us? What about Barney's boys?"

Dan Frazier shrugged his big shoulders. "Seems like the president is wanting us to stay behind. The war secretary says we're to blow the Navy Yard bridge after the militia has passed."

The flotilla men were offering hoots and whistles as they watched the farmers heading for their wagons and the militiamen and Sam Miller's marines grabbing up their muskets, buttoning their jackets, and marching smartly toward the Navy Yard gate.

☆ ☆ ☆

"He's here, the commodore!" Webster shouted, with relief in his voice.

Joshua Barney swung from the stirrup and took the steps of the brick house two at a time. The set of his shoulders and the heat in his face were evidence of his anger as he saluted the president and pivoted to face Armstrong. "What kind of fool decision is this, Mr. Secretary? Stay behind to guard a bridge? Like hell, I say to you, sir. I've got the only men in this damn Navy Yard who know how to fight."

"Just hear him now," Dan Frazier whispered to Jesse Stewart. The young coxswain from barge 112 was fingering some little shark's teeth hanging on a leather strap around his neck. He was frowning, as if uncertain of what was happening on the porch.

Barney turned to Madison and said in a loud voice, "Goddamn it, Mr. President, a corporal and five men can blow a bridge. We mean to fight. So let us fight!"

The flotilla men stamped their feet to show their readiness to march.

The president smiled his rare smile. His eyes watered as if he was moved by their vigor. He moved to the edge of the porch and called out, "On to Bladensburg, seamen! Follow your commodore, I say."

"We'll show the militiamen how to fight a war!" Barney pulled his sword from its sheath and held it high above his head. He roared, "Hell, we'll fight it for them!"

✵ ✵ ✵

In less than a quarter hour the Chesapeake Flotilla's crew—close on to five hundred men and boys—had gathered up their pikes and rucksacks. If it weren't for the damnable ships' cannons, each weighing more than a ton, they could easily catch up with the militia units. "Even pass 'em by," Jesse Stewart muttered to Frazier as they looped the thick ropes over their shoulders. When Soames came rattling up with his wagon, the foodstuffs were thrown out, and all kinds of shot and packets of powder were loaded in their place.

The drummer boy was plopped unceremoniously in the back of the cook's wagon. "I want a musket," Caleb cried out, his cheeks scarlet with excitement. "I want to kill me some redcoats!"

Standing in the back of a wagon, Mingo Jones was handing out weapons supplied to the flotilla men by the marines. He frowned down at Jason. "Where's your musket?"

"Don't need no musket. I got this." Jason pointed to his knife.

"Fool boy, that blade won't do you no good." Mingo threw Jason a musket with bayonet attached. When stood on end, the weapon was longer than Jason was tall.

Mingo spit into the grass, jerked the musket away, and gave the boy a second musket that had lost its bayonet. "You stay close, boy. That's all I say. This ain't no fishing trip. You stay close."

Jason blinked at Mingo's words. He caught a pair of shoes the marine quartermaster was handing out. He'd never had a pair of shoes before. They were man-sized and agreeable to fitting either foot. Balancing on his musket, the boy slid a foot into one shoe and then into the other. There was no way a'tall he could run in them shoes. Sadly, he kicked off the shoes and left them in the grass.

The seamen rumbled the cannon carriages over the wooden bridge and onto the packed dirt of the Bladensburg Turnpike. Stay close, Mingo had said. Jason couldn't think why Mingo would say a thing like that, but the words filled him with happiness.

Captain Jack Webster trotted his big chestnut horse alongside the marching men. A red piece of twine had been woven into Shoe Tail's mane. Seeing this, Mingo snorted so loudly that Jason heard it.

✳ ✳ ✳

"Make way for the president," someone yelled.

The seamen stumbled to the sides of the road as President Madison cantered through their midst. He was a straight-backed man, and he sat easy in the saddle. He looked neither to the right nor to the left. His brown boots were polished to a shine, and he'd buckled a pair of large, unwieldy pistols around his waist.

"Dueling pistols!" Mingo grumbled. "Now, ain't that something?"

Jason was falling behind, but Mingo didn't look back or slow his pace. How far we got to go? It seemed to Jason he might just as well sit down on the side of the turnpike and rest himself awhile. And then Soames's wagon came rattling along behind a pair of long-eared mules.

"Jason, looky! I be up here!" The drummer boy was perched on the back of the wagon, his legs swinging free. Caleb held out a hand. "Catch on and get yourself a ride alongside me."

It took a boost from Dan Frazier and a pull-up from Caleb before Jason found himself in the back of the wagon, riding the wind like a gull. He smiled his shy smile.

"We're going to war," Caleb sang out. "Look here, I got me a musket. And mine's got a bayonet too. Better'n yours!"

✵ ✵ ✵

Late morning

"An infernal country," George Cockburn called this place, this empty, wooded land, this Chesapeake country.

General Robert Ross was inclined to agree. He twisted in his saddle to watch the columns of red-coated soldiers marching behind him. Sweat was rolling down his cheeks and stinging his eyes. Still, the British officer kept his face serene and his expression steady as he surveyed the troops. His men were struggling to keep their pace steady, despite the red dust rising beneath their boots and causing them to wipe their eyes continually with the sleeves of their scarlet jackets. Ross could hear them gagging and coughing as they marched.

Their destination was still uncertain—although Cockburn had marked Bladensburg on the upper reaches of the Potomac River as a possible confrontation point with the Americans. It would all depend upon where they met up with the enemy— militiamen, scouts, farmers with rifles. Ross was prepared to react on the spot.

✵ ✵ ✵

The marching army was now descending into a wooded glade, where at least his men would find shade. Ross found the shadowy landscape surprisingly agreeable. It came to the British general's mind that this was indeed a splendid bit of Chesapeake country, with its thickly tangled underbrush and vine-encircled trees— rather like passing down the nave of a cathedral that was arched not with stone but with towering trees that gave off the scent of pine incense. The forest ceiling allowed only faint streams of light to reach the marching men, as if through stained-glass windows.

In all his travels, he'd not sensed anything quite so primitive, and yet so spiritual. When he was home again in Ireland

and done with soldiering, perhaps he'd write an account of the America mission for his wife and children. More to the point, he considered, he might write a memoir. A record that would settle his own thoughts, as this second war with America still seemed to him vaguely indecent. The opponents were not French or Spanish, but English by blood, his kinsmen. God only knew the reason they stubbornly claimed this smoldering hot land as their chosen land.

These ideas played in Robert Ross' head as his army made its slow advance through the forest. Sometimes the path ahead all but disappeared, and the forward troops were forced to hack away the underbrush with their bayonets. In truth, Ross didn't object to the sluggish pace, as a great number of his infantrymen were sick and puking in the bushes. Confined to their ships for too many weeks, they now marched on rubbery legs.

It touched his heart. As ever, his troops were uncomplaining, even jocular, adjusting as best they could to this impossible countryside. The troops were divided into three brigades. Most dear to Ross, although he'd not quickly admit this, was the First Brigade—the Light Brigade, which consisted of the Eighty-fifth and the infantry companies of the Fourth, Twenty-first and Forty-fourth. Yet, to be damnably fair, the men of all three brigades were precious to him. He was proud to lead this army, as he believed that each man carried in his heart, like a talisman, a belief in duty and discipline and an allegiance to crown and colors.

Close behind the infantrymen, a number of seamen from the Royal Navy followed. They were pulling three small pieces of artillery: one six-pounder and two three-pounders. That's all the artillery Ross could call on. In contrast, there was no accounting of the potential American cannon power, that also being an unknown, and a concern.

Adding to his worries, he had no cavalry, only fifty mounted men. The Americans were well served for horses. This countryside appeared to hold no large towns, only rural villages and widespread farm sites. A mounted enemy brigade would prove to be a disaster, as his foot soldiers were perfect targets for American sharpshooters.

Ironically, there'd been not a single attempt at ambush. Perhaps Cockburn was correct in his insistence that the American force was ill-led and unprepared. Thus far, this venture inland was proving tolerable. So Robert Ross believed this morning in the shadowed forest.

✧ ✧ ✧

Then it all changed. Emerging from the forest, the British soldiers found themselves blinking and stumbling about on a wide dirt road in a blaze of August sunlight. The columns moved quickly in their familiar quickstep, three steps at a walk, then three steps at a run. But now they staggered, some falling out to the sides of the road from sunstroke and exhaustion. Ross swung down from the saddle and walked his horse for a mile or so to share the hardness of the march.

His soldiers wore full battle dress—tight knee boots and woolen uniforms buttoned to the chin. Moreover, each man carried eighty cartridges, his musket, and a canvas knapsack holding shirts, dress shoes, and stockings. Adding to the weight were provisions for three days and a wooden keg of water intended to last the day. Since they'd left the shade of the forest, he'd watched his men lift their canteens to ease their thirst. Most of the jugs were now empty.

On either side of the road, green and pink tasseled cornfields gave way to uncultivated meadows that seemed divided haphazardly into farmland ripe with tobacco and barley. Occasionally Ross noted a farmhouse or a small plantation, all notably empty. The local inhabitants had fled, and there appeared to be no danger to his marching army. They'd come some fifteen miles since daybreak and had yet to meet a single challenge.

Rising ground appeared ahead. From the top of the incline, he could see the road descended at a gradual pace to become the main street of a village.

Obviously this was the town of Bladensburg spoken of by Cockburn. He could see no evidence of the American militia. Were they a phantom army? Did they, indeed, exist? The thought made him smile.

A brownish river lay on the far side of the town. Ross caught the glimmer of a white bridge at the end of the main street. On the far side of the river, an open meadow rose in a gradual slope toward a tree-covered crest. The turnpike—he knew it from his map—this was the Bladensburg–Washington turnpike.

An aide ran alongside Ross' horse. "See there, across the river, sir. I think it might be our own seamen have got ahead of us."

"Not hardly," the general answered shortly. The young man was delirious with sunstroke. "Pull yourself together, lad," Ross said and trained his spyglass on the far hillside meadow, for he'd caught a flash of yellow.

It appeared to be an American militia unit's flag. Figures wearing yellow jackets appeared clustered around the ensign. Ross moved his glass and glimpsed other unit clusters, men in colorful uniforms, and some in street clothes holding muskets. The Americans were spread out everywhere on either side of the pike that ran directly up the sloping meadow. He suspected they numbered at least five thousand men.

In his veins, Ross felt the rush of blood that comes to a warrior when the enemy is within his sights. True, they seemed to outnumber his army, and they held the rising ground.

Wellington had taught Robert Ross to refrain from going into battle until prodded by a decisive affront, but he wasn't dissuaded from a direct attack. He smiled just slightly. He'd brought his men to the place for a battle. And they would have it.

✶ ✶ ✶

"Almost noon," Barney grumbled to Jack Webster, who was cantering at his side along the turnpike toward Bladensburg. "Ride ahead. Be my lookout, Jack, as surely as if you've gone up the mast pole. God knows when my barefoot boys will catch up with the militia."

"It's an honor to have your confidence." Webster shortened his reins. "I'll not fail you, sir." He leaned over Shoe Tail's red-laced mane and kneed the horse into a gallop. Although he was breathing hard when they reach the top of a ridge some eight miles from the Navy Yard, the horse had hardly broken his stride.

✧ ✧ ✧

The shade beneath the trees on the ridge was welcome. Webster pulled off his hat and wiped the sweat from his brow. He could see the Pike ran down the meadow toward a thin brown river, trailing ahead into the hazy distance to the north.

More importantly, the American militia units were spread out, as if with great confidence the meadow on both sides of the turnpike, their unit flags staked in the ragged grass and dirt as if in preparation for a battle, but why here?

Why was Winder's army settling in with no enemy about? He cupped his eyes and studied the town on the far side of the river. He could see clear the red-brick chimneys and sloping rooftops. The little village appeared entirely quiet. No clatter of wagon wheels came to him. Nor clink of weapons, no trumpets or bag-pipes or horsemen. Nor a single wisp of smoke.

Webster urged Shoe Tail across a small unpainted bridge that spanned a ravine dividing the top of the hill from the meadow. On the far side of that shallow crevice, the pike widened as it descended the meadow and disappeared into an apple orchard. He gave a hard nudge to Shoe Tail.

It was his pleasure and his duty to do as Barney ordered. He'd ride into the meadow and look about. He'd make his way to the apple orchard. He would climb the mast, so to speak. When the commodore and the crew of the Chesapeake Flotilla reached this place, he'd be ready to give an account of all he'd discovered there.

✧ ✧ ✧

Horse and rider descended slowly into the meadow.

In a stubble field on the far left, a mounted militia unit had found its position. The Maryland Cavalry officers sat easy in their saddles. They were, Webster noted, joking and laughing among themselves as if waiting for a horn blast—so they could follow a pack of hounds across the countryside. The cavalry horses were glossy, festooned with blue ribbons. Their riders—he believed them to be some three hundred in number—wore light blue dress coats laced with gold. Despite the heat of this day, most had on their leather helmets, the visors trimmed with fur.

Webster glanced down at his own white trousers, wrinkled and marked by grass stains. A brown streak of turnpike dirt ran from his right knee to his boot. He was an officer, a man of the sea—a man of the stars, as Barney liked to put it—still he felt some envy for the dash and splendor of the cavalry unit. Several of the officers were swinging their long, curved sabers about, as if preparing for a joust. They were admirable fellows, he thought. He'd heard this regiment had been among the first to answer General Winder's proclamation, sent out to Maryland, Virginia, and Pennsylvania, calling the state militias to rally in defense of Washington.

Just ahead two men in waistcoats were lounging on the ground eating ham and bread, with a jug in the grass beside them. The militia troops mostly looked to be a band of shopkeepers and teachers, all sorts of soft-palmed fellows, Webster thought. He noted a few older men lying about on the ground, as if today's run from Washington had exhausted them and they'd lost interest in the whole affair.

It was only when he'd reached the bottom of the meadow and cantered through the apple orchard that he found evidence of any true readiness for battle. A sod-and-wood barricade had been constructed some yards back from the river. Some of the Baltimore boys and Pinckney's riflemen were crouching in the bushes. With their rifles in their hands, they were staring hard at the white wooden bridge that led across the river to Bladensburg.

What if the British appeared on that open bridge? Did the riflemen intend to shoot the enemy soldiers one by one as they crossed over? He knew what Barney would say as surely as if the commodore were beside him. The commodore would say, "Why in hell not chop down the damn bridge?"

✵ ✵ ✵

"Make way," a militiaman shouted down the meadow as two riders passed down the turnpike and entered the apple orchard. "The president is in the field. Make way!"

James Madison was the second rider. Aware that he was twenty feet behind his attorney general, the president grimaced just slightly. Mr. Rush was thundering ahead.

Perhaps he views himself as my advance guard, Madison considered with some amusement. Of all his cabinet officers, the thirty-three-year-old lawyer was his favorite.

"See here, sir," Richard Rush shouted back to Madison. "Pinckney's battalion is our first line of defense." He was pointing toward the men in the bushes and the riflemen clustered behind the barricade, where the muzzles of four small cannons were thrust through holes scooped out in the sod. The cannons were aimed directly at the bridge leading across the river.

Was the scout's report really true, an army of British soldiers was now entering Bladensburg from the east? Madison shuddered just slightly, aware he was moving out into the open. In the shadow of willow trees on the near bank of the river, he glimpsed a few more cannons and militiamen. Their presence reassured him, although he'd not seen troops stationed in the apple orchard. The little forest of twisted-limbed trees would offer the ideal cover to ambush an advancing army. Had General Winder not thought of it?

Rush cantered up to offer an explanation. Two militia regiments were originally positioned in the orchard by Winder. But Madison's secretary of state, Colonel James Monroe, had removed them.

"Monroe has gone about moving militia regiments like chess pieces."

The attorney general offered this information in his soft-toned voice. He flicked the edge of his wide-brimmed hat in a gesture of disdain that revealed more than his words. "I expect we shall sort it all out before the battle begins," he said, consoling Madison. "If indeed there's to be a battle. I seriously doubt that enemy troops are even in the area, sir. You recall Winder's panic at Battalion Old Field. It's said he sees redcoats at every turn, even in his dreams, I suspect."

The president thought it unwise to comment. The chain of military command appeared to him both fragile and incomprehensible. He trotted a few feet forward and stared across the river. He could see directly into the upper windows of two Bladensburg houses that stood close to the river. White curtains hung limp in the breathless air, and he sensed no movement within the rooms.

"I say, let's cross over and take a look around the town. Are you agreeable, sir?" Rush brushed a fly from his face and waited for the president's answer.

Madison squinted again at the ninety-foot-long bridge. It seemed to him rash and unnecessary to trot out there. Still, there was a certain value in a leader exhibiting courage before the troops. He couldn't falter here. And he'd have Rush at his side, broad-shouldered Richard Rush, the father of small children. Surely he'd not risk an ambush.

Madison nodded and urged his mount forward. The water beneath the low railing of the bridge was the shade of brewed tea and reminded the Virginia-born president of the Shenandoah River near his boyhood home. The image calmed him. He touched the bulky dueling pistol at his right side and kneed his horse so that he was slightly ahead of Rush when they neared the middle of the bridge.

"Mr. Madison! Go back…go back now! The enemy holds Bladensburg."

A militia scout spurred toward them from the opposite bank.

Madison struggled to turn his horse. Rush seemed more startled than Madison, and bent to catch his flying straw hat before turning his horse. Someone yelled from the sod-and-wood barricade. There was a flash of scarlet on the far side of the bridge, and now the gleam of sun on musket barrels—the call of bagpipes, scalding and fierce. The soldiers of the British Light Brigade were entering the far side of the bridge.

As the president and his attorney general raced for safety, Pinckney's riflemen let loose with a volley of gunfire. Three enemy soldiers stumbled and went down at mid-bridge. Several soldiers tumbled over the side railings and fell into the river. The advance did not falter.

And still they came on. Four abreast, the scarlet-coated soldiers marched onto the white planking. They didn't falter or break step, even at a second volley of musket fire.

Madison was still breathing hard as he watched the British advance from the safety of the barricade. He marveled at the disciplined men approaching across the wooden bridge, their muskets pressed against their breasts. He heard the echo of the American cannons and the sharp crackle of the rifles, and he smelled the keen, raw scent of gunpowder. But it was the tramping of the soldiers' boots on the wooden bridge that filled his ears and caused his eyes to smart and his throat to burn.

☆ ☆ ☆

James Madison was not a military man. The battlefield was not his arena. With Rush at his side, he retreated to the shadows of the apple trees, where he discovered General Winder and Colonel Monroe conferring with the war secretary, whose lean face was moody and dark. The three men were on horseback, their mounts pawing the ground and tossing their heads in reaction to the gunfire. The president sensed there was no consensus here. Only shock and apprehension seemed to bind them.

The militiamen positioned close to the riverbank let loose once again with musket-fire, but it was a ragged volley. Madison sensed the confusion and knew he must offer some leadership. He had appointed General Winder to this command, and Winder was urging Madison to quit the field and retire to the safety of the ridge at the top of the meadow.

"Come, General Armstrong," the president called out sharply. "Come, Colonel Monroe. Let us go and leave the battle to the commanding general."

☆ ☆ ☆

The president's party raced through the orchard and up the turnpike, galloping past clumps of men in waistcoats and farmers in black coats crouched behind barricades made from boards torn from their wagons. The riders took the most comfort from the sight of so many uniformed soldiers, so many militia units whose flags dotted the meadow.

Rush shouted to Madison to note the regiments of Colonel Schutz and Colonel Regan. Once stationed in the orchard, those units were now here in the meadow, alongside Sterett's Fifth Regiment. "This is the second line of defense," Rush said of the men in the meadow.

One or two militiamen raised their hands in salute as they swept past, but for the most part, little note was taken of the commander in chief. All eyes were fastened on the white bridge, for a jumble of fallen British soldiers now blocked its midsection. Some appeared dead or dying, others only wounded. The fallen bodies were creating an obstacle for the second wave of enemy soldiers attempting to cross the bridge. They'd begun to stumble back upon themselves, their advance halted.

The Americans in the meadow cheered and shouted out curses. A farmer brandished his bullwhip and bellowed, "We got ye on the run now, an' we're coming after ye."

Madison halted his panting horse as he neared the ravine at the top of the meadow. He put his hand to his forehead and felt blood. A branch of an apple tree had slashed his face in the dash to escape. He stared down at the bridge where the piled-up bodies made a splash of scarlet against the pale browns and greens of the river and its bank. He could no longer hear the cry of bagpipes on the far side of the river, nor the guns on the near bank.

This moment of quiet was not comforting.

For a reason Madison can't immediately fathom, Pinckney's riflemen were not advancing toward the bridge, as might be expected. Even more disconcerting, the American militiamen appeared to be retreating from their position behind the sod barricade. Some Baltimore boys were disappearing into the orchard. Others were skirting the apple trees and running toward a dirt road in the far distance.

He understood the reason for the American retreat. Above the white bridge, only a few yards upstream, a line of scarlet-coated soldiers were wading across the river like an army of red ants.

Rush moaned, "They've found the shallows."

James Madison turned away. His eyes followed the turnpike up to the tree-lined ridge. He cried out with sudden joy. "Thank God! It's the commodore and his seamen."

In the glitter of the noon sun, the president could see—as if it were a mirage—the crew of the Chesapeake Flotilla: barefoot seamen with mules and armory wagons and their five ships' cannons. At this very moment, they were cresting the top of the hill.

✵ ✵ ✵

Jack Webster had also caught sight of the commodore. Barney was standing beside his horse in the middle of the turnpike just below the top of the ridge.

Spurring up the sloping hill, Webster raced Shoe Tail across the rickety little bridge over the ravine and flung himself off the horse's back.

"The enemy holds Bladensburg, sir," he choked out, pointing his riding whip toward the town on the far side of the river. "I hear they've thousands of troops ready to cross over. General Ross and Admiral Cockburn are in command. Already their battalions are—" Jack struggled to catch his breath and directed Barney's gaze down to the white bridge. "It's Ross, for certain. Look just there; he's crossing over."

The British major general, recognizable by his majestic hat and crimson cape, could be clearly identified, for he was trotting at the head of the second battalion of the Light Brigade as they crossed the white bridge. The British soldiers were trampling over their own dead and dying. As they reached the near bank, the soldiers threw down their haversacks. With quick precision, they loaded and began firing their muskets at the few American militiamen still lingering in the high grass along the riverbank. Already, red-coated figures were following the Americans into the apple orchard.

"Pinckney's battalion, the riflemen. They've run away, the cowards," Webster exclaimed in a tremulous voice. "The first line has fallen. What if…"

"What if the second line falters, Mr. Webster?" Barney was staring down at the militiamen, who were forming a wavy line across the wide meadow. "Sterrett's men and the Baltimore Fifth haven't yet tasted war. They seem steady enough at the moment, but when blood flows, and smoke is thick in their faces, and rockets soar above their heads, they may panic. If the second line breaks, has Winder ordered a regrouping here on the ridge?"

Webster frowned, for he doubted the militiamen had considered panic. For the most part, they were firing and kneeling to reload and rising to fire again at the enemy troops who were attempting to advance up the meadow. He said briskly, "At any rate, sir, we are solid on this ridge. Major Peter of Georgetown commands a regiment of field artillery in that bank of trees to the far left. Off the turnpike, Scott's regulars are there to the left as well." Webster indicated the wooded hillside on the far side of the turnpike. "Colonel Miller's marines hold that rocky outpost to the right. Their position overlooks the bend of the river. Hood's and Beall's units are just arrived from Annapolis, seven hundred men between them. They've dug in below the marines, just above the ravine. Aye, sir, this is the third line and will hold in the event that—"

The commodore was already turning to shout to his officers, who were just now making their way down from the hilltop. "Mr. Warner, Mr Sellers, Mr. Kiddall, I'll have both eighteen-pounders positioned here on the turnpike, facing the bridge over the ravine."

Tom Warner was half-running, half-skidding down the hill toward them. He called back to the seamen pouring over the top of the ridge, "Gunners, bring down the eighteen-pounders. Now!"

When he reached Webster's side, he gave Shoe Tail a swat on his flank and muttered under his breath, "My boots are giving me fits. I'd have given a gold piece for a horse back yonder. How come you're such a lucky dog as to have Shoe Tail?"

✯ ✯ ✯

"Be this the place for it...a battle, for sure?"

Jesse Huffington, carrying his hat with its bedraggled feather under his arm, stumbled as he approached the officers gathered around the commodore. Catching sight of the redcoated soldiers darting in and out among the apple trees, he said in a voice touched with wonder, "I swan, look at them little fellers yonder, like bees in the orchard."

"A swarm of bees with killer stingers," Webster scoffed. "You don't want one of them aiming at your backside, Jesse."

Huffington shook his head. "Them redcoats ain't gonna get this far. No, sirree, they'll be horsemeat afore they make it up the meadow. All we got to do is sit tight on this hilltop and watch our militia boys mow 'em down. Thas' what I'm thinking."

A wave of disdain rose in Webster's chest. He turned away from the man's shiny face and yellowing teeth and muttered between clenched teeth to Jim Sellers, "The commodore desires this third line to be a stone wall. And we'll have it so, by God."

※ ※ ※

Joshua Barney was always definite—sometimes reckless, but always definite. It was a trait Webster had come to know and admire. Barney was pacing about on the turnpike, issuing orders. "The barge gunners will command the ships' cannons just as they did on water. The rest of my tars will act as infantry-men, as warriors. Not a single enemy soldier must come above the ravine. By God, we will hold this ridge, and we'll fight with our knives and pikes and with cutlasses, if necessary."

"Warriors...pikes and cutlasses," Warner repeated under his breath.

"Here, direct above the ravine. The eighteen-pounder must command the turnpike. Mr. Kiddall and Mr. Sellers will captain the cannon to my left." Barney indicated a clearing in the woods. "Restrain the guns with ropes and chains in the trees. Round up your crew."

Then Barney whirled to face Webster. "You, sir, will hold the battery on my right with the twelve-pounder and the crew from barge 112." He frowned as he studied the sparse trees and the outcroppings to the right of the turnpike. "A wide expanse to cover, Mr. Webster. You'll need more men. Mr. Huffington and his crew will stand with you. That will give you at least a hundred seamen. I trust you can hold the starboard against all comers."

Webster fought down a need to cough. Stepping closer to Barney, he said in a low voice, "Not Huffington, sir. If it's all the same to you, I'd choose to have Tom Warner and his crew with me."

"What the hell, Jack?" Barney frowned. "But if you wish it. Mr. Warner and his seamen will be at your side."

"Thank you, sir."

✳ ✳ ✳

The commodore was distracted, staring through his spyglass down at the white bridge. He said soberly, "Ah, he comes. It's the devil himself."

Webster looked down on the tiny figures now crossing the white bridge. He could see a British naval officer on a white charger at the head of a party of rocket-men. So that was Admiral George Cockburn.

Even as he watched, the rocket-men had reached the near side of the bridge and were making their way through the apple orchard. As they knelt to set up their launchers, Admiral Cockburn spurred up to the edge of the meadow. He was cantering back and forth as if taunting the American militia.

"My God!" Tom Warner let out a gasp. A musket ball, shot from the meadow, struck the admiral's horse and took off Cockburn's stirrup. The British naval officer tumbled from his saddle.

Huffington, standing behind Webster, cried out, "Overboard with ye!"

But the triumph was too soon. The admiral was climbing to his feet, apparently unhurt. As they watched, Cockburn raised his arm and brought it down hard. A round of Congreve rockets soared into the sky. The spear-like rockets snaked across the sky above the meadow, and then their flaming cones exploded above the American line.

"Aye, he's a devil," Barney muttered with grudging admiration.

✳ ✳ ✳

Curses and screams filled the meadow as the rockets rained down bits of fire and burning iron. An American flag tossed angrily in the smoke and then disappeared. Barney whispered through gritted teeth, "Hold on now, I say. Stand your ground against those jackstraws. Don't put to the wind. You can do it, my boys."

But the line of militiamen had already begun to waver. Men cowered to the ground, and others threw down their muskets.

"Are they running from the field?" Webster was incredulous.

"They're scared, that's what," Tom Warner whispered.

Despite the smoke in the field below, General Winder could be glimpsed astride a big brown horse racing back and forth as he tried to rally the troops. But Winder's efforts were entirely useless. The militiamen were now scrambling into the gullies and racing for the tree line to the left of the meadow.

"Buttermilk soldiers," Barney muttered. "I never cared much for militia."

✵ ✵ ✵

The battle had lasted only a matter of minutes, but the tide had turned. The British regulars were now making a steady advance up the meadow, while the men and boys in the American second defensive line were disappearing...all of them, every one.

Thousands of men were melting away from the battlefield.

"My God, not the cavalry, too." Webster could hardly bear to watch. The handsome mounted unit he'd seen waiting in the stubble field with their swords at the ready were turning their horses' heads away, racing at full gallop toward the dirt road in the far distance that led to Washington and to Georgetown.

"Why the hell?" Tom Warner murmured.

Webster tightened his hand on Shoe Tail's bridle.

"Now, my good fellows, to your posts," Barney ordered in a sober voice. "The true enemy comes. The Eighty-Fifth Foot, the king's own. They fought with Wellington. They are disciplined soldiers, grounded in courage, and loyal to the death. They'll never retreat, not with Ross as their commanding officer."

✵ ✵ ✵

In the clearing to the right of Barney's cannons on the turn-pike, Webster tethered Shoe Tail to a low branch and studied the terrain, looking for a clearing in which to station his twelve-pounder. He had to move quickly. On the far side, the smoke was thick, but already he caught shadows and glimpses of figures as enemy soldiers approached the top of the meadow.

Jack could see the tall black shakos and the scarlet coats of enemy soldiers in the bushes on the far side of the ravine. The British soldiers had their muskets at the ready. The guns were the familiar "Brown Bess" muskets. However, these gun stocks were stained vermillion, exotic in Webster's eyes. British sharp-shooters were firing across the ravine. With every spray of grape-shot in the leaves around his head, he felt a shock go through his body that was half alarm and half exhilaration.

"I'm a sailing master, Jack," Warner muttered as he and Webster crouched behind an outcropping of rocks. "I swear I never thought to see us on land, fighting behind trees and rocks like this."

"Not to worry, mate. For sure, we'll save the day." Webster had caught sight of a crew of flotilla men pushing and pulling the twelve-pounder down from the ridge.

These were his men, all from the crew of barge 112. Mostly young men. He knew their faces, sea-roughened, white and some brown or black. He knew the shape of their shoulders. He knew who was best with the oars, and who was steady on the guns. A bunch of scalawags, for sure!

Still, it filled Jack Webster's heart to see them crashing through the underbrush from the ridge.

He stepped into the open to meet them—already thinking where to place the crew for utmost safety, and more importantly, how to position the twelve-pounder. He was the senior officer in this battery, but he knew he would depend on Tom Warner to serve as gun captain. He himself had never commanded a gun crew, having always handled the duties of navigation and the overseeing of the oarsmen and the sails.

✧ ✧ ✧

A shadow fell. Webster whirled to find Mingo Jones standing behind him with his ropy shoulders, his arms shiny with sweat. "I need to tell ye, Capt'n, them redcoats is spread out. They slipping and sliding their way down into the ravine and rising up in all kinds of places. It don't matter where you aim that there cannon."

"How do you know this?" Webster challenged Mingo.

"Me and the boy was up on the ridge and looked down and seen 'em." He motioned toward Jason, who was trailing after him. "They is coming around the sides of the hill both ways. You'll see them soon enough. Like muskrats, they'll be sticking their heads up on this side of the ravine soon enough. Might as well hold fire with the twelve-pounder until they're on their feet and close enough to kill."

Webster was reluctant to give concession to this man who'd more than once proved his insolence. Still, he was struck by the certainty in Jones's voice. "You're saying we should save our powder and our shot until we see them on this side of the ravine?"

Mingo shrugged. "If you want 'em dead, you do."

Beyond the pine trees, Webster could see the commodore and Jesse Huffington and the gun crews for the eighteen-pounders. The big guns were facing toward the ravine bridge. Already the cannons' quoins had been withdrawn. Their muzzles were pointed upward, ready to receive the shot. He watched and heard the commodore cry out, "Run up," and saw the big guns rumble forward. The double roar of the American cannons shook the hillside and left a ringing in Webster's ears. He saw five British soldiers fall from the rickety bridge.

More enemy troops pushed on the narrow bridge behind the fallen soldiers. This was the Eighty-Fifth, men of experience and sheer courage. They'd never retreat—that's what the commodore said.

Webster bit his lip until he tasted blood. If Mingo Jones was right, the twelve-pounder must be shorted so that the balls would fall on this side of the ravine. "Set the mark for a hundred yards, no more," he called to Tom Warner, who was down on one knee in the center of the clearing with some of the crew, laying out the equipment for the cannon.

"Rammers, swabs, wad hooks. Where's the damn sponge?" Warner was shouting out questions even as the twelve-pounder rolled into the clearing. Aware that the gun couldn't be properly restrained, he ordered Andrews and Edwards—the faces of both young midshipmen were as red as fire—to dig away the pine needles and the soft dirt to make a trough for the gun to rest in. He shouted to one of the ship's gunners, "How many buckets we got? Where's the goddamn shot? Where's the gunner's boy?"

"Go, boy," Mingo growled at Jason, who was cowering behind Mingo like a small shadow. "See to one of these here buckets."

Mingo was carrying four buckets holding cast-iron balls packed tightly in canvas bags. Jason reached for one of the buckets. He strained at its weight and stumbled toward the clearing where he could see Mr. Warner and the twelve-pounder. This fighting on land was all a wonder to him.

It struck the boy that men's voices sounded different when they were on land rather than on the water. He could see pine trees swaying above his head, and men kneeling behind rocks. He could see the commodore smack in the middle of the turnpike and the two big cannons that looked like giant turtles with their necks stuck out.

A fallen log blocked Jason's way. He set down the bucket and leaned down to pull a burr out of his toe. He looked back, but Mingo Jones was no longer there.

"Give me that bucket, boy." Webster pushed the boy out of the way, grabbed the leather bucket, and jumped over the log.

Moving cautiously through the pine trees, he caught a flash of scarlet—too close, on the near side of the ravine. Mingo Jones was right. Already some British soldiers had made their way across the ravine. It might be the same on the far side of the turnpike. Webster could hear the far-off clack of the muskets of the Georgetown militia in the woods to the left of Barney's battery. The American militia seemed to be firing sporadically, as men might shoot at deer or rabbit spotted in the underbrush.

Something fast and dark flew near his head. Webster ducked and closed his eyes instinctively; grapeshot. He could hear the British infantrymen making growling noises in their throats as they crept up the incline toward the clearing. They were moving slowly and carefully, but snarling as they came like a pack of dogs.

He was aware of a trembling in his shoulders, and he forced himself to straighten and breathe. The snarling and growling was how the enemy soldiers held to their courage when fear might have made them turn and run. He looked for cover, any kind of cover, and crashed behind a pine tree as one of the advancing soldiers raised his musket in Webster's direction.

Beneath the tree, an oarsman from 112 was doubled up in blood-soaked pine straw. Webster could see the oozing wound behind the man's ear, matted with hair and bits of scarf. He'd turned on his side and had his hands to his face, for the shot had passed through his skull and come out his cheek. Blood was running between his fingers and out of his mouth. He was moaning and thrashing about with his legs. Webster bent close, but he was helpless, stiff-fingered, and unable to do more than put a hand on the seaman's shoulder.

"Leave him to me." Petty Officer Dan Frazier was hovering over Webster and the fallen seaman. He was breathing hard. "I'll see to him best I can."

Webster took up his bucket and stumbled into the clearing. He dropped the bucket near the carriage of the twelve-pounder.

"Where you been, Jackaroe? We ain't got all day." Tom Warner grinned. He stroked the waist-high cannon's muzzle as if it were a horse's neck. "She's primed and ready for shot," he said and lifted one of the canvas bags of grapeshot—nine balls wired together and deadly from four hundred yards—from Webster's bucket and personally rammed the bag down the cannon's bore. In seconds a crew had gathered, and the canister of powder, already in place, was pierced through the torch hole and ready to flame.

"Let's have a go at it, fellows!" Webster shouted to his crew. "These dogs are almost on us."

☆ ☆ ☆

The cannons in the turnpike were wasting shots picking off the enemy soldiers on the narrow bridge. There were only two chain shots at hand, fourteen round shots, and a dozen canvas bags of grapeshot left for the two guns.

Barney muttered under his breath, "Where the devil is Soames with the supply wagon?" He turned to his gun crews. "Not yet. Hold fire."

It was damnable hard to only wait and watch, but Barney gave the order to fire down the turnpike only when half a dozen red-coated soldiers had crossed the bridge and were massed on the near side. When the smoke cleared, he could see that it was a fair shot, ten men down, at least.

Barney motioned Huffington to step aside so that he personally could command one of the big guns. The eighteen-pounder was loaded with a chain shot, two balls attached to an iron chain. The shot was fired and whirled like a buzz saw down the pike. Barney noted with satisfaction that he'd brought down a wall of rocks that one of the British soldiers had built on the near lip of the ravine to hide behind. When the smoke cleared, there was no sign of the red-coated solder.

"Hope the poor fellow got away," Barney muttered.

Standing nearby, Mingo Jones shifted his musket and rested his hand on the leather pouch of gunpowder packets hanging on his right side. He was not afraid of dying. He'd said to himself that if he were going to die this day, it would be here at Commodore Barney's side—and not under Sailing Master Webster's command. He stood now between the two turnpike guns and watched as the enemy soldiers came on—British infantrymen climbing the meadow, spreading out along the ravine and slipping and sliding into its depth.

Somehow General Winder had made his way to the ridge. Mingo heard him shouting out orders for Scott's Regulars to retreat and praising Peter's Georgetown volunteers for having put up a strong defense. And as if in response to Winder's words, Mingo heard a last defiant volley of grapeshot from the left side of the turnpike.

He turned his head and watched the Washington militiamen racing over the top of the ridge toward the road to Washington.

"What if Gen'rl Winder tells us to retreat?" Mingo asked Barney.

"Too much noise. Can't hear a blasted thing he might say."

☆ ☆ ☆

Barney was no longer at the breech end of the eighteen-pounder. He'd turned command of the cannon back to Captain Huffington and the gunners and used the cannon's carriage for a mounting post. The commodore was now astride his roan, his jacket unbuttoned, and face flushed and vibrant as it always was in battle.

"Give 'em a hot reception, lads," he called out to the flotilla men near enough to hear his voice.

Mingo watched all this with a certain detachment. A gunner was dead at his feet. With a sigh, Mingo threw down his musket. He picked up the man's rammer and stepped in to take the gunner's place. "Get yourself down, raccoon high," he called to the drummer boy who stood wide-eyed beside the cannon. "Little white scrap of nothin'," he muttered to himself.

But Caleb had thrown off his drum and its shoulder strap. He had his musket in his hand. He bit open his cartridge packet and primed his musket with quick fingers. Caleb steadied his arm and aimed in the direction of a British soldier who'd crept up to the gun carriages and was lunging toward Barney's roan. He fired. The soldier dodged and thrust the bayonet at the horse's breast, but Mingo whacked him hard with the rammer, and the man went down on the ground, his hat rolling under the gun carriage's wheels.

"To drums, lad. Where is your drum?" Barney shouted.

"I want to fight," the boy cried out.

"A battle roll. Drum, boy!" Barney ordered.

Reluctantly Caleb threw down the musket and reached for the drum. Tears stung his eyes. Still, when he found a strong beat, it carried Barney's message across the ridge and into the hearts of the flotilla men.

☆ ☆ ☆

At the sound of the drum roll from the commodore's battery, Jack Webster rose to his feet and cried out to the men under his command, "Board 'em!"

The flotilla men leaped from behind the boulders and pine trees and raced down the slope toward the ravine to meet the British. Few of the seamen had bayonets, but their knives were clenched in their teeth, and they were brandishing their cutlasses.

Jack Webster was in the very midst of the carnage. He was the only man on horseback, and he was everywhere. He bent from his saddle to sweep a soldier's musket from his hands with a slash of his sword. He heeled Shoe Tail between a British soldier and one of his own seamen engaged in a hand-to-hand struggle.

The bold advance by the flotilla men sent the soldiers of the British Eighty-Fifth Foot reeling back toward the ravine. The ground cleared except for the wounded and the dead. Webster felt a glory in himself that was like the very pulse of life. He'd escaped death. Nothing could harm him.

"Halt, you blasted devil." He spurred Shoe Tail toward a British soldier who was about to run Dan Frazier through with his bayonet. As if sensing Webster's intentions, Shoe Tail sent the soldier spinning into the brush with a blow from his hooves.

The moment of satisfaction was passing quickly. Webster could see the redcoats had used the ravine to their advantage. They'd spread out along its dry bottom in a pincer movement to encircle the hill. Having broken the Americans' left flank, the enemy soldiers were creeping across the top of the ridge and descending the hill from above.

In desperation, Sam Miller's marines used their handspikes to turn their cannons and shower the enemy soldiers with grape-shot and a hail of musket balls. But still they came on, with the green plumes standing high on their tall black hats and their white hands holding their muskets to their chests.

"We're out of shot. Where the bloody hell has Soames gone to?" Tom Warner called in frustration.

Webster shouted back, "He's run away, the bastard! He lashed the mules like all fury, and they're skittering up the turnpike!"

Tom Warner and his gunners had fired shot after shot from the twelve-pounder, and the recoil had been brutal. One of the gunners had a broken foot, and Warner was bleeding from his nose and ears. Despite this, his eyes were shining. He said to Webster, "Wish we had some horse turds to shoot at them fancy coats."

Their eyes met, and Warner offered Webster his engaging grin. There was a grim sort of humor in the moment, and they both felt it, a comradeship deep as blood, mates from the *Rossie* to the Chesapeake Flotilla to this bloody hillside.

From nowhere came the sickening thud of a musket ball. Warner's head snapped back. His arms flew out wide. He arched his back, shuddered, and fell beside the cannon.

"Oh God, no!" Webster rolled off Shoe Tail's back and slid on his belly toward the still body of his friend. The back of Warner's jacket was already dark with blood around the jagged tear made by the iron ball. As gently as possible, Jack Webster rolled over the heavy, limp body. What he saw brought him close to vomiting: his friend's open chest of bloody, oozing entrails and cracked white bones. A two-pound ball had entered Warner's back and ripped out through his ribs. Threads of gold braid and bits of blue wool were mixed in the dark lake of blood now pooling in the grass. Tom Warner's eyes were half-open as if he were staring at the sky.

Webster's throat closed. Gasping for air, half in disbelief and shock, Jack Webster closed Warner's set and staring eyes.

When he'd scrambled to his feet, he gazed about as if uncertain where to go or what to do. His crew, aided by the marines, was holding onto a piece of ground just above the ravine. But, it looked to be a losing fight, as the Americans appeared to be greatly outnumbered. Even as Webster watched, the marine commander, a scrappy fellow and fast on his feet, took a bayonet thrust to his shoulder and slumped to the ground.

Nothing seemed real. This was a dream that a man might watch and struggle to wake from, a damning kind of dream that froze the muscles and clogged the throat and held a man's legs and arms rock stiff with fear.

"What say you, sir?" The gunner's boy pulled at his sleeve.

Jason Hayes was holding Shoe Tail's reins. The boy's eyes were wide with fright. "I don't know where to go to, sir."

Webster shook himself and grabbed the reins from Jason's hand. He grasped Shoe Tail's stirrup and swung himself into the saddle. He looked toward the men fighting in the clearing above the ravine. He reached across his chest and drew his sword. Thinking of Tom Warner, he raised the hilt to his lips in a private gesture of salute.

"Capt'n Webster, where should I go? What should I do?"

Before he heeled Shoe Tail toward the fight, Webster leaned down toward the wide-eyed boy. "I tell you—I order you, run, Jason! There's bad trouble here. Run to the commodore."

✧ ✧ ✧

Jason pulled out his knife. He wasn't sure what he would do with it, but it felt right in his hand. As he scrambled through the underbrush, he could see the cannons in the pike were still firing, if raggedly, and redcoats were lying dead in the road ahead.

"What you doing here, boy?" Mingo Jones called to him in a rough voice from beside one of the eighteen pounders. "And where's that musket what I give you?"

Jason shook his head. He'd left the musket leaning against the tree when he put down the carrying bucket. It was no use saying that he didn't know how to shoot a musket. He stared up at Mingo, whose skin was shining like the black wing of a crow. The sky was whirling above and the noise of all this shooting hurt his ears something terrible.

"Stay close, boy," Mingo ordered. "Do what I say. Get behind that rock there. Hunker down."

But Jason was staring at the bodies lying around the cannons. One of the gunners was shot dead, gone down with the linstock in his hand. And the other was a white man who was lying on the ground with his head on a rock like he was sleeping, only his leg was bent back strange-like. It was Topps lying there. Topps was not supposed to be dead. The boy drew in a shocked breath. But when he looked around, he saw more terrible things.

How could it be that the commodore had lost his roan? The handsome horse had taken a musket ball directly in his shoulder. Barney was wounded as well. Jason's eyes went wide when he saw the blood soaking the commodore's thigh and white trouser leg. Barney was leaning against the cannon carriage, but he was still on his feet, sure enough.

"Behind the rock, move!" Mingo gave Jason a hard push that sent him sprawling behind a boulder on the side of the turnpike. The drummer boy was kneeling there, his eyes dark and tears smeared on his cheeks.

"I done run out of grapeshot," Caleb whispered to Jason.

☆　☆　☆

Joshua Barney watched Jason slide down behind the rock.

He was glad of that, but it was a small matter. And there were great matters to consider. Soames and the supply wagon were gone, and the seamen were out of cartridges. There were only a few cannonballs left to load in his eighteen-pounders. Kiddall and Sellers were still alive. Huffington, as well. He looked for Jack Webster beyond the pine trees. He couldn't find Shoe Tail in the smoke and the tumble of wrestling figures near the lip of the ravine.

He drew in a shuddering breath against the pain in his thigh and said, "Spike the cannons, Mr. Huffington. Call a retreat."

Jesse Huffington's face was white as death. The men around Barney gasped at his words, then rubbed their eyes and turned their heads away as if to hide tears. The word spread quickly across the hill.

"We'll fight another day, aye; we will, my captain," Kiddall called before he hammered a hand pike into the touchhole of his cannon.

Dan Frazier whispered, "God save us."

As if a wind had come up to blow against them, the flotilla men began to fall back.

Barney reached out a hand and grasped Mingo's shoulder hard. "Help me down in the grass," he whispered. "I'm growing faint."

"I'll stay with you, sir," Mingo replied through gritted teeth. He eased the commodore to the ground. Captain Huffington came around from the cannon, tears coursing through the dirt on his face. He pulled off his blue jacket and slid it under Barney's head like a pillow.

Barney clutched Mingo's hand. "I want you to go. I won't have you fall into British hands. Go, my good man, now. The boys…take them with you. Watch over them."

Caleb stood at Barney's feet. "I'm here, sir. I want to stay here with you."

Mingo jerked the little drummer boy by the collar. "The commodore say you're going with me." He called to Jason, "Get up, you snot-nosed little pisser."

✶ ✶ ✶

But then Mingo Jones paused. He knew he should obey Barney, but he couldn't make himself walk away. He stared down at the young gunner lying on the turnpike and at the body of the white boy called Topps, who had a kindness in him. Mingo saw the twisted leg and Topps's young face turning waxy. Topps still had his dirk in his outstretched hand. Mingo could see the name *Julie* carved in the handle.

He heard the shouts of the seamen fighting and stumbling and racing their way up the hill and onto the turnpike to Washington. But Mingo couldn't leave. Not yet. He took a few steps away and looked back.

A British corporal from the Eighty-Fifth Foot had reached the American gun battery and was already leaning over Joshua Barney.

The commodore came up on an elbow and roared, "Away with you. Get me an officer! I'll not hand my sword to less than a senior officer!"

Mingo smiled just slightly and grabbed Jason's shoulder. He and the two boys watched from the side of the road as Admiral Cockburn and General Ross crossed over the ravine's rickety bridge and walked up the hill toward the American gun battery in the turnpike. There was dignity in Joshua Barney's face as he waited for the British officers to reach his side. Despite the intensity of his pain, he didn't cry out, for there was something of eternity in the moment that he knew he must stay conscious of.

Barney stared up at Cockburn, a fellow naval officer and the enemy, the demon who'd chased him so relentlessly and unsuccessfully up the Patuxent River, "Well, Admiral, you've got hold of me at last."

The British admiral was all correctness and power, his saber glistening at his side. He looked down at Barney and responded with a victor's grace, "Do not let us speak of that subject, Commodore. I regret to see you in this state."

✷ ✷ ✷

From beneath his wool hat, Mingo studied the two British officers. The major general was a fine-looking man, maybe the finest-faced man—white man or black—he'd ever seen. But it was the navy man who held his attention. The mottled color in Admiral Cockburn's cheeks, Mingo believed, reflected neither fear nor pleasure, but the thrill of conquest.

Cockburn accepted Barney's sword, which Jesse Huffington helped him remove. A surgeon bent to dress Barney's wound. Then the admiral paroled the commodore on the spot and inquired as to where he'd like to be taken. Joshua Barney was too weak from loss of blood to handle a long wagon journey. It was Huffington who said that and—being stubborn like a mule—he planted himself down in the grass beside the commodore. Mingo had to smile at Mr. Jesse Huffington taking on the admiral, sober and fierce like that.

A tavern in Bladensburg was already serving as a hospital for the British wounded, the British officers said, and that was the destination decided upon. Mingo had witnessed white men at horse races and white men hunting together. This palavering was all done like gentlemen at sport—for war is sport, or it would not be bearable—so their white faces seemed to say.

He and the boys pushed back under the trees and watched as a party of British seamen prepared a litter and carried Joshua Barney from the battlefield.

Caleb broke into tears. "I'm going with the commodore. Ain't nobody gonna notice a boy like me."

Mingo's shoulder muscles were twitching, for he too ached to stay with the commodore, no matter the consequence to himself. That lot was falling to Sailing Master Jesse Worthington, who'd lost his hat and whose breeches were slipping, but who was standing before Cockburn and insisting that it was his right to go along. And this British admiral was agreeing to it.

Mingo turned on his heel and didn't look to see if the boys were behind him. As he passed by the clearing with the twelve-pounder in it, he saw Captain Tom Warner lying on the ground dead. He didn't stop, for there was no use in it. His heart felt like a stone in his chest, although he couldn't quite say why. He'd had no sense of this battle or of any reason to be in it, except that he'd pledged to stay with the commodore as long as Barney wished him there.

Now he was free to do what he wished. He would take the young'uns to the top of the ridge and set them on the road to Washington. That was as far as he could think at this moment.

"Mr. Jones, look there," Jason called from behind him.

Captain Webster's horse, Shoe Tail, was lying dead near the bodies of two British soldiers. Mingo winced as he looked down at the chestnut. He remembered the taut, smooth feel of Shoe Tail's muscles when he was currying the handsome fellow not three days ago. He didn't see Captain Webster's body anywhere, although two seamen's bodies lay nearby.

Jason let out a second cry, for he'd spotted something on the ground. It was Mr. Webster's cocked hat, and there was a hole through the crown and a smear of blood on the gold lace. The boy's face grew sober as he picked up the hat and brushed away the dirt. "I can't see Captain Webster being dead," he whispered. "That'd be a terrible shame."

"Give it to me," Caleb said. "I'll take it. Let me keep his hat."

"No," Jason insisted. "It don't be right to be carrying it off like that. It belonged to him." With gentle hands the boy placed the hat on a nearby rock and followed Mingo through the trees up to the top of the ridge."

CHAPTER FOUR

WASHINGTON

Afternoon

On the ridge, Jason and Caleb were caught up in the crush of retreating militia and seamen. They trailed behind Mingo, who shot a glance over his shoulder now and then and offered a hard look if the boys fell too far behind.

Jason was so thirsty it hurt his throat to swallow. He squinted into the sun as President Madison and General Winder and some other white men cantered past. They weren't smiling now, like they were on the porch of the brick house in the Navy Yard only hours ago. They seemed in a powerful rush to get home to Washington.

"Out of the way, jackstraws. Give room," someone shouted.

A wagon filled with wounded marines rumbled through the throng of militia and seamen on the turnpike, and every man gave way. A burly marine, running behind the wagon, bumped hard against Jason's shoulder and almost knocked him into the dirt. The boy wiped his face with his sleeve and watched the marines pushing roughly past the seamen, even passing Mingo.

Jason carried a feeling about Mingo that was both good and bad. Right now, it was mostly bad. When Mingo jerked his head in the boys' direction, Jason wanted to call out, "Wait up, Mr. Jones." But, he knew it wasn't any use to do that. Mr. Jones did what-ever he wanted to do. Right now, it was like he was listening to something in his head. What it might be, Jason couldn't figure.

✳ ✳ ✳

Mingo was walking with his face set and his eyes half-closed. The events of the morning had left a pain in his chest that hurt like a burn scar. He'd not thought the winning or the losing mattered much. In the midst of the battle, he'd had a great wish to be elsewhere. For sure, he'd felt a surge of pride when he'd stepped in to help the commodore at the eighteen-pounder and seen Barney's eyes widen with relief that he was there. There were other feelings Mingo couldn't put a name to.

"Topps, he be dead, you think?" Jason came up beside him.

Mingo considered. "Aye, he looked dead, sure 'nuff."

"Captain Warner, he be dead," the boy said solemnly. "And them redcoats, lots of them be dead." He stared straight ahead as he stumbled along beside Mingo. "You believe they gonna bury them horses? The commodore's roan, that was one fine-looking horse, I say. I hate to see him shot dead like that. And Shoe Tail. Captain Webster put a lot of store in that horse."

"Don't know rightly. Maybe burn the carcasses." Mingo was thinking about the commodore and how he looked when the British general and admiral were standing over him. Barney's sword was off, and his hat was lying in the grass, and he had Mr. Worthington's blue coat tucked under his head. A lesser man would have looked small, maybe fearful.

The commodore had smiled, strong-faced. "Admiral Cockburn, you have me at a disadvantage."

And the British general went red on the cheekbones. "The name is Co…burn."

Then Barney had pushed up on his elbow, lifted his chin to the admiral, and said, "You're in the United States of America now, sir. It's spelled *Cock*burn, and we call it *Cock*burn."

The memory of the admiral's face flashing to color, his mouth pursing up tight, made Mingo almost laugh out loud.

"I'm hungry," the boy beside him complained. "I'm hungry fit to dying."

"We'll be at the Navy Yard afore long. There'll be grub and drink waiting for us sure enough." At least, there might be. Mingo wasn't exactly sure what they'd find in Washington City. For himself, Washington was a place to rest in for a few hours, a place to fill his belly and to sleep some. By moonlight, it might be he'd make his way north to Pennsylvania. "Follow the North Star," he'd been told. "Keep it ahead and above your right shoulder, and you'll come to a river called the Susquehanna."

He put his hand to the leather packet he wore on a thin strand of gut around his neck. If a black man's got freedom papers, he can look for farm work in Pennsylvania. That's what he'd been told by another runaway he'd come across hiding in a barn one night in Virginia. The fellow swore to it.

"I got to sit down now," Jason said in a faint voice.

The boy was limping along the turnpike like he was a brown field mouse that was close to dying. Mingo sighed and bent down. "Well, ride on my back for a'while."

✧ ✧ ✧

For a long while, they trudged the dusty road in silence, walking past tobacco fields and rail fences and stretches of summer hay lying golden in the afternoon sun. Sometimes a farm dog came out from a barn and wagged its tail, looking for a handout. No one paid any heed, for there was nothing to hand out.

When they reached the turnpike gate that marked the city of Washington, the road narrowed, city-like, and took on the name of Maryland Avenue. Caleb was walking ahead. He'd been silent for a long time. Now he stopped dead in his tracks and said to Mingo, "I ain't going farther with ye. I'm gonna wait right there." He pointed his finger at a house on the corner of Maryland and Second Avenues.

Mingo shifted Jason's weight and glared at Caleb. "Who you think you be waiting for?"

"The redcoats are coming after us for sure, aren't they? I'm waiting so as I can kill me one or two."

That idea struck Mingo as fool-ass stupid. He studied the drummer boy's face, which most times was white as milk. Now he looked to be cherry-stained beneath the streaks of dirt. It was most likely disappointment that brought it on, Mingo reasoned, not getting what you were expecting to.

"What you gonna' do when them soldiers come down this road?"

"I don't know. Guess I'll know when I see them, won't I?"

Easing Jason to the ground, Mingo looked up at the impos-ing brick house with its double chimneys and shiny black door. It was the kind of house white men of prominence owned. The place was not welcoming in any way. Planks had been nailed crisscrossed over the tall windows on the front of the house.

"Fool thing to do, white boy," he said to Caleb.

Already Caleb had turned away. He swung open the gate. When he reached the stone steps, he looked back at Jason and Mingo. There was a lonesome kind of pleading in his face.

"How he think he gonna get inside that house, it being all nailed up?" Mingo muttered. "An' what's the fool boy going to do when he gets inside?"

"He got his musket," Jason answered. "I believe he gonna shoot somebody."

Caleb was standing in front of the shiny black door with such a set expression on his face that it was obvious he wasn't changing his mind, no matter what Mingo and Jason thought about it.

"Wait up," Jason called to Caleb. "I'm coming, too."

Mingo spit in the grass at the side of the road and consid-ered the situation. He remembered the commodore's last com-mand—"The boys, take them with you." It didn't seem fitting to leave them here in the path of the British and them too addle-brained to be reasoned with.

He stalked through the gate and banged it behind him. "I ain't getting myself killed or captured 'cause of you two," he said. "We'll just get ourselves around to the back and see if there be a well. I admit to being powerful ready for some water."

A covered well stood next to an imposing carriage house. Mingo looked closely. The windows on the back of the house weren't boarded up. There was no movement inside the house that he could make out.

Still, he was cautious. "You," he ordered Caleb, "get yourself up to the back door and knock hard and ask polite like if we can have some water from this here well."

Caleb scowled. "How come...me?"

"'Cause you're a white boy, that's why."

Stiff-backed, Caleb stalked through the kitchen garden and knocked on the back door with the butt of his musket. He waited for a long minute and turned and shrugged.

"Do it again. Polite-like."

The second knock brought no response. Again Mingo studied the upstairs windows looking for a shadow, but nothing caught his eye. He approached the back door and saw through the crack that the latch would break with an upward thrust of his knife.

☆ ☆ ☆

In only a few moments, Mingo Jones and the boys were standing on the cool dark brick floor of a large kitchen. The room carried a look of disorder as if the residents of the house had departed in a great hurry.

"Well, looky there." Caleb was eyeing a platter of roasted corn ears on the table and a pie with one slice gone. He stuck his finger in the pie and licked it. "Squash pie. Mighty tasty, too."

Mingo knelt by the fireplace and fingered the blackened wood shards on the grate. "Folks what live here are two days gone, I'd wager." He looked up at the boys and said gruffly, "It won't do no harm to have some grub with our water. Me, I have a liking for squash pie."

Jason'd never seen Mingo smile, really smile so that his teeth showed. He allowed himself a grin in return, pulled his pa's knife from its sheath, and cut the pie into three equal pieces.

For sure, this was white folks' house. Rich, white folks. On the main floor was a fancy dining room and two parlors. Above stairs were some bedchambers, with tall brown chests and high beds with mosquito nets as fine as spider webbing. The feather-filled coverlets were so fluffy a fellow might sink right in over his head if he climbed onto one. In the front bedroom, Jason lowered himself onto the braided rug and rested his head on a silk pillow he'd taken from the upstairs hall settee.

Caleb pulled a heavy table up to the front window.

"You ain't gonna do any good," Mingo said. "You know that."

Caleb wiped the stock of his musket with a piece of pillow slip he'd pulled from one of the beds. He answered in a dogged voice. "It's what I got to do, Mingo. You don't have to stay. You and Jason can put out to sea now that you et and rested your legs. You jus' leave me be here. I'll be fine."

Mingo shook his head. He prowled about the room, taking in the gilt-rimmed mirror over the fireplace and the silver candlesticks at either end of the mantel. In a testy voice, he asked Caleb, "How come you think you got to prove something, boy?"

It wasn't a question the drummer boy knew how to answer.

Caleb peered through the narrow panels of plywood nailed to the outside of the windows. With the butt of his musket, he shattered the glass in one of the panes and rested the barrel of the musket on an edging of the wood. He took three paper cartridges from his pocket and placed them in a row on the table beside him.

"Who says the British be marching down this road?" Mingo asked.

"I say, that's who." There was something close to tears in Caleb's voice. "And I ain't going nowhere 'til I get a fair chance at 'em. Them British done shot the commodore, and they killed Captain Warner. An' I believe they kilt Captain Webster and kilt his horse, too. I ain't letting 'em get away with it."

This boy was orn'ry as a mule, Mingo thought. "All right, then," he said to Caleb. "It's pissing foolish. That's what I think, but we ain't leaving you."

✿ ✿ ✿

On the ridge above the meadow, all was quiet and still. No birds sang. A cloud of spent smoke from cannon fire had hung for awhile above the site of the battle. The sky was like a clean blue bowl turned upside down. Nearly three hundred British soldiers were killed or wounded in the brief conflict. Most of the wounded had already been moved to the tavern turned hospital in Bladensburg.

The afternoon sun shone on lost watch chains, black patent city shoes, and discarded knives and muskets in the meadow. There were broken wagon wheels and rumpled jackets in various colors and a forgotten flag or two lying about on the trampled grass, alongside the crumpled bodies of the dead.

From the seat of their wagon, James Biays and his daughter, Rachel, stared down at the jarring evidence of the flotilla men's final stand. The girl pulled off her sunbonnet and balled it in her hands, pressing the soft cotton to her mouth as if to stifle a cry.

They'd set out from the Biays farm shortly after a Maryland cavalry officer reined up at the Sugar Valley farmhouse. The man's face was blotched, his eyes desperate.

"Water," he'd gasped and drank his fill straight from the well bucket. "The battle's lost," he murmured. "It's all over."

He was on his way home, he said.

"No, sir," he replied to Biays's question, "I can't say where the British might go or what they'll do next."

"Do you know what happened to Commodore Barney and his flotilla men?" Biays inquired.

The cavalryman shook his head. Last he'd seen, it was only the marines and Barney's boys left behind to fight up on the ridge. They were holding fast. Maybe all were dead or taken prisoner. More than that, he couldn't say.

Rachel had persuaded her father to bring her to the battlefield. They'd come by way of Bladensburg and handed out six loaves of homemade bread and a basket of peaches to the British sentries so as to be allowed to pass through the town and over the white bridge. "To bury the American dead," Biays explained, and he pointed to the two young farmhands who sat in the back of the wagon with their shovels.

They'd rumbled across the bridge and up the meadow. Here, on this hilltop above the ravine, they could see the flotilla men weren't all dead. If so, there'd be hundreds of bodies lying under the pine trees and in the grass and thickets. James Baiys pointed that out to Rachel, who was already climbing from the wagon.

He followed his daughter, making his way through the trees toward the flotilla men's redoubt. He spotted a body lying near an eight-pound cannon some yards to the left of the road. Up close, it was the body of a young black fellow, bayoneted…rammed straight through his guts. Why hadn't he run before the British got to him?

Baiys was playing over in his head what the cavalryman told him at the farmhouse. Many of the cavalry's mounts were purchased for Lavall's regiment only two weeks ago, and the riders were mostly fresh recruits who'd never fought on horseback. When the British infantrymen came creeping out of the apple orchard and climbing the meadow toward the second line, Lavall had released his men. The cavalryman's face held shame mixed with indignation, and he'd finished with, "Colonel Lavall told us to run for our lives, claiming there was a difference between madness and bravery."

Crossing the turnpike, Biays glimpsed a twelve-pound cannon in the middle of a clearing, beside the body of a dead flotilla man. Seems this young fellow didn't take note of the difference.

Walking gingerly among the discarded canteens, rammers, and sponges, he came upon a young man in a blue officer's jacket lying on his back close to the cannon's wooden carriage. He bent closer, studied the man's face and the terrible wound in his chest and reasoned that the officer was hit full in the back and died quickly. Biays put his hands on his knees and rose with a groan.

He made his way through the trees to the main battery, two long-nosed cannons positioned in the center of the turnpike. There he discovered more dead bodies and the carcass of a horse.

The horse was a roan, sprawled forward, shot through the head.

War's a hard thing and full of terrible waste, he thought. Biays's eyes unexpectedly watered, and he blew his nose hard. He and his farmhands would burn the horses and carry the bodies of the fallen men to his wagon. They would take them home to Sugar Valley and bury them good and proper, he told himself. If it took until midnight, they'd do that. They would leave this hill clear of American dead, men and horses both.

✻ ✻ ✻

While her father considered the burying of the dead, Rachel moved about the ridge searching for the living. She didn't care if she stepped in mud or in blood. She paid no notice when brambles caught at her skirt or when her stockings were ripped by briars or sharp-pointed sticks.

A dozen Bladensburg townspeople were on the far side of the hill. They were caring as best they could for the American wounded, with water, brandy, and strips of coarse cotton they'd brought to bind up cuts and gashes and broken limbs. When Rachel came upon a dead marine with flies buzzing above his face, she flicked back her braid, pulled off her white apron, and shooed away the flies with an angry cry. "Get!" Gingerly she folded the apron over the dead man's eyes.

Near the top of the ridge she came upon her horse. Shoe Tail was saddled and bridled, lying just as he'd fallen three hours earlier. With an anguished cry, Rachel went down on her knees beside the horse.

Already Shoe Tail's legs had gone stiff. Gently she straightened out his tangled mane and stroked his neck. All the while, she was murmuring out loud in a choked voice, telling Shoe Tail that he was her "best boy" and "a handsome fellow," and it was all right, and that now he must sleep well. A piece of bright red yarn was braided in the coarse hair of Shoe Tail's mane. She released it with shaking fingers and pushed the yarn deep in her pocket.

When she looked up, she saw Jack Webster's hat lying on a large rock nearby. "Mother of God," she murmured. "No, not Jack, too!" But then she saw that he wasn't dead. He was standing under the trees close by, his face as white as death.

She could see a gash on his forehead was open from his left eyebrow to the matted hair at his temple. He was looking directly at her. Those eyes she remembered as a silvery blue-gray and full of light now appeared black. They had a glassy look in them, as if he'd just awakened from sleep.

The girl jumped to her feet and ran with hands outstretched. She put an arm around his waist and helped him sit down on one of the boulders on the ridge. She stood beside him and cradled his head against her shoulder as if he were a child. She felt the wetness of the blood on his forehead soaking into her dress.

But that was of no matter, for the truth was—and she knew it as the truth—she'd been looking for him all this time, looking for John Adams Webster and hoping not to find him dead on this shadowed hilltop.

She held him close and whispered, "You're alive, Jack. So it's going to be all right."

"No…it's not all right." He shivered in her arms. "The commodore's not here. I don't know where they've taken him, Rachel. I don't know if he's even alive. Oh God, what if he's dead!"

She thought for a moment and then replied, "He's not dead. Truly. When we passed through Bladensburg, we heard the British soldiers talking among themselves. Your commodore's alive. I heard them say Captain Joshua Barney is at the tavern in town. It's a hospital now, and one of the flotilla officers is with him. They said that Sailing Master Huffington is always at his side."

Webster let out a sob that seemed to shake his whole body.

"I tell you he's not dead," the girl insisted, "only wounded and being seen to. Be calm, Jack."

"It's not all right. Don't you see? Rachel, I failed him." Jack spoke in a rushed, slurred voice as if he were confused and struggling to sort out the story. "My commodore was shot, you see, shot bad in the thigh. And we were out of gunpowder. So he commanded us to spike the guns and run. It was an order…to spike the cannons and leave the battlefield."

He paused. It was as if Rachel's words were just sinking in. "You're telling me that Huffington disobeyed orders. He stayed with Barney. Jesse Huffington?" Webster's voice broke, but he went on. "There, you see. I should have gone to my commander's side, no matter his order. It was the thing a man should do, but I didn't. I ran."

He groaned, for the telling of all this brought back a flood of images. In particular, Jack remembered clearly the last moments of battle on the hill. The shame he felt now was like a sickness. And with the shame, he knew again the taste and smell and feel of raw fear.

He'd watched his best friend die only feet from his own outstretched hand. He'd smelled the heat of Tom Warner's chest blood and closed Tom's eyes with his own hand. Afterward, a weakness had rushed over him so strongly that he'd not been able to think clearly or even breathe. It was as if he'd fallen overboard at sea and his lungs had filled and he was drowning.

"You were outnumbered," the girl said, "and Shoe Tail was shot."

He looked at Rachel's white face, but from some kind of distance. He heard himself speaking, but it was as if he was hearing another man telling of the event. "Aye, outnumbered. The redcoats were coming from everywhere, climbing down from the hilltop and climbing up from the ravine and from everywhere. I was on Shoe Tail's back, and we were fighting, fighting hard. And then Barney said to run. But I knew...somewhere in my head I considered...that I needed to go to the commodore. I could have gone to him, you see, and carried him off the field on Shoe Tail's back. I might have saved him, or at the least, I could've remained at his side like that tobacco-chewing hick, Captain Jesse Huffington. But I hadn't Jesse's...courage."

"Maybe that was stubbornness, not courage."

"Don't try to make it right. I ran, Rachel. I heeled Shoe Tail in the ribs like I was half crazed, and we took off up the ridge." Jack Webster's voice broke again. His nose was running, and he wiped it with the back of his hand. "That's all I remember. No, I remember a musket fired close up and how the grapeshot stung my head and how Shoe Tail was jerking and stumbling. Oh, Rache, I'm sorry...damn sorry about Shoe Tail. He was your own beloved horse."

She blanched and said very slowly, "Shoe Tail was mine, Jack, and it grieves me too much to say that it's all right. I'm not the kind of girl to say I forgive you for taking him. I can't quite do that, not yet." A sob rose in her throat. "Still, it's not your fault he was shot. I know that, too."

A soldier's dropped water keg was lying close to her feet. Rachel brushed away the dirt before she took off the top and handed it to him. Webster took four long swallows and his shaking lessened. Then she tore a strip from her petticoat, moistened it with some of the keg water, and cleaned the dirt and blood from around his eyes.

He couldn't look at her. The sorrow and the shame were mixed in a sharp lump in his chest that it hurt to breathe around. He could only allow himself short gasping breaths. Her touch was gentle, and he closed his eyes and heard her say, "I'll bet you gave as good as you got, Jack. I believe you had that in you, too."

✵ ✵ ✵

James Biays came upon Rachel and Jack in a shaft of sunlight beneath the pines. He hurried off for dried beef strips and a loaf of bread from his wagon and made certain that young Webster ate his fill and drank some of the cider he'd hidden under the wagon bench.

"You'll come with us to Sugar Valley," Biays said. He took a second strip of petticoat that Rachel held out and bound Webster's head, layering green leaves between the petticoat and the gash on the young man's forehead so that the blood wouldn't stick to the cloth. "You were at sea on the *Rossie,* and these past four months aboard the flotilla giving your best. Time now, maybe you settle down and look to the land, Jack. There's patriotism in that as well."

Webster turned away. He was looking down the slope of the meadow, past the apple orchard, to the white bridge to Bladensburg, and beyond the river to the town. Joshua Barney was a prisoner there. The commodore was likely paroled, but he was still in British hands. It might be possible to ride across the Bladensburg bridge carrying a white flag and ask to be taken to his captain. But he had no horse, and worse—Barney might look at him with eyes that said, "You failed me." That would be unbearable.

"It's just one day, one hard day," Rachel whispered, seeing his eyes were glistening with unshed tears. "I promise you, Jack, there'll come another time to fight."

He turned to her...this girl with the wide hazel eyes and dark hair loosed from its binding, this girl who had a smear of his blood on her cheek and on the shoulder of her dress.

Yes, another time. He was not done yet. It was like a heat rising up in his body. He could make up for his failure at Bladensburg.

"Run now so that you can fight again." That's what Barney intended. The commodore would never have called a retreat unless he intended it for regrouping in order to fight once again. Webster stood up, felt his head swimming, but there was strength in his legs and shoulders. The thing was—how to do it? Where had the flotilla men gone to? How could he find them?

A few yards away, a company of marines was loading the bodies of their dead comrades into the back of a hay wagon. They were almost done. Already the driver had climbed to his board seat and had the reins in his hands. Webster called to the marines and received a nod back in response. He said to James Biays, "Thank you, sir, but I must go. I have myself a ride into Washington."

He took Rachel aside, uncertain of what he felt and what he would say to her. He studied the girl's face, and saw it had strength and some beauty mixed, something vivid, a wide brow, a tender mouth. She was taller than most girls, taller than Clara and more real to him, as Clara was fading now in his memory. On impulse he took her shoulders in his hands and pulled her against him until he could smell her hair and skin. She didn't resist when he kissed her long and softly on the mouth. He wasn't certain what it meant, but the kiss warmed his mouth. His heart was eased enough that he could go without looking back.

✶ ✶ ✶

The news of the terrible defeat at Bladensburg was hard to believe. There were many in Washington who'd dreamed of victory, been assured of it, counted on it. Those who lived on the hills above the city had glimpsed the flaming rockets cutting through the air above the battlefield and thought them beautiful. As far west as Georgetown, the thunder of cannon fire rattled windowpanes, causing chickens to squawk and dogs to howl. But, the clamor was short-lived.

Shortly after noon, riders had raced their horses over Jenkins Hill, galloped down Pennsylvania Avenue, and shouted out the terrible truth. The American troops were retreating to regroup for a defense of the city. And now even that fact seemed in dispute. The militiamen who'd marched out of the Navy Yard gates in the morning were now limping down the avenue in a dazed sort of way, as if they had no destination in mind except to find a spot of safety.

No one knew what the British might be up to. Most certainly, they would march on Washington, now that the city was vulnerable.

The city's mood shifted in a few brief hours from optimism to panic. There was talk of plunder and destruction and rape. Images floated of local townsmen in chains. Catching the mood of the returning troops, most of the remaining citizens in Washington, even the poorest of the Irish in Swampdoodle and Foggy Bottom, were now intent upon escape.

Escape meant a hideout in the wooded hilltops above Georgetown, or better yet, safe passage by oar or sail across the river to Virginia. With those thoughts in mind, they tumbled their children, linens, and silver candlesticks into their carriages.

☆ ☆ ☆

Jack Webster stretched his aching shoulders and climbed down from the wagon in the streaked gold of late day. He'd sat for more than an hour in the back of the wagon, leaning his head against the slatted side, and staring at the bodies of the two dead marines beside him. Sunlight had glittered on the belt of the man lying closest to his shoulder.

When he caught sight of Jim Sellers standing in the shade of the oaks at the corner of First Street, he limped toward him. He was conscious of his own filthy uniform, his blood-streaked face. Worse, he had no musket, no sword, not even his hat.

"Alive, are you?" Sellers's face broke into a smile, and he reached for Webster's hand. "You old salt, you was always the lucky one."

"And you, Jimbo." Webster was eased some by the touch of Sellar's calloused palm. He said, "Warner's dead, Jim. He's dead. I tell you that for sure." He looked away for a moment and then continued, "What of Kiddall? Has General Winder called a meeting place? What are we to do?"

Sellers rubbed his red-rimmed eyes and shrugged in a gesture that revealed his despair. "All I know is the president and some of his cabinet come racing by here awhile ago. It was like they believed a pack of mad dogs was chasing after them. Armstrong was with them, and he said…well, he said he didn't rightly know where Winder wants us to assemble."

"It must be here, here at the Capitol, for…where else? "

Webster could make out a few other flotilla men squatting in the grass near the almost completed senate and the house chambers. Barney had once shown him a drawing of the proposed seat of the legislature, two square buildings connected by a domed amphitheater. At present, the square buildings were connected only by a wooden walkway, as the amphitheater was not yet built. Scaffolding and piles of white marble marked the place where it was meant to rise—now only a sea of overgrown grass and muddy walkways.

To his consternation, only a few of the militia were lingering here. For a long moment he stood silently beside Sellers and watched the defeated, exhausted militiamen streaming past the Capitol without even a glance of interest.

"Colonel Lavall and some of his cavalry were here," Sellers offered in a weary voice. "They reined in and waited for awhile, but General Winder never showed, and they took off again."

"You think Winder's sipping tea at the president's mansion?"

"I 'spect he's hiding in the cellar, knowing Cockburn is marching hell-bent after him."

"General Ross commands the army, Jim. And he…he has taken the commodore prisoner." The thought was painful to put into words. "No doubt he'll march his army here, now that the city is open to him. But Ross has no reason to push his troops, not with our militia scattered. He has the advantage. Some commanders might advance quickly. Ross will rest his men when he can."

"But he's coming, you say?"

"Aye, he's coming. And Cockburn will be with him, that's for damn sure."

Sellers considered this for a long moment. He'd not shaved in two days. Red-gold whiskers had sprouted like fine wheat on his chin and his cheeks. "So what in hell are we to do, stand around here with shit on our faces? Where's Winder and the gol-darn militia?"

Webster grinned just slightly. "To hell with Winder. We've a crew of flotilla men waiting out there in the grass. How many do you count, say, forty? And I see some cannons, some goddamn beautiful guns." He nodded toward four eighteen-pounders resting on wooden carriages in front of the senate chamber.

Sellers furrowed his brow, "Are you a damn fool, Jack?"

"Might be. But those are American guns. I don't see leaving them for the redcoats to turn and use on our backsides."

"All right, I'll take a look-see," Sellers said reluctantly.

The four cannons appeared new and unused. Webster leaned his arms on the iron barrel of one of the guns to steady himself against the waves of dizziness that still came over him. Four god-damn beautiful cannons. What a find. But no rammers or buckets or wad hook. More importantly, no cannonballs.

"Jim…Captain Sellers, you must stop every seaman that comes along," Webster ordered, surprising even himself with the command in his voice. "Order every flotilla man that passes to wait here. I'm going to the Navy Yard. We can save these guns and deliver them to Winder."

It was a long shot, only a chance, but worth the taking. Webster hurried down the long hill that led to the Navy Yard. There was still no sound of marching feet, no beat of drums. If Ross and his soldiers weren't yet on the road, he could pull together a crew of seamen and load up a supply wagon. He'd show them that the flotilla men were not done for. He'd rather die in this effort than live another hour as a coward.

✵ ✵ ✵

The Navy Yard was a sea of confusion. When the flotilla men and the militia had marched out through the gates earlier in the day, they'd left a well-ordered place. Now, men in naval uniforms and some in frock coats were racing across the yard and running up and down the riverbank as if looking for a way to escape an approaching storm.

A bugle sounded on the parade ground, but whether it was taps or a call to arms, Webster couldn't make out. The notes were ragged and offered in segments, as if the bugler was stopping to catch his breath.

To Webster's surprise, a dozen women were gathered just inside the K Street gate. "We're a'feared Commodore Tingey will set the Yard a'fire so as it won't fall into British hands," one of the younger women explained, tears streaming down her face.

"Our homes are just outside the wall, and they'll burn as well. Pray, don't let him burn the yard, hear us, please!" the women cried out to anyone and everyone entering the gates.

Webster turned away. There was nothing he could do to help them.

He grabbed the shoulder of a marine racing past. "Where do I get my hands on some cannonballs and rammers and some canisters of gunpowder?"

The marine's face was sweaty. He shook off Webster's arm. "We're retreating, for God's sake! The gunpowder's been set about to blow the Yard on approach of the enemy. It's the president's order."

Webster looked back. The women who'd been huddled just inside the Yard were stumbling out of the gate, hurrying to save what they could from their houses before the explosion.

On the far side of the marine barracks, two young men were loading muskets into wagons. A third fellow led eight bridled horses from the stables toward the wagons. Dan Frazier's heavy build and loose-jointed walk were unmistakable. When he saw Jack Webster, the petty officer gave the bridle of the lead horse a shake.

"I was saving 'em from burning. Glad to see you're alive, sir."

"Goddamn it, Frazier, you're a sight for sore eyes! I need those horses! I've cannons on the hill, four of them! You must help me take these horses up to the Capitol and try to save the guns from falling into the hands of the British. Four cannons, Frazier, eighteen-pounders!"

It took Dan Frazier only moments to grasp what Captain Webster was saying. He stared into the distance as if gathering his thoughts. If the British should find four cannons of this size, they could blow apart the town of Washington and its few but impressive buildings with little effort. That couldn't be God's will. "I'll help you right enough," he promised Webster. "Ropes. We'll need ropes as well."

"Cannonballs, rammers, sponges, buckets," Webster cried out.

"Follow me." Frazier motioned toward one of the wooden sheds at the side of the Yard. Handing the reins of the horses to Webster, he picked up a crowbar and broke the lock on the shed door. He disappeared into the darkened doorway and in a few moments appeared again. "It ain't right to steal," he called out with a grin. "Only thing is…everything we'll need is here."

✳ ✳ ✳

Riding bareback on the friskiest of the horses, Webster led the way through the bedlam in the Yard and out the west gate onto K Street, leading a second horse behind him. Frazier followed with the other six horses on short ropes. The horses were pulling canvas sacks full of tools and serge bags of powder and cannonballs.

To Webster's relief, Jim Sellers had collected seventy or more seamen beneath the oak trees. The flotilla men were grimy and exhausted, and some were blood-streaked, but they greeted Webster and Frazier with glad shouts and fell to laying out the ropes and attaching them to the four cannons.

"Not enough ropes," Sellars spit out. "We can't pull but two of the guns, not even with eight horses and men bending their backs. We got to spike two of the cannons and leave them behind."

Regrettable. Webster groaned, but agreed.

"There's word, sir." One of the young flotilla men, whose name was Will Adams, said to Webster. "I heard tell that them what still wants to fight should head for the Montgomery County Courthouse."

"Do you know where that might be?" Jack Webster's forehead had begun to throb. A wave of dizziness made him weak in the knees.

"Rockville lies to the northwest of Washington, sir, fifteen miles or more. We can take these here cannons down Pennsylvania Avenue to Georgetown, then head north on the rolling road. It's the only road worth traveling on, pulling these here cannons." Will Adams wiped the grime and sweat from his forehead with the back of his hand. He was young, maybe sixteen years old, and there was a long ugly cut on his right arm. "My pa's farm's out there near Tenley-town. I can get us that far for sure."

It was a plan to follow. Webster ignored the pain from the gash in his forehead. He could see in the flotilla men's faces they'd follow if he acted as a strong leader, a captain, a commodore. He remounted the black horse, roped now to the first of the two cannons. He pulled the stallion's head up tight so that the horse danced about.

He straightened his shoulders as he'd seen Barney do in the past and called out in an impassioned voice, "We're seamen of the Chesapeake Flotilla. We can do what others cannot do. Aye, tars! We're men of the sea, but we'll forge ourselves into an army on land, if we must."

Jack Webster kneed the black horse, and Dan Frazier slapped the rump of another. The horses strained against the weight of the cannons, but with the flotilla men pushing the gun carriages from the rear, two of the cannons were turned into position. The little battalion of flotilla men began to roll the unwieldy guns, groaning and creaking, across the rough ground toward the dirt path that would lead them around the Capitol.

✼ ✼ ✼

Evening, August 24

Mingo woke to what sounded to him like the far-off beat of rain. He and the boys had been sleeping a long while, stretched out on the carpet in the upstairs front bedroom of this house on Maryland Avenue.

It gave him pause to wake and find walls around him, with a painted ceiling like a barrier over his head. He sat up and rubbed his eyes and looked at Caleb and Jason, sprawled like starfish beside him. He studied their thin shoulders and dirty hands and faces. Whatever the reason—and God knows he'd fought against it—these young ones were chained to him and he to them. Not for anything did he want them to know he believed this. That would be a burden he wasn't ready to carry.

He stared around the darkened room and realized the noise that woke him was not rain, but the steady tramp of marching boots. Catlike, he slipped to his feet, moved to the front window, and peered through the opening between the boards. A shadowy stretch of Maryland Avenue came into view. He couldn't see the marchers, but he suspected they were British troops and close by, maybe only a pasture length down the turnpike.

"Get yourselves up." He shook each boy's shoulder.

Jason gave a great yawn, looked up at Mingo, and whispered, "How come you waking us?"

"Open your ears, boy. They coming. But if we lie low, they'll march by us and never know we's here." Mingo spoke with authority.

Caleb climbed on the table by the window and peered through the boards. "I see a man on a horse riding slow. He's waving some kind of flag. And the tall hats, they're a'following after him." The boy put his musket across his knee, brought a cartridge of gunpowder to his mouth, ripped it open, and primed the musket.

It would take only a swipe of Mingo's hand to knock the gun from the boy's hand. Every instinct in the man's body said that to fire from this window on the marching soldiers would only bring disaster. And yet he knew there was some kind of courage in this boy that he must stand aside for. This fool-ass act of defiance was a test of manhood for the white boy.

Through gritted teeth, Mingo muttered, "Take your time now, and hold steady. Don't waste your powder."

Caleb fired, and the shot rang out in the twilight air. For a few seconds, there was silence like the crystal stillness after a strike of lightning, when a man looks to see that he is still in one piece.

The drummer boy reloaded and fired a second shot, then fell back on the table and cried, "I swan, I done hit the man on the horse. And a high hat, too. I think I done killed the general his'self." He tumbled to the floor and looked up at Mingo with an expression of pride mingled with shock and fear. "What we do now?"

"We hightail it. That's what." Mingo was already at the door. "Come on, young'uns. You got to run for it like you never run in your life." Close on Mingo's heels, the boys scrambled down the steps, raced through the kitchen, and out the back door, which they left swinging open behind them.

"I did it, Mingo!" Caleb crowed excitedly. "I shot myself a British soldier."

"You done near getting us killed. We got to find a rabbit hole to hide ourselves in."

Mingo led the boys out the back door and into the shadows of the summer trees behind the carriage house. Over his shoulder, he could tell red-coated soldiers had broken through the boarded-up front door and were already inside the house. He heard their shouts and saw the flicker of torches in the windows. It made his skin crawl to think he and the boys might have hid themselves in the house and been caught up in a fire. There were better ways to die…better to die on the run.

"This way," he ordered and pushed through the low branches of trees. They climbed through the rails of a fence and up a dry creek until they were near the crest of the hill. Mingo could see that he was right. The house on Maryland Avenue was aflame. He thought of the tin roof, how it could fall on a man or boy inside and bury him in burning metal. He thought of how the bricks could tumble and hold a body down so a man would burn slow and in pieces.

As might be expected, they were being followed. Shadowy figures were already at the tree line behind the house. He could hear their voices and see they were fanning out into search parties.

"Git," Mingo whispered and gave Caleb a hard shove as if to say, "See what you got us into."

✳ ✳ ✳

The silhouette of the half-built Capitol was above them, but an open hilltop did not look to Mingo to be a place to head to.

The British soldiers were close on their trail, shouting and calling to each other in stirred-up voices. They made him think of white men on a hunt for quail who call out to each other when they've lost sight of their prey.

"I didn't know I could do it by my lone self, but I did. Ain't you proud of me, Mr. Mingo Jones?" Caleb didn't wait for Mingo's reply, but ran ahead, disappearing into a grove of close-packed trees.

It was a welcome darkness beneath the trees. Vines scratched at their faces. Caleb was nimble, and even with his musket in his hand, he was able to scramble into the high branches of a tree. He whispered, "Climb up here. It ain't hard."

"Not if you is a squirrel," Mingo murmured. He put his hand on Jason's neck and pushed the boy into a tangle of scrub and honeysuckle behind the tree. Then he went down on his knees and crawled in behind the boy and pressed himself to the ground. Being chased was the one thing he hated most. He closed his eyes, breathed in the smell of earth and the rich scent of the honeysuckle, and tried not to lose his power over himself.

This was not the red-coated soldiers' countryside. They hadn't got dogs like the plantation masters did. Still, he could hear the thuds and jingle and the ragged sounds of a search party. He could smell a torch—just one torch, for which he was thankful—and see the flames flickering on the leaves just beyond his face.

The soldiers were swiping at vines with their bayonets and cursing the Americans who'd fired upon them. "Damn ruffians," Mingo heard one cry out. "Not good enough to face a firing squad. Let the rascals dangle in the wind for all to see."

The soldiers passed on and the woods fell silent.

"Stay put 'til I tell ye," Mingo ordered the boys, as he closed his eyes and tried to think through the problem. More British Johnnies would surely pass this way, or it might be the same soldiers would retrace their steps and he and the boys would be caught like moles with both escape holes closed. The only thing he could think to do was wait it out until something came clear to him.

For a long time, they were in darkness. Even Caleb made no sound in the tree above. Jason stretched just slightly and whispered, "Mingo, I'm thinking—"

"Lie still, boy."

"I'm thinking we be lost, Mingo."

"We ain't lost. We're on this here hill above the Navy Yard, what lies down toward the river."

"But why are we here? How come we be here a'tall?"

From the top of the hill came the echo of rifle shots, followed by the banging of muskets on metal.

Damn fool boy, Caleb, thought Mingo, shooting the general's horse out from under him and causing trouble that wasn't warranted. He felt Jason's elbow against his arm, and shook his head over this one, not knowing one end from the other and always asking questions.

As if he could hear Mingo's judgment of him, Jason gave a shiver and moved closer so that their faces were near to one another. "I got lost in the fighting today, Mingo. I went looking to find the man called Sharky what killed my pa. And then I went looking to help Mr. Webster and the twelve-pounder. Only it wasn't long a'fore there was men groaning and bleeding everywhere. I found Topps. His leg was bent back funny-like, and there was blood on his face. I wanted him to get up and run away over the ridge."

"You're soft, boy. You want more'n you gonna get out of this life."

"But Topps, he looked at me in the face like he wasn't seeing me. He was alive, I think, but he was leaving me and going somewhere in his head, somewhere I couldn't go."

"I'm sorry 'bout Topps." Mingo put his arm over his eyes. "You don't never get used to having folks leave you behind, folks you're counting on. You don't never get used to hurting inside when you recollect their faces."

The boy was crying softly. "I keep thinking about my pa being dead. It's like a hole inside I can't fill up no way."

"Fill it up with piss. I tell you, boy, fill it up with piss."

"It's me that's lost, Mingo. I don't know what to do now that the flotilla is split up. And, that white man, Sharky, I can't find him nowhere. I don't know where to look anymore."

"You ain't lost. Fill up that hole in you with gumption. You got to take care of yourself. Sometimes you got to make choices in this life."

"What kind of choices I got to make?"

Mingo felt a band of pain tighten around his chest. "Take me, I'm leading you and Caleb to the Navy Yard. I'm doing what I promised the commodore I'd do. Then I'm thinking, just maybe...I'm heading off."

The boy drew in a breath. "Where you be heading to, Mingo?"

"I can't rightly say, but a far piece from here. A man can't go along being chased and hiding in the dirt like here now. I got to go where I can stand free."

"I don't want you going, Mingo."

"I ain't made my mind up about it yet."

"Piss and gumption," Jason whispered and then fell quiet.

✳ ✳ ✳

Some minutes later, Mingo nudged Jason. The boy climbed from beneath the bush without a word as Caleb shimmied down from the tree. With Mingo in the lead, they made their way around the south side of the hill. At last they could see Pennsylvania Avenue. Some houses and taverns were alight with candles. Otherwise, the village was dark.

Jason was looking southward, where the Potomac made a bend around the Navy Yard. He put his hand on Mingo's arm, and the man bent his head and asked, "What you wanting now?"

"Look there, a ship is burning!" The boy's voice was full of amazement. Against the night sky, the burning masts and spars of a great vessel stood out clearly. It was the frigate *Columbia.*

Mingo knew this. Only last night, when they were bivouacked in the Navy Yard, he'd walked to the river's edge and studied the big ship. One of the seamen on the dock told him, "The hull's finished. Her bottom's soon to be coppered, and she's ready for launching. Aye, we can use her well to fight them Britishers." Now the mighty vessel was a burning torch. He didn't think it was the British who'd set her afire. It must be the *Columbia* was set to burning by order of Commodore Tingey himself. Mingo could appreciate that men might destroy something of great value to them rather than lose it.

Just as this thought came into his mind, the Navy Yard exploded in a flowering of red-gold flames. It was like the last days of reckoning that Dan Frazier was sometimes moved to talk about. The wooden fence around the Yard had become a quick-moving ribbon of fire. The gun carriage shops and the paint shop were just now catching fire, and a grayish smoke billowed into the dark sky like some monstrous cloud. In a great crackle of flame, the nearby barracks exploded and crumbled and fell in upon themselves.

The watchers on the hill could see that it was not just the *Columbia* burning, but the docks themselves and the storehouse of masts and ropes and spars. The schooner *Lynx* was aflame, along with the sloop of war *Argus*, which was riding in the river alongside the old sturdy frigates, the *Boston* and *General Greene*.

Mingo had never seen anything so terrible except in his dreams. "I'm thinking the Navy Yard is no place for us to be heading to," he said with a low laugh that he believed might ease the boys. This long and terrible day had no good in it, and in the glow of the monstrous fire, he could see a dazed look in the boys' eyes. Shock and disbelief. It was the same look he'd seen in the eyes of small animals that were brutalized by dogs before they were killed.

"I ain't leaving you," he said suddenly. The question had traveled with them all these hours. And now the question was answered. "You two grasshoppers are coming with me. I don't know just where…but there's somewhere safe we be going to."

☆ ☆ ☆

With the boys at his heels, he headed down the hill to the west. This Washington was not a town he wished to linger in, a slave-owning town with a slave market at its center. Not Pennsylvania Avenue. There was safety in the open land that stretched from the bottom of this hill to the president's castle on the river. As they crossed a cow pasture and pushed through the swampy grass beside the culvert that ran through the field, he could see the great mansion in the distance before him. Some of the upper windows were dark, but those on the main level gleamed and beckoned as if there were a party or ball in progress. He and the boys stumbled through the waist-high grass with their eyes fastened on the glittering house, keeping it in view as seamen might look toward a lighthouse.

A haven, a castle, so the great house appeared, not just to Mingo Jones and the boys that trailed after him, but also to the militiamen and the seamen making their way down Pennsylvania Avenue with no idea where they should go. Some paused briefly at Hughes's grocery store near the corner of Sixth Street to relieve their thirst at the water pump. A local gentleman had paid Hughes to put out a barrel of whiskey for the returning troops, but it had already been emptied by the troops that had passed by earlier.

The president's house offered little comfort.

"Ain't nobody here. The president come by for a brief time," a young black seaman in a torn jacket told Mingo when he and the boys reached the side gate of the mansion. "Only Mr. Madison couldn't find his lady. She's gone on to safety in Georgetown, and he was glad to hear of it. Everyone has run away. French John and the houseboy, Paul, they were the last to go."

"Not you." Mingo appraised the seaman. The stocky young fellow was Charles Ball, the oarsman on barge 320, trustworthy enough. He looked across the low stone wall to the dark front lawn of the mansion, where a dozen seaman and marines were standing about, as if waiting for someone to rally them into action. He frowned. "Maybe others are willing to make a stand here?"

"For sure, there be a cannon by the gate," Ball replied with some vigor. "It's only a six-pounder, but there's grapeshot canisters. And some marines got their muskets. You think it's worth standing 'em off?"

"I got my musket," Caleb whispered. "Only I ain't got but one cartridge."

Mingo put his hand on the boy's shoulder and said to Ball, "I say gather up these here men lying about and make a count of their weapons and powder."

The words sounded like an order, and for a moment the younger man stiffened and stared at Mingo Jones, a black man like himself - one who'd spoken with authority. "Aye, I can do that," he admitted after a moment. "Only it's just a pitiful few, mostly seamen and marines."

"Where 'bouts that cannon be?"

Ball pointed toward the front gate, and Mingo went on. "Maybe we could turn it round so's it points the right way."

Jason and Caleb were listening quietly, as boys do when men are strong in their ways. They couldn't help staring at the mansion, with its wide-open doorway through which candlelight flickered on soft-colored walls and the edge of a round burnished table. It crossed Jason's mind there was food in that house, something mouthwatering, for sure. It had been a long time since the squash pie, but he didn't want to bother Mingo with the idea. He whispered into Caleb's ear. "I'm aiming to take a look in that there house."

"No, you ain't," Caleb said indignantly. "We're fighting the British right now. We ain't got time to go looking around in some big house."

"What you boys mumbling about? I need you to pay mind." Mingo cuffed their heads with a hard hand. "Jason, you're a gunner's boy. I want you by my side."

Sighing his disappointment, Jason trudged after Mingo. The little cannon was easily turned so that it faced east toward the turn in Pennsylvania Avenue and a wooden building that one of the seamen claimed was the Treasury Department. A thickening of trees followed, and then the great Avenue.

☆ ☆ ☆

In the distance, a dull red sky glimmered above the trees. A dozen flotilla men from Barney's crew had gathered with Mingo by the mansion's iron gate, and to his surprise, almost as many militiamen with their muskets in their hands. Not much was said, but it was understood they were waiting for the British. For certain, this is a foolish venture, some were grumbling, but still, the little cannon was primed. Charles Ball went to the mansion for a piece of smoldering kindling in the bucket. The little band of seamen and militiamen stood together and watched as other men passed by on their way to Rock Creek and the bridge to Georgetown.

Charles Ball was at Mingo's elbow. He suggested with calm gravity, "I say we wait 'til they come close. We give them Johnnies a shot to remember, and then we skedaddle for the river."

Moonlight showed the shadows of trees. And then there came some new noises from the Avenue. To Mingo's ears, it sounded like the stealthy pad of wolves when they are about to attack a sheep crib. The sounds grew louder and signaled the approach of men struggling to move fast against some hindrance, stumbling as they did so.

He held up a hand so that everyone would pay full heed. "Men to cannon," Mingo whispered. "Take your aim. You, gunner's boy." He pointed to Jason. "You get the grapeshot canisters ready."

As the first horseman appeared around the bend, the moonlight caught the set of a man's shoulders. The man was hatless and riding barebacked, and the horse was one of four horses straining to pull a heavy cannon.

Jason stepped close to the little cannon and held up a canister of grapeshot. The gunner hesitated. Then Mingo shouted, "It's not the British. Hold your fire!"

Caleb was jumping up and down with excitement. He echoed Mingo. "Hold fire! It's Captain Webster, and he's alive!"

Captain Jack Webster and the barge gunner, Mingo Jones, stared at each other, their expressions visible in the moonlight and in the glow from the brilliantly lighted house. Shock marked both their faces. It was a moment of some kind of reckoning between them.

Mingo watched the sailing master slide from the horse's back. He noted the bloodstained strip of cloth bound 'round Webster's head. He remembered how he and the boys found Webster's hat on the ridge. "So you ain't dead," he said slowly.

"No way I'm dead," Webster retorted. "It'll take more than a one-ounce ball to kill me." He was looking behind Mingo at the six-pounder and the men positioned around it. "Were you aim-ing to shoot me?"

"Gunning for the British was what we had in mind. Didn't reckon you wuz the one coming."

"You were gunning for the British?" Webster repeated in a sort of wonder.

"Aye, we had that in mind to do."

"Damn it, man, you think you were going to stop the British army with that little cannon?" Webster smiled broadly, for he could see now that most were flotilla men and that Mingo Jones had the drummer boy and the little black lad with him. It was all too puzzling. The grace of God, Dan Frazier might say. He drew himself up, saluted, and said, "Well done, Mr. Jones. The com-modore will hear about this."

✵ ✵ ✵

"We best get moving afore it's too late," Petty Officer Dan Frazier bellowed from behind Webster.

Jack Webster shook his head as if to clear it. He looked at Mingo Jones. "The British are close behind us." He paused and then continued as if the black man was a mate worthy of hearing this information. "They've torched the Capitol to hell and back. Now they're marching down the hill. They're on the Avenue behind us, Ross and Cockburn, with a small army."

"Where you plan on taking these here guns?" Mingo stared at the cannons and horses roped behind Webster's horse.

"We're out to deliver them to the Montgomery County Courthouse." Webster paused again, uncertain whether to issue an order or make a request. He said in a diffident voice, "I'm ask-ing you to join up with us."

"We're going along, ain't we, Mr. Jones?" Caleb stepped between them and looked up at Mingo.

Mingo remained silent. All his instincts said this decision would direct his own fate. He turned and studied the faces of the men and boys gathered beside the little cannon. They were waiting for his answer.

Webster placed his hand on Mingo's shoulder, the gesture of a comrade. "I would like it, Mr. Jones, if you and your men would join with us."

A kind of energy rippled through Mingo Jones. He could feel the heat of Webster's hand flooding his shoulders and the scars on his back. He wheeled around and waved a hand at the men and boys around the little cannon.

"We be heading out with the sailing master." Turning back to Webster, he mumbled, "I'm sorry about Shoe Tail. I sure 'nuff am."

"Aye, Shoe Tail was a stouthearted fellow, a great loss." Jack Webster rubbed his chin and said with an effort toward a smile, "But as the commodore would claim at this hour of some desperation, we'll fight with what we've got. Will we not, Mr. Jones?"

✧ ✧ ✧

"Buildings a' burning brightly make a pretty show." Vice Admiral George Cockburn sighed with satisfaction as he and General Robert Ross trotted along Pennsylvania Avenue at the rear of two columns of British soldiers. Behind them, the American Capitol on the crest of Jenkin's Hill was as brilliantly etched against the sky as if it were a painting of buildings outlined in flame. "A sight worth all our efforts," Cockburn continued with a sigh of satisfaction.

"As you say, Co'burn," Ross responded abruptly, aware the naval officer was defending his insistence on destroying this symbol of the American government.

Firing the Capitol's two completed wings had not proved easy. The solid limestone exteriors proved to be the devil to burn. After numerous attempts, it was decided to set the buildings ablaze from the inside out. Ross' infantry troops piled together the desks and writing tables, chopped up the shutters, and tore the crimson drapes from the windows. They lighted the lot with rocket powder. So, it was done. Stone walls had smoldered and cracked, and in less than an hour, the handsome rooms and staircases and galleries were turned into prisons of fire.

"This Capitol of America was Greek in design, but now I'm reminded of Rome burning," Cockburn offered with a chuckle. "Pretentious to my eye, a bit swell for what they call 'a democracy.' The scaffolding for the unfinished center gave promise of height and grandeur. And, to be fair, the legislative chambers were uncommonly handsome, those Corinthian columns and masterful carvings and friezes...fine glass windows, eh?"

Ross hadn't expected such architectural awareness on Cockburn's part. "I agree. Rather astonishing to look upon."

"One might have expected a simple edifice befitting a self-pronounced republic," Cockburn finished with asperity.

They rode in silence. Ahead of the two officers marched a single battalion of British infantrymen, less than two hundred men. Their faces and hands were blackened from the firing of the Capitol. They moved without drums or fanfare, a party of fast-moving shadows. In truth, they expected to be attacked at any moment by a party of snipers waiting behind the fences or in the dark houses that lined this Avenue.

Cockburn joked under his breath, "My kingdom for a horse."

Ross wasn't in the mood for jokes. He himself was riding a fresh horse. His last mount, the third shot from under him on the day, had been brought down by some fool patriot hiding in a brick house on Maryland Avenue. He flicked the reins and did not answer Cockburn. The admiral was ever at his side, a thorny burr that he'd not been able to shake since that night in Upper Marlboro when he'd agreed to this attack on Washington. The man was indomitable...but also insufferable.

At present, Cockburn rode astride a bony white mule, purloined from a Bladensburg merchant. The mane and tail of the mule hung as long and yellowed as a crazed old woman's hair. She wheezed as she trotted beside Ross' horse. Behind the mule, her young black foal followed. Cockburn appeared not in the least embarrassed by his pathetic mount and her accompanying foal.

Perhaps, Ross considered, he's relieved that his choice of mounts proved too unworthy to be shot at on Maryland Avenue. That event occurred some three hours ago. At that time, he and Cockburn were riding at the head of the detachment. They were in full-dress uniform and were traveling behind one lieutenant, who carried a long pole with a white flag attached.

This dignified and cautious approach to the village of Washington was part of the plan. Ross had brought a single brigade with him from Bladensburg. Some of the infantrymen chosen for this maneuver were soldiers of the Eighty-fifth Foot, but most were soldiers of the Third Regiment, who'd not taken part in the battle at noon.

The white flag held high on Maryland Avenue was a clear signal to the citizens of the capital city that the British commander wished to parley with an official of the American government. He'd intended to demand a settlement fee, a commitment of funds from the city. When that prize money was placed in his hands, he would have given his word that Washington—its official buildings and the houses and business establishments of its inhabitants—would be spared destruction and shame. If the money were delivered, there would be no plunder or rape. He'd have put his word on it. Cockburn had scoffed and thought him soft, but agreed.

Despite the slow and careful approach of the British soldiers and the white flag at the head of the line, no official of the American government rode out to meet them – even when the British drummer repeatedly beat out the call for parley. They waited. It was growing dark, and they'd no choice but to resume the march. And then had come the two shots fired from the brick house on the corner of Maryland and Second Avenues.

It was Ross' good fortune that, when he'd gone down with the horse, he had clambered to his feet unhurt. His officers were incensed that their commander had been shot at and had escaped death by only a hairbreadth. The forward troops raced toward the brick house, intent upon capturing the brigand who had the audacity to shoot at Major General Robert Ross, traveling as he was at a walk, erect in his saddle, and in full-dress uniform.

George Cockburn was almost jocular that this generous approach to the American capital city was interrupted in so crude a manner. "The rowdies deserve a leathering," he crowed. He'd dismounted from the mule and taken a personal interest in the search of the house on Maryland Avenue. Even more so in its burning. The light from the flames had shown his fine-featured, weathered face in animation, the gleam of excitement in his hooded eyes.

"Now their admirable Capitol building will take a blow in retaliation," he'd promised. He had been standing in the red glow of the burning house, staring at the crest of the hill and the Capitol's completed twin chambers. And so it had happened. Ross had not attempted to defuse the anger that fueled his troops and the sailors under Cockburn's command. He'd personally authorized the burning of the houses of legislature. He rationalized the destruction in his mind: his white flag had been ignored. A stand must be taken, all weakness disavowed and honor upheld.

After the dastardly attack on Maryland Avenue, they'd moved with caution. Ross had chosen to bring only a small force down the Avenue, leaving the remainder of his fifteen-hundred-man brigade on the hill. If the Americans mounted a counterattack, he would have troops in reserve to call on.

To his left, a great field or meadow stretched out into darkness.

If he looked hard over his shoulder, the night sky was reddened like the roof of a great cauldron. He knew it was the American Naval Yard. His point men reported the Yard was set ablaze shortly before he and his infantrymen reached the Capitol. He heard the explosions and suspected as much. He'd have done the same before allowing ships and gunpowder and supplies to fall into enemy hands.

✻ ✻ ✻

"What a pathetic excuse for a town," Cockburn murmured, "shabby and full of empty space, without the charm of the simplest of English villages. I'm curious to see what lies at the turn of this avenue. Shall we find the palace of their president, think you? Can you see its turrets through the trees?"

He couldn't. Clouds were moving across the face of the moon. When they passed over, Ross caught glimpses of townspeople huddling behind trees. Dogs were barking, and some tavern windows shone bravely with candles and lanterns. Without bearings, he didn't like to move his men at night.

When they rounded the bend on Pennsylvania Avenue and passed beyond the low wooden building that was said to hold the republic's treasury department, Ross could see the lighted windows of the president's house. The two-storied house with its hospitable appearance: flat-roof, and full windows reminded him of a gentleman's manor house in Dorset or Ireland. The front door stood open, and he could make out a large entry hall and the shining floor of the foyer.

The very lack of a defensive force here made Ross wary.

He ordered his troops to creep across the grass and surround the house. He murmured to Cockburn, "It staggers the mind to believe the militia would leave this house undefended. Yet, so it appears."

"Cowards all. Shall we pay a call on that dwarf, Jemmy Madison?"

Ross put his hand on his sword as a caution and entered the house beside Cockburn. In the front hall he paused and listened. He heard only the clatter of his aides following behind, their quick, excited calls. To his right was the archway into a handsome hall that ran the width of the house. Drawing rooms opened across the back of the house, one into the other. Everywhere candles shone on silk, brocade, mahogany, and fine paintings. Jasmine and roses scented the rooms, and books and papers lay about in some disarray.

In the dining room on the southwest corner of the house, Cockburn pointed upward toward a large gilt frame, the painting cut from it. He raised an eyebrow and then turned to the long table. "I say, Ross, they've set a feast for us." Bread and sweets were waiting on silver trays, the wine decanted. There was the aroma of roast beef and hams cooking on a spit somewhere nearby.

Ross enjoyed a release from the day's tension. He unbuttoned his high collar and joined the admiral and their top aides at the table. He reached for a biscuit and slathered it with butter, added a slice of ham, and downed it with a glass of Madeira. And then he accepted a second glass to accompany the cigars found in a humidor on the high chest.

As the British point men peered into corners and climbed the stairs to search out the upper floor, Cockburn moved a candelabra on the long table so that he could see Ross' face more clearly. "You feared it would be more difficult, my dear fellow. You thought the rascals would confound us and put up a defense we could not overcome. You see how wrong you were."

"I overestimated their command. They had more than one opportunity to take us." Ross stared into his glass. "They could have felled trees in our path in the woods as we marched from Upper Marlboro and then attacked my army from all sides. It would have been a massacre, and I feared it. But they did not."

Cockburn gave his scoffing laugh and reached for a plum in a silver dish. "Why, I would ask, did General Winder and his militia not position themselves in the town of Bladensburg? Fortified there, the defenders could have held out for days, until we, without provisions, wearied and withdrew. No, they left the town for us like a gift and positioned themselves in an open meadow like idiots.'

"The flotilla men…"

"Aye," said Cockburn. "The only real fighters we've encountered in the Chesapeake. I thank God for the capture of Barney and the disbursement of his men, those cocksure seamen, those damnable blacks. But I doubt they'll fight without Barney. No, my good general, I suspect they've not the wits to regroup without the old black-guard to lead them."

☆ ☆ ☆

A tall clock in the hall struck ten before the two British commanders were done with the dining room and walked again through the reception rooms. They would burn this handsome house. The words were not said; it was understood.

"A souvenir of the little apple-john president." Cockburn pulled a beaver hat from the hat stand and squashed it under his arm. "Everything of value must be destroyed, but look here… one can imagine that Queen Dolley's plump *derriere* has heated this cushion more than once." He took up a satin pillow roll from a sofa in the parlor and tossed it to Ross. "May it warm your bed tonight."

Ross laughed and threw the pillow down. Gazing around the parlor, he noted bits of silver and a few china figurines here that his wife might like him to bring home to her. Perhaps he would take some small thing, a memento. But no, he could not choose. Being in this house with the imprint of its occupants so clearly visible—and a feeling of a rare grace about it that he'd not expected—caused him to hunger once more for his own life, his house and possessions and the sight of his children.

In a cubbyhole of the mahogany desk in the yellow-walled drawing room, he spotted a packet of letters. He believed the letters might be of some significance. But when he ruffled through the packet, he found they were love letters exchanged between James and Dolley Madison. On impulse he unbuttoned his tunic and thrust the packet against his heart. On the rack of the pianoforte was music sheet for Bach's complex Fugue Number 1 in C—perhaps, in Ross' opinion, the most beautiful piece of music in the world. Seeing it sent a throb of delight through his chest.

"Another edifice of limestone." Cockburn had a keen look on his face. "So we torch from the inside, say you?"

"Agreed." Ross turned from the pianoforte and signaled to his second in command. "No looting; that is my order." His infantrymen knew what was expected. Sofas and cabinets were soon piled in the center of the rooms, along with Dolley Madison's bed linens and fine dresses thrown on the piles in the upstairs bedrooms.

Ross remained in the oval drawing room. He listened to the thump and crash of furniture and watched as the red silk draperies were pulled from the long windows and heaped over the piled-up furniture. Two of his infantrymen knocked over the pianoforte in the parlor next door and dragged it out into the hall. When he saw a soldier raise his musket to smash the ivory keys, he turned away and left the room.

✲ ✲ ✲

The house must burn quickly and decisively. Ross sent a detachment of soldiers down the Avenue in search of torches to ignite the house. They returned after a short while with long pine poles wound 'round with wads of blazing cotton.

"The Treasury Building is next. I'd see it burn as well," announced Cockburn, who was standing with his aides at the iron gate. Nearby, a British seaman held the bridle of the white mule.

Ross was reluctant to leave the great mansion until the torching was accomplished as it should be. Staring through the house's windows, he watched the shadows of his soldiers moving from room to room, setting fire to the furniture and the paintings that were torn from the walls. He watched the first flicker of flames dancing on the ceilings of the upstairs rooms and thought of the love letters in his tunic.

When the soldiers were done and safely outside, the charges of powder he'd ordered laid in the basement were set off. Again, loud explosions filled the night, and the smell of gunpowder rent the humid air. Within moments, white smoke began to seep up from the lower floor of the mansion. With a curl of flame, the furniture piles caught fire. The red glow reflected on the faces of his soldiers, who stood with him on the Avenue just beyond the gate.

He'd ordered houses burned before. He'd watched great buildings and castles and handsome houses brought to rubble on the continent. The destruction of this house may prove to the good of all concerned, he told himself. With its mansion and its Capitol buildings destroyed, the raw young country could well fall to its knees. After all, the Americans were English in bone and sinew.

If humbled sufficiently, they'd align themselves again with the mother country in trade and alliances. The thought brought him comfort. He told himself that he must push aside all misgivings and personal discomforts. It was his duty to his king and to the great empire, which stretched from the small green island that was Great Britain around the globe to India and Australia and to Africa and Canada and the islands of the Caribbean. America should be proud to be the friend to such an empire… as he was proud to serve it.

CHAPTER FIVE

DEFIANCE

Nearing midnight, August 24

Jack Webster rode bareback on the lead horse, a black stallion. Jim Sellers followed, mounted on a speckled mare. As they made their way into the Maryland countryside, Dan Frazier and Mingo Jones traveled on foot struggling with ropes that burned their hands as they urged on the horses pulling the two heavy eighteen-pounders as well the little brass cannon discovered at the gate of the president's house.

The cannons were a great prize. Webster was proud of them and proud of the horses he had purloined from the Navy Yard. The exhausted battalion passed under the trees, and the horses and cannons splashed across creeks and struggled over rocks and fallen logs. Webster looked over his shoulder constantly. Once, when the crew attempted to pull and push the cannons up a steep incline, he had called out in an encouraging voice, "Heave to, my lads. We won't let the bastards win, will we?"

He'd heard only a few groans in reply, for the strongest of the men were straining against the weight of the cannons and the softness of the soil, and all were hungry and drained of energy from the long, discouraging day. Now and again, a curse rent the night when someone stepped on a sharp rock or cut himself on the briars that lashed out across the way.

Webster didn't know how to help them. He knew himself to be in command of this little squadron. He and Sellers were equal in rank, but he was the senior officer. Almost from the moment he'd dropped from the wagon beneath the oaks on Capitol Hill, he'd taken the power. Still, the weight of this command was heavy. He'd never captained men without Barney to turn to for direction. Now he had a single goal—to deliver the cannons to General Winder. No matter the pain. No matter how hard the effort, the capital city must be taken back from the British.

✻ ✻ ✻

"Tenleytown lies ahead," young Will Adams called out as the little army of men and horses and cannons descended into deep woods, headed for the wooden bridge over the Rock Creek.

Once across the rippling creek, they were on the ascent again, but the going was difficult. They weren't alone on the road. Webster glimpsed old grandfathers carrying children on their backs and women wrapped in shawls, despite the heavy heat of the night. Some carried lanterns, which appeared like large flickering moths under the trees, but most of the citizens fleeing Washington were simply stumbling along in the shadows of the night.

An occasional farmhouse sat close to the road, with a sodden cluster of refugees huddled on the porch. It was all strange and unreal, the reddened night sky behind them and the jolts of musket fire that inexplicably sounded in the far distance. Once, a campfire revealed a ring of frightened faces. A dozen folks were gathered around a pot of soup set on smoldering stones. A child was crying.

Webster hated it, hated it all...hated that the battle was lost and the militia had run from the battlefield and that the commodore had been shot and taken prisoner by the British. And the insolence of the enemy, he hated that, too.

An image flashed in his mind's eye of the British general cantering up the meadow at the very height of the battle. Ross had his whip in his hand. He was rising in the saddle to post with his shoulders straight, sitting tall and secure in himself, as if he had no fear of being shot. He hated Robert Ross for not being afraid.

Even more, he despised the admiral. What was that seadog Cockburn doing on a battlefield, anyway? And those dogged infantrymen in the scarlet coats with their red-painted muskets and the bagpipes that went everywhere with them. He hated the fact that they won so easily. Webster's anger was like a fever alternately heating and chilling his body. He hated most that he'd panicked on the battlefield and left Barney wounded and on the ground. The shame of that was almost more than he could bear.

☆ ☆ ☆

Webster whipped the stallion, who tossed his head and fought the second hilly climb through the woods. The boy Jason rode the back of one of the horses pulling the second cannon. Caleb was trudging along behind Mingo. Boys were of good use aboard ship, but on land, Webster wasn't so certain. Caleb was a drummer. Perhaps there was some value there.

A sudden clearing revealed Tenleytown. It was hardly a village, only a scattering of wooden houses near to a creek and a general store. There were no militiamen or horses about that Webster could see. He slid from the stallion's back and entered the dimly lit store, where a few men were sitting in the flicker of a lantern around an upturned barrel. The shelves behind the proprietor were almost empty.

"I ain't giving nothing away," he said before Webster spoke. "They been here already and cleaned me out. A parcel of men, all hungry and wanting a handout."

"Was General Winder in command?" Webster asked.

"He was. In a dither, I'd say. Word is he's regrouping the militia units at the Montgomery County Courthouse for another try at the British."

"Where is this Montgomery County Courthouse?"

"The way you're headed now, some five mile."

The clatter of a fallen chair and the scrape of boots caused Webster to whirl, a hand on his sword. One of the men sitting around the barrel in the corner was on his feet and had moved deeper into the shadows. The man's hat was pulled low, but the slope of his shoulders was familiar.

"You should hide yourself in hell, Soames," Webster said coldly.

The barge cook stepped out of the shadows.

"Hold your horses, Mr. Webster. You're thinking I cut and run back there on the ridge. Well, it's not so. The mules were spooked by the cannon fire. They ran near a mile down the turnpike before I could halt them. When I turned their heads back to the ridge, the seamen were retreating toward me on the road. I knew that the battle was finished."

Webster's instincts said the man was lying. "Where's the supply wagon now?"

"That old wagon hardly made it to Washington. I junked her near to the Capitol. Hadn't a choice, you see."

"We could've fought on if you hadn't run, Soames."

"Them mules took off. Nothing I could do, I tell you."

"The commodore was shot," Webster said soberly. "He's alive, but he's a prisoner of the British."

"I heard that for a fact." Soames paused. "Do I gather you are in command now, Mr. Webster?"

There was something of a smirk on the cook's face. Webster turned back to the proprietor. "Have you some live chickens out back? I'll give you a receipt for them. My word is good." Over his shoulder, he gave a curt nod to Soames. "We'll build a fire down the road, and you can make a spit to cook them on."

The cook moved back a step. "Who says I'm going with you?"

"You're not released from the service of the flotilla."

The men around the barrel shifted their legs, and one man drained his glass.

Soames shrugged. "If there's chickens to be had, I'll cook them."

The price charged by the storekeeper for a half-dozen live chickens was outrageous. Still, the gnawing in his own belly reminded Webster that his crew, sprawled in the grass outside the store, had no bread or meat. They were hungry as well as tired. Five miles lay ahead, and he must push them. He couldn't allow Winder to attack the British without Barney's boys in the forefront. It was now a matter of honor. He studied the proprietor's face and saw the man's eyes were red-rimmed and suspicious. There'd be no bargaining. Bending over the wooden counter, he signed the receipt: *This bill to be paid in full when Washington is retaken, John Adams Webster, Sailing master, the Chesapeake Flotilla, August 24, 1814.*

✵ ✵ ✵

Morning, August 25

At dawn, the rain began, the sullen leaking of an overcast sky. Webster and his battalion of men and boys had reached the Montgomery County Courthouse in the small hours of the morning and slept for a few hours in some haystacks on a farm close by. Most were still asleep, buried under the sodden hay.

Webster woke with blood caking his eye, as the cut on his forehead was bleeding again. He pulled himself from the hay and walked with his head lifted up to the rain. When the crusty blood had lessened, he tied his scarf around his forehead. It stunned him that the courthouse grounds were virtually empty. He could see only a few fellows in muddied militia uniforms standing about.

In the shelter of some dripping pines, a party of flotilla men was huddled, thirty men at least, the young coxswain, Jesse Stewart, among them. Captain John Kiddall was there, with a blanket wrapped around his shoulders. He threw both arms around Webster in a fierce hug. "You're in one piece, I see."

Tears were close behind Webster's eyelids, to come upon Kiddall here, and alive although disheveled, his eyes dark with exhaustion, all but closed down Webster's throat. He returned Kiddall's embrace without words.

"I was fearful you was dead, like Tom Warner," Kiddall said, regret in his voice. "By God, Jack, it's good to see you here."

Webster drew in a ragged breath. "Where's headquarters? Sellers is with me, and we've brought cannons and horses."

"There's no headquarters. General Winder has gone on."

"Gone on where?"

"Hell, nobody knows. Most of the militia's took off for home. Some of the feisty ones, they've made for Bal'imore, thinking the British will strike at the port, now that they've scuttled Washington."

The news was shocking, hard to absorb. So there was no talk at all of taking back Washington, no talk of an American attack on the British. What stunned Webster most was the fact there was no command here. No fire, no coffee in this place, nothing to eat. The eyes of the flotilla men standing with Kiddall appeared glazed, and they walked about under the dripping trees with their shoulders slumped.

"We'll on to Bal'amore as well. That's what I'm thinking," Kiddall said in a hard, gruff voice. "We sign in at the dock with Lieutenant Rutter and find out what the devil's what. We'll take them horses and cannons you got, and we'll hit the road this morning."

It was a plan and a fair one. "Aye, mate. I'll tell Sellers and my crew." Webster felt his chest ease. He went on, "We had five cannons, but we had to spike one at Tenleytown. We still have four guns and eight good horses. That's the one success I can claim."

But he was wrong. There was no success to claim. Sellers was waiting for Webster at the haystack. He bellowed out the fact: the eight sturdy horses they'd struggled through the long hard night to bring to this courthouse were gone.

"Stolen from the courthouse stables," Sellars said bitterly.

"My God, the horses! Stolen…but how? Who could have?"

"Militiamen took 'em out before dawn and rode off home," Sellers told him and looked away. "Jack, the men are powerful low. And hungry, too."

✳ ✳ ✳

It was a bad morning and getting worse. Every man and boy in Webster's small army was worn-down and miserable and struggling with aches and scratches and foot blisters. The handsome flotilla uniforms—donned so eagerly in April before the flotilla sailed down the Bay—were now torn and filthy. "We're as dirty as pigs long in mud," is how Jesse Stewart put it, fingering the sharks' teeth on the strap around his neck. And they were hungry, belly-twisting hungry.

Soames stood about with his arms folded over his chest and watched the despair of the flotilla men. "There ain't nothing I can do about it," he muttered. "There ain't nothing to cook." One of the militiamen hung his head and murmured that he was going home to his wife and baby on the Eastern Shore.

If Barney were here, it would not be so, Webster thought. The commodore would rally these men and give them hope and find a way to fill their bellies. The thought that Barney was a prisoner at Bladensburg was a constant concern, an ache that would not go away. He looked around for Mingo Jones. "We're heading out to Bal'imore, Mr. Jones. We made it this far, we have to go on."

The words were said crisply, but Mingo Jones could read Webster's face. Captain Webster was low in spirits, riding on his nerve. He was most likely thinking on the commodore.

Joshua Barney was heavy on Mingo's mind as well. He'd like to see for himself that the commodore was being treated all right, that his wound was being seen to. And more, he wanted to look Barney straight in the face and ask him about the boys. He'd pledged he'd not leave them behind, but what was he to do with them? Caleb had no ship's berth waiting, and Jason was a lost boy, with a heart as frayed as his shirt and a mind not yet settled on being a man.

Mingo walked with Webster to inspect the cannons. "You thinking we be pulling these here guns without horses?"

When Webster finally spoke, it was in a dull and exhausted voice. "I was counting on finding General Winder with a regiment of militia, an army fit to fight. But where'd they all go? I count only twenty men from Stansbury's regiment here and less than a hundred with Colonel Beall. As for the rest, I never thought to see so many cowards. It shames me to see it."

The word *cowards* sat uneasy on Mingo's mind.

He looked away for a moment. "It ain't fitting to run, but I can reason why. Ain't no man gonna hang around without no coffee or bread, no cover and no gunpowder. An' more, no command."

There was a pause between them, a shifting of ground. Webster sighed and continued in a calmer tone. "So, I'm thinking, Mr. Jones, we leave the cannons here. The commodore is paroled, so he's bound to show up in Bal'amore one of these days. We'll wait for him there. This war is like a storm that's gone fierce, and Barney is the only man who can command the ship."

A smile touched Mingo's face. It was a rare smile, the kind that seemed to crack the lines around his mouth and bring a shine to his dark eyes. "You got a truth in that, but I say...why we gonna wait around in Bal'amore? How 'bout you and me, we seek the commodore out in that tavern in Bladensburg? He'll tell us face to face what we oughta do."

Webster's eyes widened. "You mean, go into the British encampment? You and me? What if we get ourselves caught?"

Mingo drew his mouth down in a droll way. "Them British got other things to think on now. I say we ease up on 'em and act like what we're doing is natural and right, delivering foodstuffs, things like that. You and me can do it. We can watch each other's backsides, that's what I say."

☆ ☆ ☆

There was a roll of thunder from the southeast, an odd darkening of the sky. Lightning cracked with a sudden strange brilliance above the trees. Mingo eyed the vivid and threatening sky and said, "A'fore we be heading to Bladensburg, we got to get the flotilla men to Bal'amore. Them young'uns I got following after me, they be tuckered out. I'm gonna scout me up a mule what to carry 'em."

Webster stared into the blur of rain. The idea of going to Bladensburg to see the commodore and maybe to rescue him was a fine one. It was the right thing to do. As for himself, looking Barney in the eyes would be hard. He was not sure he could do it just yet.

As for Mingo Jones, Webster was turning over a new judgment in his mind. It might be he'd misjudged Jones. If courage was the mettle of a man—and he believed that to be true—the oarsman might well be a better man than himself.

☆ ☆ ☆

Night, August 25

Joshua Barney lay in a tangle of sheets in an upstairs bedroom in the largest tavern in Bladensburg. All day he'd listened to the howling wind lashing against the windows and the continuous pound of thunder that reminded him of the crash of waves during a hard storm at sea. Now the storm seemed exhausted. The air—cooled some by the rain—was mournfully and ominously still. Even the wasps nesting in the high corner above his head were quiet.

In this stillness, he could hear voices. Two men in the room next door, British officers with leg wounds, were exclaiming in their crisp and haughty British accents that the storm had been a "bloody riot" and "a grand finale" to the capture of Washington.

Barney closed his eyes and let himself ride the pain in his hip and leg. The iron ball buried in his thigh was removed yesterday at sundown by a ship's surgeon from Cockburn's navy. He'd cursed but once, grasped the back of a chair with both his hands, and borne the pain as stoically as possible. His leg was now hot to the touch and throbbed with an intensity that even the occasional shot of brandy did not alleviate. Every second-floor room was filled with downed officers, and the main floor held some sixty or so cots, he'd been told. The cots were for the British soldiers wounded yesterday on the Bladensburg hillside. All night long, Barney had listened to groans and cries echoing through the timbers of the old tavern.

The capture of Washington. The words grated on his ears. He'd not believed it true until a messenger banged open the door to the tavern shortly after dawn with the news that General Ross and his army—not even a full army, at that—had taken the city last evening without a fight. Indeed, without even the smallest skirmish, the man claimed. The men on the cots let out cheers and whistles and shouts of "Hurrah!"

He'd reached for the stick by his bed and banged the door closed. He lay with gritted teeth and a hand over his eyes, for he could hardly bear to hear their shouts of glee. Where the devil were Winder and the militia? Why had they not regrouped and ambushed the British troops as they made their way toward the Capitol? And his own seamen, his tars? Where the devil had they gone to?

The failure lay in the American command, he'd told Huffington when the sailing master came in to arrange his tangled sheets. James Madison seemed an honest man, an admirable political philosopher, but he'd failed miserably as commander in chief.

Would that General Washington was in charge, Barney thought to himself. One of the *first* president's gifts was the ability to choose talented, loyal subordinates. Not so Madison, whose cabinet was easily confused and ineffectual. In particular, the war secretary. Armstrong was an arrogant man who was so contemptuously wrong in all his assessments that his refusal to arm the militia or to prepare the city for attack could be called treasonable.

It was Madison's weakness, Barney concluded, his weakness that he'd lacked the gumption to discharge the man. As for General Winder, the Maryland lawyer's heart was in the right place, but he was not a leader of men, and he was undermined by Armstrong. Moreover, Winder's orders on the Bladensburg battlefield were overridden by Monroe. The secretary of state, trailing whip and spurs, was an apt fellow, but self-important, a fatal flaw in Barney's eyes.

On top of all that, the militia was untrained and unprepared. It was as if a ship had put to sea with a crew of men who'd never hoisted a sail nor battled a wave—which brought his thinking around to his own seamen. He couldn't fault them, officers and men alike. They made him proud. Consoled by that single thought, Barney allowed himself to sleep.

He didn't wake when Huffington placed a tray holding bread and cheese and a tankard of buttermilk at his bedside.

✻ ✻ ✻

Shortly after midnight, Barney woke to the rumble of wagon wheels, the trample of hooves, and the rhythmic tread of a marching army. He went up on one elbow. "Huffington...what the devil?"

"Ross and Cockburn are returning," Jesse Huffington came in to tell him. The sailing master was breathing hard, and his collar was undone.

"What's all that damn noise? Sounds like oxen trampling."

"Sure, and it is oxen, sir. I hear tell that on the march back here from Washington the army took on a herd of cattle, claiming their men was 'ongry. 'Prizes of war,' they call the taking of 'em."

Through the open window floated the hot scent of cattle. Barney heard the stomp of men on the wooden porch of the tavern-turned-hospital and the jingle of officers' belts and spurs. He waved Huffington away and struggled to pull himself higher against the pillows, for he sensed the officers would soon pay him a visit—if for no other reason than to gloat over their victory. He'd not be caught lying flat on his back.

Cockburn held the lantern high as he entered Barney's room. The flame illuminated his features, his glittering eyes, and more than anything, his smile, which reminded Barney of a cat that has just feasted on a nest of mice. "Rested well, Commodore?"

"So you have taken Washington, have you?" Barney rejoined in an effort to ward off having this noxious information forced upon him by the British admiral he so despised. "What of the president? His cabinet?"

Cockburn's face twitched just slightly. "Had we the time or the inclination to do so, Commodore, we would have captured the lot. The destruction of your Capitol is humiliation enough, do you not agree?" He paused and turned toward the open window. "It was General Ross' decision…it was our decision to return the troops to their ships without delay."

Barney's ear, attuned to nuance, picked up the fact that the two British commanders had disagreed on this issue. As he considered this interesting point, Ross entered the room. Despite their differences, Barney couldn't resist a wave of admiration, even affection, for the Irishman. Even in wrinkled, mud-spattered battle dress, Ross was as distinguished a man, as impressive a military officer, as ever he'd witnessed.

"I say, Commodore, are you fit for conversation?" Ross threw himself down in the nearby chair and rested his muddy boots on the footstool. Barney watched without speaking as Cockburn set down the lantern, clicked his heels in a formal salute, and left the room, as if a conversation with a captured American naval officer was not worthy of his time.

"Destruction," Barney echoed Cockburn's word. "Was it necessary, and to what extent, if I may ask?"

"Your Capitol is burned, and that's a pity, for it was handsome beyond all expectation. I regret the burning of the library belonging to the Congress. To destroy books is a travesty, and I take no pleasure in it."

"The burning was necessary?"

Ross flushed. "We were flying a white flag as we approached the town, asking to parlay, and we were fired upon. My men were enraged. A major riding by my side was killed. I agreed that retaliation was necessary to regain our honor."

Barney nodded. "The Navy Yard?"

"Burned by American hands."

"What of the president's mansion?"

Instinctively, Ross put a hand to his breast where the Madison letters rested within his tunic. "Also burned. A regrettable situation. I'd not have allowed my men to torch the house if Mrs. Madison had been there. Cockburn sent a letter ahead offering Mrs. Madison safe passage from the city. We heard nothing in reply, for she'd fled the mansion…already fled, along with your militia. Only vandals and looters were lurking about."

Barney winced at the inference to the militia's cowardly behavior.

"There's a tide that cannot be stopped, as well you know, Commodore," Ross continued. "So it was with the affairs of last night. It was decided to burn the house, as we had not taken the man who lived in it."

The president was still free. Barney smiled slightly.

"I allowed no looting by my troops," Ross continued, "on pain of death. To my knowledge, not one honest citizen, no woman or child, was injured by a British soldier. It has always been my belief that war offers hardships enough."

"I don't take to plundering or to murder. On that we agree, General."

Barney could see exhaustion in the ruddy handsome face, along with a soul-weariness that he understood, if he did not share. He was aware the British general had been fighting in the service of his king for the past six or seven years and had been wounded several times. He'd won a gold medal in the battle of Maida and a Peninsular Gold Star. Military service had taken its toll on the man's spirit, but not on his ideals. For that, Joshua Barney had only admiration.

The British officer rose to his feet and stood for a moment by the window. He murmured as if to himself. "The men of the Eighty-fifth have walked the battlefield, so I can be assured we've properly buried our dead before we move on. We'll stay a brief hour here in Bladensburg to gather those of our wounded fit for travel. I'd have my men aboard their ships by dawn, if possible."

Ross stepped closer to the bed and addressed Barney in formal tones. "Commodore Barney, a favor. I would ask a favor of you."

"I'm at your service," Barney responded gruffly.

"There are eighty-three men among my wounded too ill to travel. I would commit them to your care, if it's possible. It grieves me to leave any of my soldiers behind. I'll rest easier knowing they are under your protection."

Barney flushed. "I accept the responsibility. Your men will be treated with respect. You have my word on it." He would have chosen to rise from the bed, but he could not. He held himself straight against the pillow and studied the man who'd paused in the doorway, the lantern throwing his shadow like a dark bird in flight against the wall.

"Might I ask where you intend to strike next?" Barney inquired.

The general's smile was courteous and amused. "You may ask, but I'll not tell you. Would that your recovery be swift, sir. Good night."

As the door closed behind Ross, the dark room seemed to press down, and the pain throbbed with greater intensity in his leg. With a groan, Barney rearranged his limbs as best he was able and allowed himself to close his eyes.

✬ ✬ ✬

For two days Barney did not wake entirely from a fevered sleep. He was vaguely aware when the bloody bandages on his leg were changed and when Huffington attempted to bathe and shave him. He waved away food and drink. In his dreams, he was at home on his Maryland farm with his second wife, of whom he was hugely fond. He heard her laughter and saw the way she dashed up her skirts to show her ankles when she climbed the stairs. He heard her light footsteps, and he called out her name in his sleep.

When the fever began to abate and he opened his eyes, he believed she was bending over him, holding a basket filled with peaches. He could see her hands were tanned and long-fingered. The vision steadied. Hazel eyes…not blue…gazed down on him. Here was a slender face with wide-spaced eyes, a girl's face with a braid down her back and a cluster of careless curls showing beneath her white cap. A townswoman, perhaps? He closed his eyes to stop the swirling of the room beyond her face.

"Commodore," she whispered, "I bring a message from Captain Webster. He asks if you are safe and well treated, if it is possible to send you a note."

Slowly Barney felt his senses clear. It was midday. Sunlight fell across the foot of his bed. He recognized the room in which he lay, and he could hear the voices of the men on their cots below stairs. Ross and Cockburn were long gone, and the army with them. Of that, he was certain.

"Who are you, my girl? Where is Webster?" His voice was raspy from the fevered sleep and harsher than he intended.

She put her basket on the table and said, "I'm Rachel Biays, Sir. My father has a townhouse in Baltimore. Captain Webster came to our door and asked that I pack eggs, loaves of bread, and a basket of peaches and bring him to this place. We thought to use these gifts for the British wounded as a ruse to find you. And I did find you here…sleeping and alive. Praise be to the heavens for that."

"And Jack…Captain Webster?"

"He lingers in the wood behind the tavern with my father and another seaman from the flotilla. We have a wagon waiting, and it's Captain Webster's hope to deliver you to Baltimore."

"Why didn't he come to me himself instead of sending you?"

"The British. He wasn't certain."

Barney responded with exasperation. "This tavern is safer than a flat-bottom rowboat on calm water! Scarce five British soldiers are on their feet in this place. Bring Webster to me. I'm eager to set my eyes on him. Hurry, girl. Scat."

The girl wasn't offended. She offered a hearty laugh, unseemly in a female, but the sound of it was pleasing to his ears. With a quick smile over her shoulder, she left the room. He heard her wooden clogs clatter on the stairs. Something of her freshness and energy remained in the close room.

✭ ✭ ✭

Barney lay with his eyes closed, remembering with keen nostalgia the years past, when he was brimming with young blood and as frisky and as fearless as Rachel Biays. More fearless, never afraid of a battle, no matter the size of the foe. Three times he'd escaped by wit, sword, and bribe from British prisons in the years of the Revolutionary War. What a bold fellow he'd been, foolhardy for sure. And a lover, God, yes, as eager as a young stallion where pretty girls were concerned. With what audacity he'd kissed the cheek of Marie Antoinette and then the lips of half the ladies in her court. How monumental it was to be young and carefree, quite certain of the future, alive to dreams, and how damn regretful to be old and in pain and, more, to know one's limits.

His efforts in the defense of his country in this war were done. There was some satisfaction. His seamen had proved their worth at Bladensburg. Faces flashed before his eyes, Kiddall and Warner, Sellers and Huffington and the boys from Baltimore. An image of Jack Webster with his reckless sweet face caused him to smile. The young captain was alive, thank God. When he opened his eyes, he saw Webster standing in the doorway, along with the oarsman, Mingo Jones.

"We've come to get you," Mingo whispered, moving on his silent bare feet closer to the cot. "I'm gonna carry you down the stairs. We got a mattress in the back of the wagon."

Barney considered for a moment before answering. "Hand me that pitcher of water, Mr. Jones. My throat is right parched."

When he'd wet his lips, he leaned back and studied the two men. He found it odd to see them together. Webster still lingered in the doorway. It was only the black barge gunner who'd moved close to the bed. Mingo's clothes were as ragged as ever, his old wool hat still pulled low, but his eyes shone clear, and his voice was impassioned and hungry in a good way.

"I didn't expect you and Captain Webster to come after me... and together," Barney managed to say.

"It was in both of our hearts to do. It was enough of a binding." Mingo's tone was stoic.

Barney felt the pain surge once more in his thigh. "They tell me the militia has most all gone off home, run away scared like bastard pups. I swear I wouldn't have thought it. Have we no defense? No damn men strong enough, brave enough?"

Webster stepped closer. He had a French pistol stuck in his belt. "It's only that no one knows what to do or where to make a stand. We need you, sir. We'll get you out of here and take you to Bal'amore. We need you in command most desperately."

"No need for your pistol, my man." Barney waved an arm in a gesture of impatience. "There's only a few guards about. Where is your sword?"

"Lost at Bladensburg...my hat, my horse. I don't remember..."

"Shoe Tail downed." Barney sighed. "My horse as well, a great loss."

"We have blankets in the back of the wagon, and Rachel—"

It appeared to Joshua Barney that Webster wasn't faring well. His voice was strained, and he wore a dirty bandage around his head, with dark blood stained through. He looked like a man washed out hard in a storm at sea. "No need," Barney said. "No need to show up here with a wagon and blankets. I'm proud to think you'd come for me, the both of you, worthy men, I say, and I thank you for it. But I'll not go. I can't leave this tavern. I gave my word to General Ross to stay with his wounded until they are well and properly exchanged, and by God, I'll do so."

Webster stepped back from the bed as if he'd been slapped across the face. "I don't understand, sir. You made a promise to a British general?"

"I did. He's a man of honor, and I gave him my word."

"Captain Webster, he needs you to come with us," Mingo bent close and said with all the honesty he could muster, "We all needs you. We be having hard times now." He struggled to say more. "If you don't come now, I'm thinking we ain't got nothing to fight for. I'm thinking the flotilla men are 'bout ready to head off on their own ways."

Joshua Barney studied Mingo Jones, studied the set of his shoulders, his face. He could tell there was a new strength in this man standing beside his bed. "Damn it, that mustn't be! I say this to you, Mr. Jones. You and Captain Webster are good men. God's truth, man, you can do this without me."

Mingo narrowed his eyes. "Do what, Commodore?"

"I've been listening to the British officers in the rooms around me, hearing their talk. They say that their ships will leave the bay directly the men are boarded. General Ross wishes to give his men a long rest in Rhode Island, and then, after a month or so, it's their plan to take Newport by surprise. In the spring they'll attack the Carolinas and Georgia."

"In the spring? What are we supposed to do now?" Webster asked in an anguished voice.

"Hear me out." Barney leaned forward and spoke harshly. He was trembling and aware that he was using the last of his energy. "That's what I heard *said*, I tell you. But I know the devil Cockburn. He has other plans. Baltimore will be his next target, for it's the homeport of the privateers that shamed the British at the beginning of the war. Cockburn's a proud man with a long memory. He'll not rest 'til Baltimore's taken and destroyed. I believe that with all my heart."

"Then, sir, you must come with us," Webster insisted and went down on one knee beside Barney's bed. "We'll take you straight to Bal'amore. Already we've delivered more than fifty men to the docks. I swear there's a score of flotilla men gathering. We must have you with us! Without you there's no heart, no command."

He paused as if he could not think of how to put his anguish into words.

"Mr. Webster," Barney snorted just slightly. "Have you not heard me clear? I gave Ross my word. I'd not leave this place until his men are returned to him."

"You were ill when you said it, a prisoner."

"It was my word."

"Does that make sense…to try to kill a man one day and give him your promise on the next?"

Barney paused before answering. "Every man must choose the setting of the sails for himself, Mr. Webster. Every man chooses what to stand for, to be accountable for and what to die for."

"We fight. We die to defend our country against the enemy. Isn't this war what we're about? What we're willing to die for?"

Barney considered, then said slowly, "We're men of the sea, Mr. Webster, and not the decision makers. It's not ours to decide who is the enemy and who is our friend. We trust in the good sense of our leaders and in the stars. We've only our squadrons, our battalions, our blessed foot-stinking, stubborn crews to hold to and to stand up for. We rag on them, our jacktar seamen. We pull them close; we push them onward. Maybe…what the hell, we die for *them*."

"This British general, Ross…he would?" Webster was frowning now, unsure of his stand.

"Die for his soldiers? Or with them? Aye, he would, and I must honor him for that." Barney turned from Jack's white, grief-stricken face, gave one last look at Mingo Jones, and grimaced. "I'm tired now and in pain. Call Mr. Huffington to me."

"Can we?" It was only a whisper from Webster.

"No." Barney waved them away. "My heart goes with you. Go now and find your way. These are desperate times, but you will know what to do. When the time comes, Mr. Webster, you will know what to do. I swear it."

✢ ✢ ✢

He didn't hear the two men leave his room. He closed his eyes, oddly content. He heard the voices of the men on their cots downstairs. He pictured the fine-eyed girl named Rachel with Webster and Jones as they rumbled the wagon from beneath his window. It was a damn fool idea to come to fetch him. But a worthy one, by God. He'd been right about Jones from the start, damn right to fight to hold on to him. He sighed, partly from the pain. He meant to ask Jones about the drummer boy and the black lad, Jason Hayes. He hoped to hell they were faring well.

Barney put a hand over his eyes. And Jack Webster, struggling with his own demons, finding himself dirty and sword-less and chased after. It hurt him to see the young man in such despair. Aye, he was all glory, all valor on the *Rossie,* and for sure he showed good sense as the captain of barge 112. As for courage, he'd glimpsed Webster through the trees at Bladensburg, fighting like all the furies in that last battle just above the ravine.

Aye, that was courage. But these were the young man's darkest days, his self-respect gone ragged. If he could, he'd tell Jack Webster that now was the testing time, that a man is only a coward if he quits when he's behind.

✤ ✤ ✤

"I don't understand," Webster said to Mingo Jones. "Sometimes he talks like that, profound and profane, at the same time. If Barney's willing to die for the flotilla men, why wouldn't he come with us?"

"He said his piece. The commodore, he know what he's doing."

"He sent us away."

"Aye, he did."

They sat side by side in the back of the Biays wagon. Webster groaned his discouragement. Was it a slap across my face for leaving Barney on the hillside at Bladensburg? Has he lost all faith in me? He didn't say this aloud to Mingo, but bent into his cupped hands and coughed hard and felt his chest closing. He moaned, drew in some hard, ragged breaths through his mouth, and wished for his lost flask of brandy.

As if she'd heard his moan and his muffled cough, Rachel turned on the high board seat. "I say you were right to try," she offered and studied the shadows in the back of the wagon. When there was no answer, she finished, "It was worth the effort, I think, even if—"

"Worth the effort, I say." James Baiys flicked the reins, and the horses broke into a trot. Webster threw himself back against the pile of blankets and closed his eyes. Everything he'd believed about himself had changed in these past few days. It was as if a strange door had opened, and he'd been forced to walk through it into hell. For a few hours on the night of the burning of Washington, he'd taken new hope. Finding the cannons at the Capitol and the eight horses at the Navy Yard had filled him with something like power. He'd believed himself redeemed from his failure at Bladensburg but that feeling had faded away. Now his breath came hard and scarce in his chest, and he was filled with only exhaustion and regrets.

✻ ✻ ✻

When they reached dockside in Baltimore, it was almost dawn, and Rachel was sleeping, her head on her father's shoulder. The horses halted in front of the old harbor hotel that served now as naval headquarters and the seamen's quarters.

Jack Webster climbed from the wagon behind Mingo and stood for a long moment as if coming to a decision.

"I'm not coming in with you, Mr. Jones," he said finally. "There being no duty-call and no need for me at present, I'm thinking to go on to the Baiys farm and help bring in the last of the harvest. They're shorthanded. I see it like a payback for their help to me. A payback for giving me Shoe Tail. You'll know where I am. I can be sent for if needed."

This pronouncement from Captain Webster took some thinking over. Mingo looked up at the farmer driving the wagon and the girl sitting beside him. She'd waked and pulled her shawl around her, and she was looking back at Webster with quiet, thoughtful eyes. Webster's face was the pasty gray of a dead gull's wing, a sign of a dead spirit. Something happened up there on that ridge that weighed heavy on him. If there's one thing that Mingo understood, it was that laboring in the fields could clear a man of his thoughts. It might be the hard work of bringing in the harvest was what the captain was needing most.

He watched the wagon pull away. Then he turned, yawned, and studied the sheen of sun rays on the waters of the harbor. Morning was fast coming on. He could smell cooking in the morning air—it might be bacon and biscuits in a fry pan—and, he reasoned, he might as well go into the seamen's quarters and fill his belly. While he was at it, he'd see how the boys were doing.

Caleb and Jason, them two rascals, they weren't worth nothing but a handful of spit. He'd meant to talk to the commodore about them, but it hadn't seemed the time, and not worth the commodore's concern. Nor his own concern. Still, the thought of the tadpole boys filled his head, and he moved with quickened steps toward the old harbor hotel.

☆ ☆ ☆

September 3

The burning of the nation's Capitol and the president's house, the violence of the storm, and more than anything, the American militia's humiliating defeat at Bladensburg—a defeat some newspapers referred to with scorn as "the Bladensburg races"—shocked and demoralized the people of the Chesapeake.

General Ross and the British infantrymen had boarded their transport ships, and the fleet was now standing off in the river. Cockburn's lead ship, the *Albion,* and the frigates under his command were already making their way down the Patuxent into bay waters. It was said he was headed out through the capes to the Atlantic and on to Bermuda.

The citizens of Washington City, who'd fled with such anguish and fear upon the approach of the British troops, had returned to find their homes and businesses undisturbed. But the government appeared to have lost all control; whispers spread that a slave rebellion was brewing, this fear always the first rumor to fly when times were out of joint.

It hadn't happened. There was also talk in parlors and taverns of unruly gangs—mostly the Irish and the marble cutters, the day laborers, and boat hands from Foggy Bottom—looting the ruins of the Navy Yard and the Capitol and the president's mansion. Looting and plundering, theft of all kinds, and drunkenness, as well. Those rumors were true. In desperation the city fathers, including the mayor, strapped on pistols and patrolled the streets themselves. It was disconsolate work, for the stench of the fires still smoldered on the hill and at the Navy Yard. The remains of the great house on Pennsylvania Avenue was a constant reminder of what had once been…and was now lost.

James Madison had given up all thoughts of joining General Winder and the remnants of the American army, wherever they might be. They were not at Montgomery County Courthouse when he'd arrived there. At the secretary of state's urging, he'd returned to Washington on August 27 and immediately penned a letter to his wife, which began, "*My Dearest…*", who was at Wiley's Tavern near Difficult Run in Virginia. They'd met up briefly and she was still there waiting for word of his safety.

The next day Dolley hurried to her husband's side. As First Lady, she was still in danger of being kidnapped or even killed. So she was warned. She traveled in borrowed clothes, trailed by a single guard, and in disguise she'd crossed the river by ferry, and walked on foot into the still-smoking city.

His wife's return was the only good thing in Madison's life. His home was gone. His government was in shambles. Newspapers throughout the thirteen United States were heaping insult, blame, and condemnation upon him. There was now a general resentment in the nation against the rush to war that brought such horror.

Impeachment was suggested by more than one influential opponent. There was one thing he could do, and he did it, if belatedly. The war secretary had returned to the city. Madison paid John Armstrong a call and relieved him of his duties. "A temporary retirement" was the phase used, but much more was meant. Armstrong had often expressed his preference for New York City as the site of the nation's capital. There were those who believed Armstrong deliberately allowed the British to destroy Washington so that the capital could be moved to that northern city. Madison didn't call Armstrong a traitor. He simply relieved him of his appointment and ordered James Monroe to assume the duties of the secretary of war. It was a start in regaining some kind of control over his administration.

✵ ✵ ✵

September 9

Word spread quickly that the British fleet was moving down the Bay toward the Atlantic. Along the coastline, men climbed church towers and watched from the decks of their fishing vessels, eager to witness the last of the British in their waters.

At the top of the bay, Baltimore seemed secure from attack.

It's just as well, reasoned Jack Webster, as there was no longer an army to defend the shore. And no ardor for it. He himself felt no ardor, only a need for physical work and mental rest. Why had he chosen to not go home?

For awhile, that question was in James Biays's eyes.

Webster couldn't give an answer, but he knew. There'd be many questions and too much succoring at home, too much praise he didn't deserve. Letters were sent to The Mount reassuring his family that he was alive and well. The Biays family seemed to accept him as he was: difficult, withdrawn, quiet. Rachel, in particular, watched his face, but asked no questions. He would not sleep in the main house at Sugar Valley. He agreed to take his meals with the family. But he preferred to sleep outside.

"What if it rains?" Madam Biays asked.

He accepted a throw of blankets for the high loft in the barn, where he could see the stars through the rafter beams. After a day's labor in the fields or digging potatoes in the farm's vegetable garden, he slept best there. It was like lying in his hammock aboard the *Rossie* or aboard barge 112, his body tired and warmed by a day in the sun, his mind stripped of thoughts except for an idle study of the stars. He'd heard once that the stars are bits of fire broken off from earth by God. He felt a kinship to them, for he was broken off as well. Broken off from everything that had ever mattered to him.

✵ ✵ ✵

"You're so sad," Rachel said to him when she brought a jug of water to the fields one day. He was sprawled beside her in the shade of a poplar tree. "What is it that holds you sad, Jack? Not Shoe Tail. For sure I've forgiven you that. He died in a good cause."

For a moment, he didn't answer. Then he gathered the energy to respond. "Aye, Shoe Tail's a part of it. He had a great heart and soul, but you know that better'n anyone. My heart bleeds over him, I give you that."

"But it's more," she said.

More, so much more, he thought. Words came to him because her eyes were kind. "My friend died in my arms. I closed his eyes with my hand. I'll never forget that and I see the commodore all the time in my head, Rache. He's lying there in that bed in the tavern in Bladensburg, and he won't come with me. He gave his word to the enemy, he says, gave his word to stay until the British soldiers are paroled. But I think he hasn't forgiven me for running away on the ridge. He has no trust in me. I failed him. I had no courage when put to the test."

For a long moment, there was the silence of shared contemplation. She stared out into the soft glaze of the sun. "I would like the test of courage."

"You're a girl. How can you say that?"

Rachel leaned forward so that her braid fell over her shoulder. "I think it would be a good thing to know what it is you're willing to die for. I think you have to love something...or someone...a great deal."

"What would you be willing to die for?" he asked her.

Her profile was lovely, he noted, the shadow of dark lashes on her cheek, the curve of her chin.

"I'd risk dying for the people I love...that, mostly, and without hesitation, and this." She put out her arm as if to encompass the newly cut cornstalks and the thick bower of trees on the sides of the fields. "These fields, you know, and the trees and the dogs and horses. Maybe for all this."

"I always believed I'd be willing to die for the commodore."

It was a truth Jack Webster had been wanting to say, the words bottled up inside him. "God's truth, I still would. Given a second chance, I'd never have left his side."

"I've met your commodore." She turned to him then, and her eyes were wide as if to acknowledge the passion in his voice. "I saw his face, white against the pillow in that bed in the tavern. When I said your name, something in his eyes came alive, as if he knows your worth. I'm certain he knows you didn't run out of cowardliness."

"Then why then did I run?" He put a hand over his eyes as if trying to look inward. Something terrible was there behind his eyelids, huge and dark, but he saw it only in shards and images— the glint of sun on a cannon and Tom Warner on his back with his chest ripped open, the dappled light and shadow of the pine trees on the ridge. And then, clearly, the face of a British soldier. Brilliant blue eyes staring at him from beneath his shako, a silky black mustache, a young man's mustache, the flash of his saber.

With a groan, Jack rolled over and pressed his face into the grass. "There's something that keeps coming into my head, Rache. I killed a man up close, too close. He came out of nowhere, and I was on Shoe Tail's back, and he looked up into my eyes, and it was like…well, for just a moment, we knew each other. In another circumstance, we might've lifted a pint in a tavern together. But I leaned from the saddle and thrust my sword in his chest, and the blood spouted out. Oh, Rachel, the look in his eyes…the surprise in his face. And the blood…everywhere, even on the arm of my jacket. I think it was then that I took off up the hill."

"You were surrounded, fighting for your life. The commodore said for you to run. You know that's true."

"I once knew everything, everything I needed to know. And now—"

She laid her hand gently on his back. "It's only that you must learn new things, I think, to find your way."

✵ ✵ ✵

On the deck of Admiral Cochrane's flagship, the *Tonnant*, General Robert Ross stood with legs braced, eyeing the scrubby shoreline He breathed in the hot, salty air and sighed his relief that the convoy was leaving the bay. He'd no wish to see his men to remain in these waters a day longer than necessary. A year ago a mysterious fever had swept through the British naval force assigned to the Chesapeake, felling five hundred of two thousand men. He couldn't imagine why and, indeed, how civilized men and women existed on these lonely shores. It could be endured, yes. He could appreciate the fine interplay of water and sky, a bountiful sea catch at the throw of a pole or net. But the land was unruly and marked by mists, evil vapors that rose from the brackish waters and swamps.

He now had the agreement of Admiral Cochrane to depart these waters.

His transport vessels would soon make the hard sweep at Solomon's Island and head out to sea. The fleet would follow the American coastline north and find a suitable location in which to establish winter quarters. It was his intention to find agreeable surroundings so that his men could regain their health. They suffered too much from dysentery and heat sickness and odd and mysterious rashes.

Of course, Cockburn argued otherwise. He'd pressed heatedly for an immediate attack on Baltimore.

Ross had held firm, aware that too often he'd given way. Only by good fortune and the misadventures of the American militia had the British advance at Bladensburg been successful. With a fighting force of only twenty-six hundred men, he'd routed twice that number. And captured ten long guns and taken one hundred twenty prisoners. Even with the march on Washington, his losses amounted to only two hundred fifty men killed. Could such good fortune hold?

Cockburn had argued persuasively. "Consider, Ross, the Americans are in despair over the burning of their capital. They are demoralized, and more importantly, as confused as goslings. Their newspapers claim we head for Rhode Island, so let them think it, by God! Let them go soft at Baltimore, and we shall deliver a blow to that mob town more devastating to this illicit nation than the burning of Washington."

Cockburn was bending over a map of the upper Chesapeake when he said this, a familiar stance. His cheeks were reddened by the day's heat and by his own passion.

"Look here, Ross." He'd rattled the map. "Baltimore lies at a fork in the Patapsco River. On the point of that fork stands the city's main defense. I've heard Fort McHenry is nothing extraordinary, a modest affair, being aged some fifteen years. It's our only impediment, Ross."

Cockburn had grinned then, that old, confiding, confident grin. "See here. On the left as we approach the fort by water, the river narrows and becomes the Ferry Branch. That concerns us not. It's the right branch that matters, as it is the thoroughfare into Baltimore harbor. They call it the Northwest Branch, though God knows the odd thinking of the Americans, as the branch heads in the eastern direction. What's important is that this branch leads directly to the shipyards and the docks. Damn it all, there's our target, that den of pirates, Baltimore."

☆ ☆ ☆

Cockburn had made it sound so easy—a land assault to be led by Ross with a company of his crack infantrymen, while a simultaneous naval attack was carried out against Fort McHenry—which the admiral insisted could not hold against a barrage of rocket and cannon fire from the British warships.

"They'll panic as they did at Bladensburg and hoist a white flag," Cockburn had argued. "Then our light-hulled barges will make their way into the heart of the harbor and meet with your troops to take the city. It shall be as easy a victory as the taking of Washington."

Ross had only listened. It was his opinion that Cockburn's passion to attack Baltimore came from his personal antipathy against the Americans. In this instance, revenge. In the first year of the war, Baltimore commissioned more than a hundred privateers that captured, or sent to the sea's bottom a score of British merchant vessels. To destroy the Maryland city, or force it to pay a heavy contribution, would give Cockburn enormous satisfaction.

He'd listened, but stood firm. Thank God, Admiral Cochrane was in agreement. Within hours dispatches had gone off to England with assurances that the British fleet would not attack Baltimore. Without the support of the higher command,

Cockburn had reluctantly given way. Grudgingly he'd accepted defeat and was now aboard the *Albion,* on his way to Bermuda, his consolation being that he was carrying a prize load of rich tobacco, for which he would receive personal gain.

For the first time in weeks, Ross slept soundly in his berth.

He'd sent a letter home with the dispatches. He thought of Ly's face when his note reached her hands and she read his words of love. It would please her to read that the assault on the American capital was successful. Even more pleasing to his wife would be his assurance that he was safely aboard his ship once more.

Chesapeake Bay

North Point

Patapsco River

Fort McHenry

Whetstone Point

Fort Babcock

Baltimore

Fort McHenry

CHAPTER SIX

FORT McHENRY

Afternoon, September 10

Mingo was restless in Baltimore. He was giving considerable thought to heading out for Pennsylvania. The old dream still nagged at him. When it did, he put his hand on the oil-skinned pouch that hung over his heart and contented himself that the freedom papers were there. No one would ever question the scrawled signature of Commodore Joshua Barney. He was a free man, and he could go wherever he chose.

Still, his belly was full, and he had his half pint of grog every day, rum or whiskey. He had a place to sleep in the seamen's quarters, and there was work to do that put coppers in his hand every day. More importantly, no one paid him any mind, as Baltimore was like a town in a constant storm.

Last week it was reported the British fleet was descending the bay. Early this morning a new rumor raced through the town claiming the enemy fleet had reversed itself and was headed north.

The rumors came and went. All the while, the city streets surged like swirling water with militiamen from Virginia and Pennsylvania. Every day, and even far into the night, the air rang with drills and shouts. The stench of horse manure filled the streets, and the taverns were packed with boot-stamping soldiers. The stable hands and the blacksmiths were hammering away, day and night. Even the bakers kept their ovens going all the time, for there was a fear the city would run out of bread, with all the newcomers about.

Mingo felt safe in this confusion, safer maybe than if he were out on the road by himself. For one thing, he wore the black scarf and stiff-brimmed round hat of an American seaman, and for the first time in the six months he'd been a flotilla man, he took a certain pride in that allegiance.

Pride was not a feeling he'd ever known. Nor had he ever cared to ally himself in such a way. Still, he took personal satisfaction in seeing that more than four hundred of Barney's flotilla men had straggled into town. They'd made their way by foot or in wagons to Baltimore. Although he didn't mingle or talk much in their presence, he knew himself to be one of "Barney's Boys." He didn't mind the feeling of it.

Jason and Caleb had grown frisky with pudding and fresh meat and eight ounces of bread to eat every day. They scampered about town and brought the news and rumors to the seamen's barracks. Caleb told Mingo that a new military man was in charge of the city's defense.

Major General Samuel Smith was now the commander of the Third Maryland Militia, a tough-minded fellow in his early sixties. "Older than the commodore," Caleb related. General Winder was said to be sorely struck by the news of his demotion. Even his uncle, the governor of Maryland, had gone along with the choice of Smith. Now, Caleb reported, Winder was just one of the seven generals who served under General Smith.

That mattered little to Mingo. Barney's flotilla men reported directly to Mr. Rutter, and Lieutenant Rutter reported directly to Commodore John Rogers, the senior officer of the Navy. There were other naval units about town, including the Sea Fencibles, two sea-going companies that made up part of Fort McHenry's garrison.

"They're assigned to the defense of the port and harbor, an' they service the cannons at the fort's water batteries," Caleb explained. He added with a rueful face, "Us jack-tars being sorta left out, with the commodore ailing."

Jason and Caleb stayed in his mind like burrs caught on a wool blanket. He puzzled over them, believing that Caleb was too full of himself, striding about town in his old black boots, and staring up, so innocent-like, from under that cornstalk hair that was always falling in his eyes. The boy was likely to amble into barracks, like the one on Piper's ropewalk, where the Fifty-sixth Virginian unit was stationed, and help himself to a mug of coffee and a handful of biscuits, and just as likely to hang about at gatherings of officers, where he had no business being. As for Jason, he just trailed after him like a puppy dog, something wistful and lost in his face.

Mingo mulled over this as he swung a pickax on a hilltop above the city. The flotilla men had been working all this day alongside the militia and a score of city men to set some sixty cannons in place behind newly dug earthworks on the hills that looked down, most particularly, on the harbor. General Smith gave the orders.

The sun was low now in the western sky. He was alone on this hillock by choice. He was about to head over to where Dan Frazier was working on the far ridge and say, "We needs a resting time," when he heard his name shouted out. Looking over his shoulder, he caught sight of Caleb racing along the ridge of Hampstead Hill, waving his arms like a bull was chasing after him.

Mingo cupped his hands and called out to the boy, "Here, over here, you whippersnapper. Where you been, an' where's Jason at?"

Caleb's words tumbled out between hard gasps. "They're coming! The British! They're coming here, for certain, Mingo."

"What you mean...coming here? Where's Jason be?"

"I've come to tell ye, Mingo, there be signal fires up the coast, and two horsemen come riding in less'en a hour ago to find General Smith and tell him. It's for certain now. They done reversed course. There are white sails coming right up the bay, and we are going to have a fight! I know it, Mingo. I just know it!"

Mingo straightened his back and shaded his eyes. The town of Baltimore carried the golden glow of late day as he viewed it spread below Hampstead Hill. It was a fine-enough looking town, the largest and proudest he'd ever seen, made rich on tobacco and wheat and the shipping trade. He could make out half a dozen great merchant vessels anchored in the Northwest Branch, along with a score of schooners and smaller fishing boats bobbing in the waters of the harbor.

When he looked west toward Fort McHenry situated at the break of the Patapsco, he could see a faint glint of silver river beyond the red brick fort. He stared hard at Caleb. "Them British coming all the way here to Bal'amore? You say this for sure, boy?"

"Can't say nothing for sure." The boy was dancing about, his eyes bright with excitement. "Two frigates been sighted below Plum Point, and the fleet is following after. They're carrying a full press of canvas. I come to get you, Mingo. We got to go to Mr. Rutter and find out where's we're supposed to be."

"Jason's down there with Mr. Rutter?"

"Can't say for sure. Last I saw, he was moving around on the dock, studying them ole white crewmen like he does. You know how he does, moving around quiet like and searching for the man what killed his pa."

Mingo threw down his pickax and gestured to Dan Frazier and the two midshipmen, Edwards and Andrews, who were working with him on the far ridge. They'd heard the news as well, for they were waving back at him and pointing down toward the docks.

"All right, boy," Mingo sighed. He spit in the grass and cuffed Caleb on the shoulder. "Let's take oursel's down there and see what's happening and what mischief Jason has got himself up to."

✧ ✧ ✧

The sign over the swinging doors read Nardin's Tavern. Inside the bar, dust-covered men leaned against the rail or sprawled at the rickety tables. They were red-faced with excitement or had their heads thrown back to drain down the tankards of ale in their dirty hands. The fact that the British fleet was no longer heading out the Hampton Roads to the Atlantic but was indeed moving up the bay toward Baltimore must be absorbed. That was done best with whiskey in a man's belly.

Jason crept in, unnoticed. The tavern was loud with voices.

"Stud sails set...moving past Annapolis...ships of the line, frigates, schooners. They're steady on for Bal'amore," he heard one man say.

The dim-lit room smelled of whiskey and sweat, and even of fear that sweat could catch hold of and give out, like the scent of animals in danger.

The boy rested his hand on the handle of the knife that barely showed beneath his oversized seaman's shirt. Scarce an hour ago he'd laid eyes on the white seaman he'd been chasing for all these months. And maybe it didn't matter so much after all, he'd decided. It was like the pain that had made the flame of anger in him burn like a candle had gone low, and there was only the wisp of smoke left, and the smell.

But then someone on the dock called out, "Sharky," and Jason had turned his head and seen a white man standing clear in the sunlight. His heart had leaped with the same sort of feeling he'd known once before when a bolt of lightning struck the mast of barge 112.

"Over here, Sharky," someone had called again, and the old man stepped closer to the water to help move a mess of ropes.

Sharky had a mess of stringy white hair and was wearing a vest that showed his arms plain enough. Jason had slipped around Mr. Kiddall's elbow so that he could see the tattoo up close. It was sure enough a shark with teeth bared and pointed, coming out of a wave.

Now he stared into the back corner of the tavern where Sharky was sitting with two empty tankards before him and his knotted arms stretched out on the table, his head hanging low. The boy stepped across the sawdust-strewn floor, not letting himself think about the danger in what he was about to do. He grasped the back of the seaman's vest. The man's head rolled back. His eyes were red-rimmed. He was an old man, the boy sensed, not so much in years, but worn out and slack in his muscles.

He stared into the man's toothless, twisted face. "Do you be Jake Simpson, what's called Sharky off'en Barney's flotilla?" His voice was soft, only a whisper.

"What's it to you, boy?"

For a moment Jason wished Caleb was beside him, but the drummer boy had gone off somewhere, and it was just as well, for he knew this was something he must do for himself.

"I've a message for ye," he said in a stronger voice. "Come outside." He pulled the old seaman to his feet and grabbed his hand. The man swayed as if uncertain why he was standing. Jason led him toward the swinging doors of the tavern. On the wooden sidewalk, Jake Simpson put up a hand against the sun. He was drunk and unsettled by the boy's action. He stared down at Jason and a smile of awareness touched his face.

"Who are ye? Ben Hayes's boy?"

Jason drew a deep breath to push down his fear and said the words he'd been waiting for so long to say. "Aye. I'm Jason Hayes. You sailed with my pa on the *Constitution* when she fought the *Guerriere*. And when she docked in Boston, you drank with my pa and stole his prize money and stuck a knife in his back outside the Black Dog Saloon. I know it's true. It was told to me on the dock at Norfolk by a seaman what knew Ben."

"Not true, lad. Not true, I say." Simpson staggered back and caught himself against the wall. "I heard you wuz looking for me. What's that about, I sez to myself?" Now the man's voice grew hard, and his smile was cunning. "Stinking little black rat, always on my tail, are ye?"

Jason struck out with his fist, giving Simpson a hard blow in the belly. The old man doubled and fell, bumping his head hard on the mounting block, a spurt of blood staining the corner of his mouth. He rolled to his knees and pulled out his seaman's curving knife. A crowd of men had begun to gather, some having followed them from the tavern, intrigued by the sight of a black boy commanding a white man. They were murmuring among themselves and jostling each other for a spot to watch the fight. Jason was smaller, but Simpson was unsteady and breathing hard. The boy leaped back as Simpson, still on his knees, slashed out with his knife.

"Good for nothing black boy!" one of the watching men cried out. "Get yourself up and fight like a man, Sharky. Ram the nigger boy's gut, I say!"

"You killed my pa," Jason screamed and pulled out his own knife.

Simpson lunged forward and landed hard on the boy's chest. Jason was pressed flat on his back, his head banging against the plank sidewalk. With a desperate surge, the boy wrenched his right hand free and thrust upward with the knife, slicing the man's face as if it were a loaf of bread.

"Me throat's cut," Simpson cried out.

The line of blood came from the long slash, but was not so deep a cut as all that. Jason pulled up both legs and kicked out hard as if he were underwater and drowning. He threw himself on top of Simpson, whose drunken state evened the difference between them. They struggled, but the boy was wiry and slippery as an eel, and finally the older man lay still.

Simpson groaned. "Be it God's truth, I never killed your pa."

Jason sat astride the man's belly. He flinched when Simpson belched in his face. Then he sobbed out, "I say you did and you stole his pay and you left him there bleeding to death."

"We were mess-mates, Ben Hayes and me," Simpson gasped. "Sure'n we was. Aye, we drank at the Black Dog, like you tell it. And he won my prize money offen' me with one throw of the dice, 'cause I was that gone with whiskey. But that's all the truth in your story, boy. I swear it."

"My pa was kilt," Jason repeated through gritted teeth.

Sharky struggled to push Jason from his chest. "Me and Ben, we came out of the tavern, still the pals we always was. And the first we knowed, a handful of thieves was upon us. They being wise to the fact we was off the *Constitution* with prize money of our own. When I came to, I was lying in the gutter with me pockets ripped and Ben on the street there alongside…dead as a mackerel."

Murmurs rose in the crowd, some agreeing with Simpson's version, others not.

"You are lying to me, ole man. You killed my pa, and I'll make you sorry for it. I aim to kill you dead." Jason pressed the knife against Simpson's chest just above his vest. He could see the throbbing of the vein in the old man's neck. He had only to press with the knife.

A hand came down firm on Jason's shoulder. A familiar voice startled him. Mingo Jones bent close to his ear and whispered, "It ain't gonna bring your pa back. Hear me now. Ain't nothing gonna do that."

The crowd of men tightened around them. Jason could hear the stamp of boots and the muttering of drunken men. The smell of whiskey was strong in the air, like the hard salt breeze before a storm at sea. A small runty man shouted, 'Go on, boy,

finish off the ole boozer." But it was only the taunt of a militiaman inflamed by the fight, and Jason could hear other cries and
whispers, stronger and angrier. He knew they were coming from
militiamen who were not on his side and who'd as surely stomp
him to death as not. Him and Mingo, too.

"You found Jake Simpson like you set out to do," Mingo
whispered in his ear. "You said your piece. Now let it be. He
ain't worth your killing. You free-born. You strong and proud
like your pa, ain't you? An eagle, he don't mess with flies,
boy."

Jason looked down at Jake Simpson, saw the man's dirty, gray
beard and the bloody cut on his cheek. Some kind of pleasure
came in him, a power he'd not known before. He bent closer so
he could stare directly into the man's eyes. "I ain't saying your
story be true or not. But me, not knowing the truth of it, I choose
to let you live."

When he looked up, he saw Caleb standing close by, his face
red as fire, and Lieutenant Rutter with his saber in his hand, and
Mr. Kiddall and Mr. Sellars, who had his elbows out and his hands
on his hips like he was willing to take on any comers. But it was
Mingo who pulled Jason off Simpson's belly and threw the boy
over his shoulder like a bag of sugar. They set off down the cob-
blestones, a wedge of flotilla men ignoring the jeers and threats
and catcalls and pushing through the disappointed onlookers. It
was Mr. Rutter's sword that cleared their way.

"Is the lad all right?" John Kiddall asked as they neared the
seamen's quarters on the dock. He was eyeing Jason, who was still
on Mingo's back. The boy's eyes were closed. He sagged against
Mingo's shoulders as if he were exhausted. "What was that all
about anyway?"

Mingo shifted Jason's weight in a way that was both rough
and affectionate. "It weren't nothing to speak of, sir. Just something weighing on the boy's mind what he had to tend to. Had
to have his say, he did. But it's done now. Jason Hayes, he gonna
be all right. He got the piss in him, that's the truth."

★ ★ ★

Early evening

Vice Admiral Alexander Cochrane's decision to change course and attack Maryland's major port city came as a shock to Robert Ross. By this hour, he'd been expecting to see dark ocean water. Instead, the sun was setting over tobacco and cornfields, throwing a soft sheen of gold on the water as the British convoy, some fifty vessels strong, climbed the Chesapeake Bay.

As their ships passed the village of Annapolis, the bells in the church towers began to ring out the alarm. The frantic pealing reached Ross as he stood on the *Tonnant* at mid-deck. By rights, the townfolk should be warned, he considered. Cochrane's commands were known to veer with the wind. It could well be he'd order the ships' cannons to fire on the town of Annapolis for the pure hell of it.

★ ★ ★

A fair wind billowed the sails of the *Tonnant.* Ross was thinking of his wounded men left behind in Bladensburg. A few days past, two Americans—a Georgetown lawyer, Francis Scott Key, and his companion, Skinner—had come aboard the *Tonnant* to ask for the release of a prisoner.

That prisoner was Dr. Beanes, a dastardly sort of fellow in whose home Ross had stayed the night in Upper Marlboro. Gracious with his hospitality and his brandy, Beanes pledged not to engage in hostile acts against the British. A few days later, he went back on his word and captured two of Ross' soldiers who were straggling back to Benedict after the burning of Washington.

It was Ross's tenet that such a man was entirely without honor. He had no intention to release Beanes from the dungeon in the hold of the *Tonnant.* "He better deserves a rope at his neck than freedom," he'd told Key curtly. But then the American lawyer thrust out a handful of letters from the wounded men left under Commodore Joshua Barney's protection in Bladensburg.

He'd taken the letters below to his quarters to read in private. The scrawled notes spoke of the kindnesses of local people and the good medical care the British soldiers had received. His relief in receiving these assurances and his high regard for Commodore Barney had caused Ross to rethink the situation. One fair turn deserved another. With some reluctance he agreed to the release of the doctor to Skinner and Key, who both appeared, in fact, to be admirable gentlemen.

Still, Key and Skinner had learned too much of the British plans in their hours aboard the *Tonnant.* Cochrane concurred in his decision that the Americans could not be allowed to return to shore immediately. Until the assault on Baltimore was over, the Americans would travel, under guard, in their sloop behind the convoy. No doubt Key and Skinner were, at this very moment, staring with longing at these bonfires along the Maryland shoreline.

☆ ☆ ☆

A creak of the boards and Ross sensed Admiral Cochrane at his elbow, the spread of belly and a gold-braided shoulder. As well, he was acutely aware of that devil, George Cockburn.

Cockburn was now aboard the *Tonnant.* He'd stationed himself, with some casualness, ten feet down the rail from Ross and was joking with some half-dozen fleet captains and junior officers. Ross could feel the eyes of the adjuncts and younger officers flickering in his direction. They were watching him covertly, curious as to his reaction to Cochrane's reversal of plans. It was known that the assault on Baltimore was, in General Ross's opinion, a terrible mistake.

☆ ☆ ☆

"Remember the cowardliness of the Americans at Bladensburg," Cockburn kept insisting. Those words had not changed his mind. Men react differently in different situations. Ross had it on good authority from his spies that the "mob town" was now teeming with eager militiamen hoping for a chance to redeem their honor after "the Bladensburg races."

To capture this American city with its recessed port and extensive docks would not be as effortless as the taking of Washington, he'd stated to Cockburn. The entrance to the harbor was said to be guarded by a small but deadly dragon, a star-shaped fort called McHenry—surely well armed and fortified. So he'd argued.

"Not to worry, old fellow," was Cockburn's response. "McHenry is an aged fort that will run down its flag as soon as we show our guns." Admiral Cochrane had patted his white wig and smiled his agreement. It was Ross's opinion that Sir Alexander Cochrane was thinking of the prize money. The city fathers of Baltimore might well offer a great prize of silver to keep Baltimore from burning. Cochrane, and Cockburn as well, would benefit handsomely from the victory.

✿ ✿ ✿

From the corner of his eye, Ross could see Cockburn's hawklike profile. Only by luck—or by the hand of God—was the *Albion* overtaken on its way out of the bay and Cockburn informed of the monumental reversal of plans. Within hours, the *Albion* was back in signaling distance of the convoy. Since Cockburn's return, tensions had risen, as well as voices in argument concerning the plan of attack on Baltimore.

"I'm giving consideration to the landing of my troops," Ross turned from his study of the shoreline and said to Cochrane. He waited for the senior naval officer's reaction.

Alexander Cochrane nodded. He was some ten years older than Ross, the younger son of an Earl. More importantly, as the captain of this eighty-gun frigate and indeed commander of this impressive fleet, he had the power to set policy and targets for attack, but there was a subtlety here. He and Ross both knew it. General Robert Ross could express his opinion on all operations from the military viewpoint and, more importantly, he carried complete veto power over any orders from Cochrane concerning the army troops.

George Cockburn appeared beside Cochrane. He wore a smile, but his eyes were cool as he nodded to Ross. "Aye," he said. "I concur with a two-pronged attack." His words were directed to the senior admiral, but his eyes remained fixed on Ross. "We've talked for hours, General Ross and I, aboard the *Albion,* and gone over plans to land his troops on a spit called North Point, which lies some fourteen miles south of Baltimore harbor. As the fleet commences the bombardment of Fort McHenry, the army will approach by land and by stealth. I intend to march with General Ross." For a long moment, there was silence. "Aye, an attack by sea and by land. That is, unless the city fathers offer a weighty prize to save their city from destruction."

Cochrane grinned and muttered his approval.

Ross stiffened his shoulders and spoke precisely. "A land approach is not yet entirely decided upon. Certainly Admiral Co'burn is aware that a score of my men suffer from dysentery. I don't relish marching them out to face an enemy force of which we have little intelligence concerning their numbers and cannons and inclination."

"Inclination?" scoffed Cochrane. "They're spaniels." It was the word he used most often to describe the Americans, and it brought no response. Still, he stared hard at Ross. "Not gone soft, have you?"

Ross flushed and fingered his sword. George Cockburn responded in a quick, soothing voice, "He's not gone soft. He'll come round, sir. General Ross is a man of honor and of duty."

☆ ☆ ☆

For an hour after this interchange, Ross strolled the *Tonnant*'s deck. He'd waved away his aides. He wished to be alone in order to think clearly. He had serious doubts about the attack on Baltimore, but they were the doubts of a seasoned military officer. Cochrane's implication that he was soft toward the Americans was an insult. The flow of blood was hot in Ross's neck and shoulders. He paused and stared out across the bay, which had narrowed considerably as they approached the mouth of the Patapsco River.

Already the moon was rising, heavy and brooding, a full moon. How he hated this place, this war. He reached into his tunic and fingered the miniature of Ly that hung around his neck on a thin gold chain. A man's honor was his character and his worth and a gift from God.

✯ ✯ ✯

September days can be long and golden in Chesapeake country.

The sun rises early beyond the bay and does not dip beneath the horizon until after eight in the evening. Even before night darkens the waters and closes over the flat farmland and the long stretches of wheat and tobacco and corn on the inland farms, a harvest moon appears.

Those field hands available to bring in the harvest at Sugar Valley on Saturday—the tenth of September—were working under the full-faced moon. Jack Webster was chopping rye behind the barn, his shirt stuck to his back. There was a piece of straw caught in his hair. Now and again he looked up at the moon and noted how it rode the sky near to the planet Mars.

If the commodore were here, he'd look at the sky and say, "The god of war, Mars," and Barney would smile and raise an eyebrow. Sleeping alone in the loft above the barn, he'd dreamed each night of the flotilla and sometimes of Barney. More than once, in his dreams, he'd felt the heat of a saber in his hand and stared into the face of the British soldier with the mustache and the startling blue eyes.

Once he dreamed the soldier was alive and here at Sugar Valley. He'd waked, certain the man was standing in the corner of the loft. Or was it Warner standing there? Tears had streamed from his eyes, and he'd climbed down the wooden ladder and wandered out of the barn, letting the coolness of the night dry his sweat and calm his thoughts. The soldier in his dreams was the enemy. How can a man so sterling in character as Joshua Barney stand behind his cannon, hold aloft his red-tasseled sword, and cry out, "Give 'em hell, boys," and scarce a day later, make a pact with the enemy general?

Was that not relativity? Did life not depend on judging things true or false, right or wrong, honorable or dishonorable? And if honor was not as clear as that, what was a man to do?

He'd wrestled with this question as he'd bent his back to hoe potatoes under the noon sun and lifted a knife to slaughter a pig. He'd watched the pig's blood run down his hands, and an image of Warner lying in the pool of blood on the ridge came fresh into his mind. When he and Tom had joined Barney on the *Rossie*, it was not because they had any great understanding of the reasons America had declared war on Great Britain. For sure, they'd talked with indignation of the arrogance of the British in impressing seamen from the decks of American merchant ships. More than once Tom had delivered some choice curses at the embargo the American government had put on shipping because of the war between France and Britain but mostly their feeling was righteous indignation.

The truth was something different. Neither had gone aboard the *Rossie* for anything more than the great adventure of it. They'd joined the crew of the Chesapeake Flotilla to follow Joshua Barney and to face a worthy adversary, whatever enemy it might be; to know the challenge of sword and cannon and life, vivid, gritty life, at Barney's side.

There was more to puzzle out. He could still see Barney straining to lean upward on his elbows on that bed of pain in Bladensburg. Those things the commodore said while talking of the crew, his men. He claimed he'd die for them. And Rachel had echoed those words. What would he, Jack Webster, die for? Or live for?

As the harvest was mostly gathered in, there was to be a bonfire tonight, with cider and cakes set out on a plank-board table. Already he could hear shouts and the rise of fiddles in the meadow behind the tree line. He rested the hoe and pitchfork in the corner of the barn. Drawing a bucket of water from the well, he stripped off his shirt and poured the cool water over his head. He washed himself with a cut of hard lye soap and rubbed himself dry with a strip of coarse linen until he could feel his shoulders tingle.

When his hair was wet-combed and pulled to the back of his neck with a knot of rawhide, and he was wearing his clean white shirt, he wiped the dirt from his boots and went down the meadow to the music.

✧ ✧ ✧

"Jack, it's time for dancing now. There's whiskey aplenty." James Biays greeted him, two warm hands enclosing his. The farmer was smiling broadly. "Last I heard say, the British have gone down the bay. All that bother and fuss of preparation in Baltimore was unnecessary. Now they're leaving the bay. Thank the good Lord." He paused and asked, "You'll stay with us, won't you? Having you at Sugar Valley is maybe something I've always hoped for."

"You're kind to offer it, sir." The music was loud, cutting the air with the squeak of fiddles. A feeling came over Webster like the press of a blanket, and with it the familiar choke in his throat as if he'd been thrown in deep water, a tightening of his nostrils so that he could barely breathe. He coughed hard into his palm and turned away from James Biays's eyes.

The answer to that question had to be no. It was not his destiny to live on this farm. To live out his days with wheat and rye and the bleat of oxen would be a little death. Each man must find his own. James Biays would risk his own life to hold this land safe, to keep it for himself and for his offspring. For sure, he'd share it with the right son-in-law. That was the way of men who loved the land above everything.

Webster poured a tin cup full of rum and turned away from the music and the dancing. He walked past the shadowy, laughing faces toward an outcropping of dark woods on the side of the meadow. His heart hungered with a feeling like homesickness, but not for his father's comfortable house and the land in Harford County. He wished himself aboard the *Rossie* or even the crowded, clumsy barge called 112. To stand in the bow of an open boat and watch this same round moon laying a golden pathway across dark water. To hang his hammock under the stars and to face a storm at sea.

"My father's wrong. They're not gone down the bay."

Rachel appeared with the dogs, Bones and Daisy, trailing behind her. She slid onto the rock beside him and said emphatically, "I say they're not. I say they're moving up the bay, a flock of vessels."

"We're miles inland, Rachel. How can you say that?"

She scratched Daisy's ear. "Not so far inland as all that. I see it in the birds, especially the gulls. Something's disturbing them out on the bay. It's got to be something big...like a fleet."

For a long moment, he sat still beside her. He stared out at the meadow and heard the fiddles, and breathed in the heavy sweet scent of cut wheat. He felt the girl's shoulder brush his arm, and he considered her words. "The commodore claimed it was to be Bal'amore next. He said Cockburn will have his way and they'd not leave before they conquered Bal'amore. Maybe you're right, Rachel."

"I *am* right."

"Are you saying I should leave Sugar Valley and go up to Bal'amore? You think I want to go, don't you? You think I want to go there?"

"The moon's full tonight, Jack. See those shadows on it. I think it's like a place you'd want to go to. The place you want to be, not here where there's farming and daily work to be done. Me, I like being here on the land. I love the smell of the pines and the baying of hounds and the feel of a horse beneath me roaming the woods. A good horse is..."

"Shoe Tail's dead," he retorted and drained his cup of rum. Then he asked her in a rough voice, "Is that why you want me to leave here? You're still angry, aren't you? Don't you know I grieve him too?"

She seemed surprised at the quickness of his response, surprised and touched by his emotional response. Her voice was gentle when she answered. "I know that about you. I know you're grieving about a lot of things you treasured and lost. Shoe Tail's only one of the things you lost on that ridge at Bladensburg. There was more. You lost something of yourself, I think."

She'd said that right. An emotion that was almost like relief flooded through him. An answer wouldn't come, not even straight clear thoughts that he could put into words. He wanted to tell her of the anguish in his heart, the great sense of failure that he felt inside. If there was anyone in the world he could admit his pain to, it would be this girl, but he hadn't the words to tell it.

"Grieving is right, Jack. It shows you've got a heart and a soul, I think." She'd turned now so that she was facing him. There was a directness in her that forced him to meet her gaze. "But after the grieving, you have to go on, and it's the going-on that shows you who you are."

"I'm a man of the sea. I don't know what else to say."

"A long time ago, when I was just a little girl, you used to come out here to Sugar Valley with your father, and I'd watch you when you weren't looking. You had the bluest eyes, and you sat a horse better'n anyone. So I thought maybe you were a prince or something...that's what I thought about you. And then I heard you went to sea. It seemed fitting to me that you would do that. I knew you weren't a man who'd ever be satisfied with the seasons and the crops and the quietness of a farm. But I didn't really know who you were...inside yourself. And now I do, and I like it that you can grieve so hard. It's maybe the best thing I know about you, and I won't forget it when you go on to where you have to go."

It was a long speech, and she gave a little sob as she finished it. He took her hand and laced his fingers with hers. Maybe it was the feel of her hand, maybe her words. Something inside him loosened, a knot that had been tied so tight he couldn't breathe. A kind of peace came over him.

"Where is it I have to go?" he asked as if teasing her. "Shall I go to the moon? You're right, I'd like that...to take on the stars."

"I think to join your mates...to meet the British."

He knew she was going to say that. For a moment the faces of Sellars and Kiddall and Warner, and even Huffington, flashed into his mind. He frowned and said nothing. He sat quiet for a long moment, as if considering the inevitability of her words and testing his own commitment. "Maybe it's not true about the British moving up the bay. Maybe you're reading the gulls like a fairy tale. I know you, Rachel. You could do that. No way I'm aiming to walk—"

Pulling her hand from his, she struck his shoulder with her palm, the old Rachel, the feisty Rachel. "If it was me, John Adams Webster, I'd go see for myself. I'd walk there if I had to. Only you haven't got to. There's that old mare in the barn. She's not good for much, but she'll carry you to Baltimore. Only it's you that's got to choose."

✲ ✲ ✲

Morning, September 11

"What does she want of me?" Jack Webster asked himself as he trotted the old mare through the woods and up the long dirt road to Baltimore. He could still feel the sting of her slap on his shoulder, and that made him grin. But even more, there was the taste of Rachel's mouth.

She'd come out with him in the pale darkness just before dawn to saddle the horse. She was wearing a shawl over her nightdress. Her hair was loose, and her feet were bare. Those white, slender feet. He'd glimpsed them beneath the hem of her gown and been filled with tenderness. Even a shade of happiness. And some confidence in himself. It was a feeling he'd not had in weeks, and he knew the bad time was lifting—like winter passing and seeing the birds in the sky. It was this girl and her words, even the challenge she offered him, that was giving him the right to go on.

He hadn't any words to say what he was feeling, but he'd pulled her into his arms and buried his face in her hair. "Will you kiss me again, like you did on the ridge?"

She shook her head in that way she had of not agreeing to anything until it was right and true with her. Then she'd whispered, "Not a sad kiss with tears in it, like on the ridge. I'll kiss you again, Jack, but this time, it's going to be a fierce sweet kiss between us."

He'd closed off her words with his own mouth. And there'd been a fierce, sweet delight—incredible, that pleasure—in their kiss.

✲ ✲ ✲

Rachel was right about the gulls. As he trotted down Calvert Street and breathed in the familiar scent of guano, the salty smell of the fish market, and the pungent odor of horse manure, he

could tell something big was happening in this town. It was well
past noon on this Sunday, and the church bells were still pealing,
as if offering up a cry to God for safekeeping. Wagons rattled by,
filled with women and children on their way out of town. Twice
Webster was forced to pull the old mare onto the grass at the side
of the oyster-shelled street. Men and boys surged past him, some
in their Sunday clothes, and he could see a whole party of militiamen wearing the plumed hats and yellow cuffs they'd worn at
Bladensburg. They were bumping into each other and cursing
at the redcoats. Naturally, they damned Ross and Cockburn, the
latter in particular.

"Straight to hell with him, I say," a young cavalryman was
shouting as Webster trotted past.

Two militia units went by to the cadence of a lively band, pacing out toward the fort at Whetstone Point, while a disorderly
trail of city men with muskets scrambled east toward Hampstead
Hill. A fever ran through the excited voices of the marching
men, and he heard their shouts above the beat of the drums and
the whine of the fife.

"What the hell's happening?" Webster shouted out to a young
militiaman.

"The British fleet is fast upon us," the young man shouted
back. "They're already at the mouth of the Patapsco. Bal'amore's
out to defend itself against the bastards. They'll not take our
port. That's for bloody sure!"

⋇ ⋇ ⋇

"The work of the Lord, it's Jack Webster," Lieutenant Solomon
Rutter cried. The grizzled sea captain had been Barney's second
in command on the Chesapeake Flotilla and now he served as
the commanding officer for the flotilla men in Baltimore. He
pushed back from his cluttered desk in the front room of the
seamen's hotel. "I prayed for it, and here you are. I knew you'd
come in time for battle."

"How'd you know that?"

Before Rutter could respond, Sellers slammed into the
room and cuffed Webster on the shoulder. "You were sighted on

Calvert Street. The bo'sun from barge 112 saw you. He gave us word you was coming."

Sellers smelled of sweat and salt water. He offered his mocking grin. "We wuz thinking you were holed up with some purty little lady friend and forgot all about us and this here war. 'Bout time you showed, mate. We've set up our own battery against the British invasion, Commander Rodgers' orders. Barney's boys, we'll be the first squadron to take on the bastards when they come upriver. We'll give 'em hell, like the commodore always says. We'll do it for him, what say?"

The promise in that was like wine in Webster's veins. He asked eagerly, "Where's our battery...at Fort McHenry?"

"Acros't from Whitestone Point at the mouth of the Northwest Branch. We're at the Lazaretto, the old fever hospital on the point."

"I know the place. Have we enough men? Who is here?"

"Kiddall...most all the crew," Sellers said. "They've been showing up right regular for days now—the watermen, the old coots, and black rascals, every last one. Excepting, you know, the dead ones. Warner got it at Bladensburg, but you know that. And Martin's laid up with a busted shoulder, and Huffington is with Barney in Bladensburg. But a fair lot are here. And now you're here, ole Jack Webster, come lazing in. We figured you'd show up once you got the word of it."

Webster walked with Sellers onto the wooden dock outside the hotel. Jesse Stewart and Dan Frazier turned to salute him, grins wreathing their sunburnt faces. Two young fellows in ragged jackets were stumbling over their feet as they loaded cannonballs.

"Andrews and Edwards! By God, I'm surprised those two made it," he muttered under his breath.

Sellers told him in his gruff, singsong voice that the enemy vessels would surely try to storm this Northwest Branch. "Commodore Rodgers has seen to that. A line of vessels is sunk now to snag up any gun barges and rocket boats that might slip by us at the Lazaretto. Oh, Lordy, there was shouting and grumbling from the city men when such a fine merchantman as the *Chesapeake* was sunk. And the brig *Father and Son* and the schooner

Scudder. Still, they're Marylanders and patriots sure, and fierce to defeat the scum British. They was grumbling, but they went along with it." Sellars snorted and slapped his knee, and Webster laughed, but he was hungrily seeking out more familiar faces on the dock.

Loading a skiff with cannonballs were some black seamen he recognized. Charles Ball was among them, and the drummer boy, young Caleb, was standing on an upturned barrel near to the water's edge.

"How do I get out to the Lazaretto?" Webster asked eagerly.

"Mr. Webster." Rutter loomed behind them. "I said God sent you to rejoin the flotilla, and I meant my words. I've a command for you. Commodore Rodgers has just now signed the orders. You will captain your own crew of flotilla men and establish a separate bivouac on the riverbank."

A command of his own was unsettling, but he welcomed it. Webster took the order from Rutter and smoothed out the paper with his fingers. "On the Patapsco, sir?"

"Aye, Mr. Webster, a mile north as the river bends past the fort and becomes the Ferry Branch. You'll lead a small crew of your choosing and establish a battery. It's a cleared place close on the water called Fort Babcock. Six cannons will be spared for you." Solomon Rutter paused. "However, I doubt you'll have a need to fire them."

Sellars shuffled his feet and looked away.

No need to fire the cannons? Webster looked up at Rutter and saw the quiver of nerves around the older man's eyes. He sensed the lieutenant's exhaustion, the pressure of command. This man was once skipper of a packet. He was a man of God, like Dan Frazier, and this war was wearing him down.

"Aye, aye, sir," Webster responded crisply and struggled to hide his disappointment. His command post would be out of the line of action, somewhere on the lazy turn of the river above Fort McHenry. Babcock would serve only as a backwater's battery and see no activity when the British began their attack.

"Damnable luck," Sellars whispered.

"Will you serve with me?"

"I'm promised to the Lazaretto." Sellers refused to meet Webster's eyes. "I'm sure sorry about this, old man, but I'm set to command one of the cannons there."

"Kiddall?"

"Like I say, he's at the Lazaretto as well. Bad luck, Jack."

"I'll sign on with ye, sir." Dan Frazier appeared at Jack Webster's elbow, loyalty and maybe pity in his eyes.

Something stubborn and fierce rose in Webster's chest. He walked out on the deck and studied the men working there. The coxswain from barge 112 was loading barrels off a schooner. Webster watched the waterman for a long moment, saw the young man's soft brown hair and soft brown eyes. Also, the strong arms and sturdy legs. On the barge he'd never given him much consideration, but there was something steady about Jesse Stewart. He looked to be the kind of fellow that would be good to have at your side. Within a half hour, he'd signed Stewart on for Fort Babcock and then the four black gunners from the crew of barge 112. Also, Charles Ball and Will Adams. And, finally, and with reservations, the midshipmen, Edwards and Andrews.

Standing before him was the drummer boy. Caleb announced, "I got me a musket, sir. I'll go along with ye."

"I like your spirit, boy, but I won't need your drumming at Babcock."

"I wasn't thinking of drumming. No, sirree. I can be a fighting man with a musket for ye."

"Sorry, lad. I can't use you."

"But I'm a fighting man." Caleb's voice took on a whining tone. "I ain't just a drummer. Me, I done already shot a redcoat."

Giving the boy's shoulder a gentle press, Webster turned away.

✲ ✲ ✲

In the seamen's barracks, Webster discovered half a dozen flotilla men, young watermen from the Eastern Shore, mostly oarsmen from other flotilla barges. They listened to his words and scratched their heads and shuffled about. Finally, a few agreed to join his command.

"Fort Babcock," he told them in an assured way, then forced himself to honesty, although he hated the words as he said them. "Only a battery of guns and some earthworks, I hear. Not a fort at all."

An old seaman with a dragging foot signed on and whispered, "Most of the hardy fellows are at the Lazaretto, or they're waiting for the enemy on the gun barges in the shoal waters below the fort. Me, I'm not so able as I onc't was. I can handle the backwaters with ye."

☆ ☆ ☆

Late day

When the sun was low in the western sky, Webster mounted the old mare and rode to Fort McHenry to search out the six cannons assigned to the Babcock Battery.

He noted a tavern just outside the fort's walls packed with men. He could hear singing and the thump of mugs on a bar. The fort itself sat on a slight rising overlooking the break in the river, with a drum moat circling it. Crowded into that grassy moat were dozens of tents, wagons, horses, and townspeople. He could see women leaning over the cook fires, stirring pots of stew to help feed the throngs of militiamen at the fort. Maybe a thousand men with muskets and packs stood about, staring out at the glittering water, where as yet there were no enemy sails to be seen.

Within the fort's wooden palisade, he found more militia in the parade yard. Above their heads—on a pole some ninety feet high—hung an American flag of such great size that Webster gasped.

More than once Webster had heard the story of that flag from Barney. Major Armistead, the commander of this fort, wanted a tall pole and a flag so large the British could see it clearly from a distance. That was a year ago. Where or when the British might make an assault was unknown. Barney himself, along with General Stricker and the Maryland militia colonel, William McDonald, approached a Baltimore woman known for the stitching of flags for merchant vessels. The three men laid out Armistead's wishes: fifteen white cotton stars—each star to be two feet in length from point to point—to be sewed onto a field of blue, and that material to be cut out so that the stars would show on both sides. Barney emphasized the flag was to hold eight red stripes alternating with seven white strips, each stripe to represent a state in the Union. Four hundred yards of bunting to be used, no less.

Mrs. Mary Pickersgill accepted the assignment. With only her young daughter to help her, she completed the task. Now the great flag was high on its pole, fluttering in the September breeze like a massive shield of defiance.

☆ ☆ ☆

Webster paused to get his bearings. He was disconcerted by the clamor of boots and swords and shouts and the clank of metal and the stomping of horses. This crowded yard was like a wild sea, and he didn't know in which direction to swim. With a flash of relief, he caught sight of Mingo Jones sauntering through the wooden gates on the near side of the yard. The boy walked with him. Jason was wearing a seaman's scarf and a well-fitting blue flotilla jumper. He seemed older than he had in past weeks, as if he had stretched out and grown older.

"Mingo Jones." Webster cupped his hands and shouted across the clamor.

Like a hawk hearing a musket shot, Mingo's head jerked.

He lifted a hand toward Webster and grabbed the boy's arm. They pushed through the crowd toward him. "Capt'n Webster, I been thinking I best go down to the farm and fetch you." A glimmer of a smile touched Mingo's face. "I'm also thinking you gonna show up on your own if you've a mind to it."

Webster took in the man and the boy with hungry eyes: their roughness and their vulnerability, the dark satin skin of the man and the soft gold brown of the boy, and more, something warm and alive in their eyes. He asked Mingo, "You assigned to any command...maybe to the Lazaretto?"

"Not yet we ain't." Mingo spat into the grass.

"Then I need you, and I need you bad. Come with me, the both of you. We have to find cannons and horses to pull them."

"Where we be taking 'em?" Mingo folded his arms over his chest.

"We coming," the boy cried. "We coming to help you, Mr. Webster."

☆ ☆ ☆

Evening

Near the spit of land called the North Fork, some fourteen miles downstream from Baltimore, the British fleet rode at anchor in the Patapsco River. In the dusky haze of early evening, Ross could see the frigate, *Surprise,* swaying to the wash of the tide. Sir Alexander Cochrane was aboard, having left the *Tonnant* to make the lighter vessel his command ship as he led the convoy of warships upriver toward Whetstone Point.

Ross himself was aboard the *Fairy,* a small sloop that could maneuver close to the flat sandy shore when it was time for the troops to disembark from the transport ships. He'd spent the day giving orders and overseeing the preparations for the landing of his soldiers. Three days' provisions had been handed out to each of his infantrymen, along with eighty rounds of ammunition, twenty more than the usual. Having learned a lesson on the sweat-drenching march to Bladensburg, he had ordered a minimum amount of personal baggage to be taken ashore: a change of shirt, a pair of shoes, and a blanket. Hairbrushes and sundries must be shared.

Each man was ordered to eat heartily and to sleep in his clothes tonight. Ross himself would have biscuits and wine in his quarters, he told Cockburn. He had letters to write before he slept. He gave an order that he was to be awakened at midnight.

But he couldn't bring himself to eat or to put words to paper. What's more, he couldn't sleep. Just before midnight he left his quarters and walked on the deck of the *Fairy.* He called into his mind the notes of a piece of music he once liked to attempt on his violin. It was Beethoven's *Jupiter.* One day soon he would take up the violin and play it again and master the piece this time.

The thought pleased him. He signaled his aide. The night was balmy. There was no reason to wait. Orders were given.

☆ ☆ ☆

September 12

At two in the morning, the clang of the ships' bells sounded on the transport ships. Within minutes the British infantrymen began to clamber down the swaying ladders to the barges and cutters that would transport them to shore. Ross watched a gun brig glide past like a shark in the dark waters. Cockburn had assigned the brig to keep watch against an attack by the Americans during the four hours necessary for Ross's men to be safely landed on the sand and rocks of the promontory called North Point.

What's more, Cockburn—no doubt restless under Cochrane's command on the water—had insisted on going ashore as well. He joined Ross at the rail as six cannons and two howitzers and the horses needed to pull them were lowered, without incident, to the landing barges by Ross's able soldiers.

"So, let us see what these Baltimoreans can put in our way," Cockburn said, flashing his warrior smile as Ross buckled on his sword and prepared to go down the ladder. As if for reassurance, both men turned for the last time to view the British armada spread upon the waters of the Patapsco.

Somewhere in the rear of the convoy floated the little American sloop, the *Minden,* carrying the three Americans, plucky fellows—Skinner and Key, along with Dr. Beanes, newly released from confinement by the generosity of Ross.

"They shall see a splendid show," predicted Cockburn as he climbed down the ladder behind Ross.

☆ ☆ ☆

The landing of the British troops at North Point went well, and the morning march, mostly through a light forest of pines, was entirely without incident. Robert Ross found himself in good spirits.

An advance guard unit led the way, and the infantrymen paused only to burn a deserted farmhouse. Excepting this bit of nonsense—one of the advance guards carved the Union Jack into the wooden mantel at the urgings of his companions—the British infantrymen moved at a quickstep. Ross sensed their energy was high.

A halting for lunch set the cooks to frying chickens and boiling corn. During the hour-long stop, three young American dragoons were captured in the nearby woods and brought before Ross, amusing him with their insolence and indignant, flushed faces. He questioned them as to the extent of militia troops in Baltimore. He was told by one bold-faced young fellow that the number was "about twenty thousand."

The afternoon sky turned overcast, yet the air was still surprisingly pleasant as the army resumed its march. The notes of the Mozart symphony still resonated in his head as Ross cantered the shady dirt road with his aide beside him. He allowed himself to think with a pleasant sense of nostalgia of past campaigns, of the glint of snow on the Alps, and of the grit of sandy deserts. And more, of the great good fortune he'd had, and the men he'd loved and the men he'd lost in battles.

The advance guard had moved ahead of the light companies, perhaps too far ahead, he considered. They were lost from sight beyond a turn in the narrow road. Still, there'd been no activity of note, not a single threat by cavalry or snipers, no sign of a strong defensive force in the area. He heard only the call of mocking birds. Once he'd spied a red-winged blackbird in the tangle of forest on the side of the road. There was only the sweet smell of pine and honeysuckle.

He allowed himself a favorite pastime, to wander in his mind through the grounds of *Rosstrevor*, the great manor house that belonged to him and his family in Ireland. The gardens must be in the soft full bloom of September, the roses he'd planted years ago trembling on their stems. How good it would be to go there with Ly and his children upon his return—perhaps in the spring—for it might be that this war would soon be over.

It seemed possible Cockburn was right. The Americans appeared to have no resolve. The fall of Baltimore would be the turning point, the surrender of this fragile American government to the Crown. He turned and smiled over his shoulder at his aide.

At that moment, he heard the commotion ahead.

George Cockburn was riding on a brown horse some yards behind Ross. At the clatter of musket fire beyond the turn of the road, he came up beside Ross. Again they heard the clear, sharp rally of muskets firing.

"Sharpshooters," cried Cockburn. "I say, Ross, your advance guard is too far ahead."

He didn't need to be told that. Major Brown, who'd led the advance guard at Bladensburg, was wounded in that battle. His replacement was an inexperienced young officer. The Irishman flushed and rose in his stirrups. He'd been daydreaming, and now he noted the marching army was too far behind as well.

"Stay here, Co'burn," he said crisply. "I shall go back and hurry the light companies."

He turned his horse and galloped along the dirt road beneath the shady trees. Usually careful to a fault, he'd let his army string out too loosely. A mistake in this America, Ross considered now.

A shot cracked, and he felt the arrow. It was as if an arrow has pierced his right arm. No, it was his chest that was stinging so sharply as if from the bite of a snake. He gasped at the fierceness of the pain. A spread of blood appeared on his tunic, and he felt a great heaviness and burning in his side. He tried to grasp the pommel, but lost his sword. He heard it clatter, just before he followed, diving head and shoulders first onto the hard crust of dirt on the side of the road. No, no, he thought, not again. So many times he'd been wounded in battle. But this was the only time he'd ever felt as if the pain itself might kill him.

His aide-de-camp heard the shot and was now thundering down the road, calling out his name. A handful of the First Brigade troops ran toward him. Their faces were white, and some were already in tears as the horse Ross was riding had gone tearing past them, his distinctive saddle and housing stained with blood.

Ross couldn't acknowledge them as he didn't want his troops to witness his moaning from the fierceness of his pain. He allowed his aide to go forward and alert Admiral Cockburn. A few of the infantrymen slashed at the nearby trees and built a canopy of blankets to give him privacy, but the agony was growing more unbearable. Surely he could stand it until the surgeon arrived with whiskey ... that blessed whiskey.

Ly would know of this. She'd know of his wound, perhaps of his death. No, he must not die. He drifted off, as if in sleep, and heard voices calling with great urgency for a cart. His eyelids fluttered. He was aware that George Cockburn was bending over him, his eyes huge and dark with emotion. Men lifted him, easing him into the back of the cart as if he were made of glass, so gentle their hands. Tears fell on his face. He hadn't the strength to thank the soldiers.

But the jolting of the cart finally made him scream out for it to stop.

He whispered to Cockburn that he must be still. He must die here.

"Ly..." he whispered, "her picture, take it."

As gently as he'd ever moved, George Cockburn opened the stiff white collar and unhooked the gold chain and miniature from around Ross's neck.

"Rest, old fellow, you mustn't fade on me now. Rest awhile and we'll get you to the ship's surgeon." Cockburn's voice was a hoarse whisper, an attempt to rally the dying man's spirit, but there was such anguish in the whisper.

"Co'burn, bend close. You must tell the king...the old king, the one that I have served so long...given my best to. Tell him I commend my wife and children to his protection." Ross was spent and closed his eyes.

He didn't want to die, not here on this American soil. But it was done. All his service and all his dreams were over, finished. He'd have liked to have taken Baltimore, the last regret, a mission unfinished. But there was Cochrane, and the frigates and gunboats. They were moving upstream in the river. He could see the glint of blue water, the billow of sails, a black seabird with its wings stretched overhead.

✼ ✼ ✼

Morning, September 13

The bombardment by the British fleet started shortly after seven in the morning. In the Babcock battery, a third of a mile on the far side of Fort McHenry, the roar of British cannons woke Mingo Jones. Like the rest of the flotilla men under Webster's command, he'd spent the night wrapped in his blanket under the stars. The roar of cannon fire brought him up sharp. He went up on an elbow and stared at the sky.

A light breeze was blowing from the east, and the morning smelled of rain. The explosions were great white blossoms that made him think of exploding stars in the sodden sky above the trees. Not in the sky above Fort McHenry.

Mingo could see the fort clearly upriver on the left bank. It looked to him like the bombs were exploding short, brightening the sky between the fort and the British boats he'd seen out in the river yesterday.

Jason crawled closer and asked Mingo, "You hear that?"

"I hear it. You stay put. There ain't nothing for us to do."

Most of the flotilla men had leaped up, startled at the loud burst of explosions, and were now climbing the low hill behind the open battery so they could see the fire-bursts in the sky. Mingo jumped to his feet, relieved himself in the bushes, and went in search of coffee.

✼ ✼ ✼

Soames had laid out a pile of hardtack biscuits on a piece of canvas some feet behind the battery. The cook handed him a cup of coffee without any milk or sugar and complained. "We've gone through what supplies we were issued. Finished 'em up yesterday. Wasn't much to start with. And I've got nothing to cook for later, neither."

Cookee's apron was dirty, and he was staring at the southeast sky, where the explosions were appearing with great regularity, brilliant and sharply etched against the grey of morning. "I shouldn't have agreed to this," he muttered in a mournful voice. "Shouldn't have allowed Captain Webster to bring me out here to this godforsaken spot." Soames wiped his hands on his trousers as if to show his distaste for this makeshift battery.

Mingo said nothing, for he had no use for the Englishman with his constant complaining, his bloodshot eyes, and his droopy mustache. A rat, sharp-eyed, not to be trusted, is how he saw Soames. More importantly, he was not to be cottoned to. He downed his coffee and turned back to the battery in search of the sailing master.

On Sunday afternoon, in the arsenal at the Fort, Mr. Webster's face had turned the shade of fresh-baked bricks when they'd finally come across the guns assigned to Babcock. The six cannons, all being eighteen-pounders, were rusty and corroded with hard grease and dirt. The runners of their carriages were clogged up stiff.

Captain Webster had cursed under his breath, stared at the dirty guns, and told Mingo to find him some horses. It wasn't easy moving the guns up-shore. It took Mr. Frazier with his big shoulders and all forty-six men assigned to Babcock to move the cannons across the sand. They'd strained their backs as well and set the horses to slobbering.

✳ ✳ ✳

Now, in the morning light, Mingo considered the Babcock battery, which in fact was not much to consider—only a floor of rough-set bricks perched on a sandy hillock a few yards back from the riverbank. Masses of briars were covering the spot when they first got here. Mr. Webster ordered the crew to chop away the briars with their cutlasses and clear a path through the underbrush to the dirt hill some sixty feet behind the battery. Then they'd dug out a hole in the hill to hold a powder magazine.

Will Adams had led a team in building a four-foot-high breastwork of tabby bricks to front the battery. As if expecting action, the rammers and swabs and buckets were laid out around the cannons. Mingo knew for a fact—being as it took several trips to the fort—that a store of cannonballs was now in the magazine in the hillside, along with canisters of grapeshot. For most of yesterday, the men had their shirts off, working over the guns. They scraped the rust off, swabbed the cannons, and oiled them good. Now the guns were in place with their aprons stretched over the low battery wall so that the six guns faced the shoreline of the Ferry Branch.

If fired, would those old guns shoot or blow up? That was the question.

✫ ✫ ✫

Mingo grunted to himself and ambled down to the battery. Captain Webster was wiping down the truck carriage of one of the eighteen-pounders. His shoulders had lost their tightness, and his face has gone back to its usual color. He's righted himself, Mingo thought.

Webster's eyes lighted some when he saw Mingo Jones approaching. He nodded toward the fireworks in the distant sky. "Sounds a racket...like hellfire, only most of the bombs are bursting in the air before they reach the fort."

"How come?" Mingo squinted at the sky.

"Their bomb boats are too far out. Makes a pretty show, don't it?"

Mingo frowned at a fresh explosion. "And us out of the action here at the Babcock. You minding that?"

Something curious, even knowing, in the black oarsman's face caused Jack Webster to step away from the battery and indicate that Mingo should follow him. They headed down the slope to the riverbank.

When they were standing close to the slow ebb and flow of the river, he said curtly, "I'm minding it. Aye, Mr. Jones, I'm minding it bad. I'd give a lot to be at the fort right now or at the Lazaretto—" Webster's words broke off in a fit of coughing.

"You done lost your flask, I recalls."

Webster wiped his mouth with the back of his hand. "Aye, I lost my flask, and I'm minding that. And I'm thinking about

Captain Warner dead, and I'm minding that. We could use him here sure enough."

Mingo said nothing, but something like sympathy flickered in his dark eyes. "Captain Warner was a steady man on the guns. Pity you ain't got any other officers to serve as gun captains."

"I've got a fair crew. I've got Dan Frazier and Will Adams and Jesse Stewart and some strong hands. Mostly oarsmen, I grant you. And there's Soames and a few old-timers, and the midshipmen Andrews and Edwards. We'll make do if need be."

"That young Edwards ain't worth shit. Cookee no good, neither."

Webster picked up a white stone and spun it into the current. "And there's you, Mr. Jones. I don't rightly know why you're here, and that puzzles me."

Mingo stared into Jack Webster's eyes. Blue eyes, searching eyes, mostly shading toward gray, they were looking back at him straight on as a man looks at another man he thinks of as worthy.

"It's not the pay or the food keeping you here," Webster said, going on in a musing tone, as if thinking the question out. "And it's not 'cause there's some pretty gal waiting for you to prove yourself for. At least, I think not."

Mingo saw the stubble of a beard on Webster's face and the dirty rim of his shirt beneath his blue jacket. He squinted, and said slowly, "Can't rightly say. The way I see it, there's folks here that needs me, you mostly. And them boys." He looked out on the water. "They needs me here more'n any other folks I can think of. Is that a reason?"

Jack Webster laughed. It was a full-bodied laugh that he felt in his chest and was glad for it. He kept his eyes steady on Mingo's face and said, "It's a fine reason, and I thank you for giving it." He started to turn away and then said, "You know for a fact, Mr. Jones, it eases my mind to have you here with me."

✠ ✠ ✠

When the captain had gone back to the battery, Mingo walked the shoreline. There was no woman waiting for him. Not anywhere. Once there'd been Minna, that's all. She was only a girl, and he not much more than a stripling, but they'd married proper and slept snug in a cabin under the willow tree. And along came the baby. A hard time she had birthing him, and in the days afterward, both Minna and the baby sickened. The old master came down to the quarters himself. He had Minna bled twice, but it did no good. When she died, and the baby boy, too, they'd given Mingo a day off from working in the fields so he could tend to the burial. It had rained, and the casket he'd made himself had sunk in the mud, and he'd gone back in the dark to cover it again with dirt. It was like his blood went into every shovelful of dirt; all that was part of the closing of his heart.

"Mr. Jones, what you doing out here on the river?" Jason was standing on the breastwork of the battery.

Mingo didn't turn at the boy's call, because tears were burning his eyes. Why he was crying, he didn't know.

"I been looking for you everywhere." The boy jumped from the breastwork and came running toward him. "I'm thinking 'bout Caleb up at the fort. I'm thinking he might be scair't. It might be we take us a horse and go get him and bring him here where it's safe."

"I'll think on it," Mingo said without turning his head.

✲ ✲ ✲

Afternoon

He wasn't scared. Caleb liked the fort, liked all the smells and noise, the gunpowder that made your eyes burn, the horses, and the men laughing and shouting. He'd been hanging around with Captain Joseph Nicolson's company of Baltimore volunteers, who called themselves the Artillery Fencibles. They'd taken Caleb into their tents as if he were their mascot, and allowed him to help with the cleaning of the muskets and the few rifles and the two pistols that belonged to the Fencibles.

"I can handle a musket," he told them proudly. "I done shot a redcoat already. Maybe two or three. I got a good eye on me."

The men laughed and slapped him on the back. Sergeant Clemm gave him a company scarf to wear and shared with him some fried chicken legs his wife in Baltimore brought out to the fort. Another tall fellow with a gold tooth rubbed Caleb's head like he was a good fellow and gave him a spare blanket and a slice of gingerbread.

He was standing close with the Sea Fencibles on the parapets this morning when the firing began. He'd watched the explosions in the sky and laughed to hear the men say, "Them British upstarts better not move any closer in, or we'll blow them out of the water."

As they watched, the bomb boats glided in toward the fort 'til they were scarcely two miles out. He heard the men murmur the names of the vessels, the *Volcano*, the *Meteor*, the *Erebus*, and a little schooner called the *Cockchafer* that some of the men were making jokes about. The fort's cannons fired back. Only it was too far a distance, and the American cannonballs fell in the water.

The laughing on the parapets stopped. Even Caleb himself got the jitters, until he saw the British cannonballs were still bursting out over the water as well, and not raining down fire and iron bits on the fort at all. He'd thought about Mingo and Jason and wished they were there to see the sight, for it was pure glory to watch.

In truth, the firing on both sides had slowed, like drops of water emptying from a leaky bucket. It seemed to Caleb the British vessels had lost heart, as their forward boats were pulling back. He'd climbed down from the parapet and slept in a ditch under the southwest bastion.

✭ ✭ ✭

He had been dreaming he was walking with Jason in the woods, and they were looking for the flotilla camp. Then he'd clutched his chest and bounded up on his knees. He'd heard a crash, and now there was rumbling above his head and the crackling and thump of bricks as part of the bastion fell around him. Men were screaming around him as he crawled from the ditch.

A bomb had landed on the big cannon on the southwest bastion. Dead men were sprawled about. Other men, their faces burnt black, were the ones screaming. The cannon was knocked off its mount. He crept up to the bastion, thinking to help, but he was pushed aside.

"Out of the way, boy." Someone gave Caleb a hard shove.

Caleb could see that he was only trouble to the Fencibles, only in their way. He didn't hold it against them. The bombardment was on again. Bombs were exploding above the fort, and shrapnel was flying all around, fizzing and sizzling down like burning rain and causing the men in the embrasures to duck and swear. The shells landed helter-skelter, splintering the brickwork, although most weren't causing any real harm, their fuses being already spent. But each one was a threat. It was like being in a storm at sea, Caleb decided, when lightning was threatening to strike.

He was beginning to shiver. He stumbled down the steps and saw they'd taken down the big flag with all the stars and stripes on it and only the garrison flag was flying. He hid under a wagon in the yard alongside a parcel of dogs which were panting and whining out of fear from the noise. It wasn't much later that a second shell crashed through the roof of the armory. The very air in the fort seemed to tremble. The bomb didn't explode, but everyone looked to be scared shitless, and a sergeant cried out that the powder barrels had to be moved across the yard. Caleb ran as far away as possible from the barrels and climbed up to stand with Nicholson's men, who were peering over the parapets. The bomb ships and the little *Cockchafer* appeared to be moving in close again. Caleb held his breath as the militiamen and the volunteers waited for the fort guns to fire on the British ships. For a long moment, the guns remained silent.

"Armistead's waiting," the tall fellow with the gold tooth said to him. "No use firing a fourteen-pounder at a target less'en eighteen hundred yards. Nor a twenty-four-pounder at less'en twenty-eight hundred yards."

The British vessels are closer than that already, Caleb thought, but he didn't say so.

"We're sitting ducks if the British fire first," the tall fellow added.

As he spoke, the big guns at the fort let fire. Armistead had finally given the order. Every cannon let loose with its charge. Some of the cannons carried extra charges of powder. As Caleb and the man with the gold tooth watched, an iron ball filled with explosives, and now another, and then another cannonball, five in all, tore into the sides of the *Volcano.*

The mast of the *Volcano* disappeared in a cloud of smoke. When the smoke cleared, she was still afloat. It was the *Devastation* that was listing to port, having taken a direct hit. Her mainsail was down. The militiamen standing in the embrasures and on the parapets cheered. They cheered even more wildly when they saw the British ships withdrawing to a safer distance. Small boats were towing the *Erebus* out toward the frigates clustered on the blue line of the horizon, like mother ducks awaiting the return of their ducklings.

Caleb cheered with the others. But he felt suddenly very young and very lonely. The man with the gold tooth told him something terrible. Sergeant Clemm was killed when the twenty-four pounder on the Southwest bastion was bombed. He wanted to tell someone about Sargent Clemm giving him the scarf and the chicken legs. But the man with the gold tooth had moved off, and everyone was busy and in no mood to pay him any mind.

He went down again into the yard and looked for the wagon with the dogs huddled under it. Only someone had moved the wagon. For a moment he stood forlorn in the yard. A light rain was falling.

✳ ✳ ✳

"Caleb, is that you, boy?"

The drummer boy turned and saw Mingo and his old wool hat. There was rain glistening on his black arms. Jason was with him, sitting on the bare back of a big brown horse.

"We come to get you," Mingo growled. "We need you at the Babcock. You coming with us? Or maybe you too busy up here at the fort to help us out."

A knot of pure joy exploded in Caleb's chest. He couldn't stop grinning. He called out, "Sure 'nuff. I'll come to the Babcock and help you out…if you want me. I shore will."

✳ ✳ ✳

Evening

Tuesday was ending, as gloomy and rain-spattered as it began. Jack Webster walked the riverbank with his eyes fastened on the fire-streaked sky. He watched the rockets fly and the bombs still exploding out over the waters and sometimes above the fort. The bomb vessels had renewed their fire since the afternoon lull.

This was a war, a battle of conquest and defense, and he ached to be part of it. There was a second battery farther up the Ferry Branch, and he imagined the men in that battery, which was called Fort Covington, were restless and dispirited as well.

He'd led his crew—awkward but willing—through the firing of the six cannons, and he'd seen to it that the slow matches were under cover from the rain. He'd personally checked that a worm, a sponge-rammer, and a hand ladle were placed beside each cannon.

Most of his crew was sitting cross-legged on the ground with their blankets shielding them against the rain. Yesterday, Webster would have given anything to be at the Lazaretto with Sellers and Kiddall. But in the last twenty-four hours, he'd come to feel differently. He was charged with some kind of warmth that had to do with his crew. It was like Mingo Jones said: these Chesapeake watermen and dock boys were here because this was where they were supposed to be.

It humbled Jack Webster to think on that, humbled him to command this crew. Huddled in their blankets, the men and boys had begun to sing: *"Our ship she lays in harbur, just ready to set sail..."*

He heard their fine strong voices, and it touched his heart. Walking among them, Webster bent to speak to Jesse Stewart and saw the coxswain's nervous fingers fiddling with the sharks' teeth hanging around his neck. He'd squatted then, with the rain falling on his face, and talked to Jesse about the time a few years back when he too had climbed to the cliffs near to Solomon's Island and found some sharks' teeth in the clay. How they got to be there was a question he still pondered.

For the first time, he looked at Charles Ball and saw the scars from a neck iron. Ball was once a slave. He knew that now, although he'd not thought about it before. These were his mates as surely as his fellow officers. He smelled their sweat and saw the dirt on their hands, just like on his own. Does a man go to war because he's born in a place and must fight with his brothers? Or do men become brothers because they fight together and are willing to die together, and for one another? This crew—watermen and dock hands, black and white together, even the farm boys—they were his brothers, and they would fight side by side in this place. They would die to save one another, and that was a good thing and a true thing. It was an honor to lead such men.

Earlier in the afternoon, the sky cleared for a brief stretch, and the Eastern Shore boys set up a game of horseshoes on the beach. But the rain came again, and the jostling and the good feelings didn't last. To make matters worse, there'd been no meat all day, no grog and no whiskey. Soames spent all his time with his hands behind his back, staring at the explosions upstream. The crew grumbled and settled for hard bread and molasses. They drank Soames's bitter coffee until that was gone as well.

It was raining hard as evening settled in. Webster pulled up the collar of his blue jacket and spread his blanket on the brick breastwork between cannons five and six. He stretched out and put his arm over his eyes against the rain. He could see Rachel's face, her smile, and the freckles on her nose. Strange how he could muster up the scent of her hair and her body, how it lingered with him and pleased him. Rachel smelled like fresh corn and honey. He liked her mouth and her white teeth, her dark eyelashes and the spirit that flashed in her eyes. Rachel had a face he could look at and study for a lifetime, he thought. There was the taste of her mouth when she kissed him that held him content to think on. Even here, in this sodden, wet place.

☆ ☆ ☆

A few yards away, Mingo used the blanket to tent himself and the two boys. He thought about going into the garden behind the hill to see if he could dig up some radishes or such. But he concluded it was hardly worth the effort in the rain and the dark.

Jason stirred against his shoulder. "I been thinking, Mingo."

"What you troubling yourself about, boy? Not that old Sharky?"

"I wanted bad to kill him. But I didn't, Mingo. And now I'm fuzzed up in my head. I don't rightly know what living's all about."

There followed a silence. Then Mingo said, "Hard to know about living. Me, I don't know. Only you got to rise to the best in yourself like your pa would want, boy. Takes gumption."

The boy chuckled. "Takes piss, don't it?"

"I got piss," Caleb broke in. "I shot me some redcoats already."

"You got piss enough." Mingo chuckled. "I'll say that, for sure."

✫ ✫ ✫

Robert Ross was dead. It was the way of war. George Cockburn had seen death in many forms—having been orphaned young and given to war as long as he could remember, as a midshipman and a captain and now as an admiral—but he was deeply distressed.

At midday he recalled Ross was in unusually high spirits, convinced his army could easily handle the land approach to Baltimore. His cheeks were ruddy, his shoulders taut. Now his body waited in a wagon, wrapped in the Union Jack.

So men go to battle ... so men die, Cockburn reminded himself. For most of the afternoon, he'd listened to the bombing. Cochrane's vessels were shelling the fort at Whetstone Point. Now all was silence. That was not good news. An hour ago, an attaché' came with a letter from Cochrane. The fort had not surrendered. Nor had the British bomb boats and barges been able to slip into the Northwest Branch.

He had nothing positive to send back to Cochrane. When Ross was killed, the command of the land forces had fallen to a young colonel named Brooke, who had proceeded cautiously with the army toward the Northwest Branch. Meeting a defensive force out of Baltimore, they'd engaged in several hard skir-mishes. At this moment the British army was some four miles from Baltimore. However, the rain was slowing their progress and threatening to render their gunpowder useless. What's more, Brooke's advance scouts reported American earthworks and newly dug ditches in their path.

☆ ☆ ☆

Cockburn shielded his candle from the rain and read again the vice admiral's most recent communication. Cochrane urged the infantrymen to retreat to their transport ships waiting at the North Point. To cap his argument, he emphasized the navy could lend no support to Brooke's land assault on the city, as the mouth of the Northwest Branch was entirely blocked with sunken vessels.

Frowning, Cockburn twisted his signet ring. It was his most cherished possession, Nelson's own ring, given to him in per-son by the great man. He must send this note on to Colonel Brooke, but he'd also respond directly to Cochrane. Earlier, Brooke had suggested a diversionary action by the navy up the Ferry Branch of the Patapsco. This diversion would draw the American troops, at least a portion of them, away from Brooke's line of advance. Cochrane had not been adverse to the idea. That was still a fair plan. If not a direct naval attack on the Northwest Branch, then a diversion up the Ferry Branch might prove to be the answer.

He would send back a note to Vice Admiral Cochrane, care-fully worded so it might appear the idea was Cochrane's own. He wrote quickly. "It's true, sir, that a force of three hundred or more seamen and marines might be sent from your vessels in the dead of night—dressed in black and in barges with muffled oars—in a daring and bold attempt to slip by the fort and up the Ferry Branch." Of course, the men must be well armed and carry scal-ing ladders, for—and Cochrane once pointed this out himself—the fort could be taken from the north as well as from the south.

"What is needed is a force of twenty-two gun barges armed with carronades and rockets and a long schooner to carry an eighteen-pounder," he wrote. "Perhaps Mr. Napier might be given the command." George Cockburn put this all down on paper. He bent over his writing desk as his aide shielded his candle and quill pen from the rain. He folded the note and handed it to a messenger, who would deliver his message to the small boat waiting to carry the reply to Cochrane.

Brilliant! Cockburn rested his face in his palms and remembered the way the city of Washington burned most gloriously. What a night that was, a marvelous night, and the Irishman's face, seen in the glow of the burning Capitol. A gentleman and an officer, a marvelous fellow, Ross. What a loss, his death.

☆ ☆ ☆

Midnight

The boys were wet and cold. He could feel them shivering. Mingo shifted his weight so that each boy could nestle close against his chest. Body warmth was a good thing. He remembered being a boy and how painful it was to be cold. He remembered the harsh flax shirt he wore as a small child and no trousers and the dirt caked on his body. Just lately, all kinds of memories had been flooding into his head: memories like driving the cows home in the evenings, his bare feet in the warm grass, and the overseer, name of Cawley, who went about with a heavy cudgel in his belt just to remind the slaves not to get uppity. And the blood whippings. It only took one beating to crush a man's spirit to lamb-soft or to turn him mean as a rattlesnake, one or the other.

He had another memory that was good to think on. When the master carried the tobacco and wheat to the pier on the Rappahannock, he'd once gone in one of the wagons to help with the unloading. Afterward he'd stood on the shore and watched the white sails moving off. He was about the size of Jason then, and he'd studied the gulls rising and dipping and gliding on the river breeze. His heart had soared like one of the gulls. He'd wanted to be loose and free and going somewhere.

Jason fidgeted under Mingo's arm. As if aware the man was awake, he raised his head and asked in his dreamy way, "How old you be, Mingo?"

"Don't rightly know. My momma said I was born in plant-ing time. She used to come to me at night and lie with me and get me to sleep. I was raised by an old woman too old for field-work." Corn stripped off the cobs and ground into mush, Mingo was thinking, and bacon drippings and sometimes molasses on a piece of shortbread, the smell of the whitewashed cabin, the singing in the evenings, and the dogs barking in the moonlight.

"What kind of boy was you like?"

Mingo laughed shortly. "I was mean and always in fights. Nothin' to live for, nothin' to lose, I guess." He rubbed Jason's head with a rough hard hand. "The overseer, he don't mess with me after a while 'cause it shamed him. I wasn't rightly tamed, I guess that's the truth of it."

The truth was that after Minna and the baby boy died, he'd run away in the dark of an October night and climbed for weeks in the Virginia hills, working whenever he got a chance for a farmer who'd asked no questions. He was running, listening always for the dogs, until he reached Baltimore and came upon the commodore and the Chesapeake Flotilla.

"My pa is dead." The boy sighed and rested his head on Mingo's chest. "I got that straight in my head now. He ain't never coming home. Where you call home, Mingo?"

"Ain't got no home. I ain't got no need for one."

Jason raised his head again to study Mingo's face. "So we ain't got no home, neither one of us?"

Mingo thought for a long moment. He struggled to find the words that would comfort the boy. "Maybe home is being on this here riverbank. It's Barney's boys working together for some-thing...something you can't put your mind on, but you know is right. The commodore, he was the only one who could put it into words, but it's something real that binds us."

Now that he'd said it, a feeling of pleasure flooded Mingo's heart and filled him with contentment in a way he'd not known since he was young and newly married and sleeping in the cabin under the willow tree. He'd not gone on to say that when you take care of somebody or something, that's like being home, too.

"I'm cold, too," Caleb said and plucked at Mingo's back.

He pulled the boy into a huddle with Jason, and they giggled and squirmed and poked each other to find comfort places against Mingo's chest.

✫ ✫ ✫

The noise was like glass breaking, or like someone or something splashing in the water. Jack Webster sat up on the breastwork and listened. It was long after midnight. Maybe he was dreaming. Considering the moonless night and the rain, it was likely that no man or bird or boat was out on the river. But there it went again. His heart leaped in his throat, for he recognized the sound as the sweep of muffled oars. He stumbled to his feet and called out in a hoarse voice to the men sleeping around him.

Mingo heard him and pushed the boys aside. "Stay put," he ordered and crept across the wet grass to the battery, leaning beside Webster on the breastwork.

"I believe there's British barges on the river," Webster whispered. "Not more than two hundred yards offshore, I figure."

The crew was awake, mostly whispering among themselves and a few were already moving toward the cannons in the battery. Someone kicked over a bucket.

Mingo asked, "We got dry fuses?"

Webster didn't answer. He began to slide down the bank toward the shore. Mingo was close behind him, along with Dan Frazier and some of the crew. They were breathing hard and still not certain this was really happening and not just some dream, some odd noise. The river looked like an inky black ribbon, and the men stood silently on the shoreline, listening to the soft wash of water on sand.

A light—as small as a lighted fuse—flickered and then was gone on the river.

"What that be?" Jake Edwards was shivering. The young midshipman stood close by Webster. He choked out his question, "You think it's them British?"

"Shush." Webster sensed Mingo Jones also at his elbow. "To cannons," he breathed. "Let's give them a royal welcome."

But would the rain-drenched cannons fire? That question consumed his mind as Webster felt his way along the line of eighteen-pounders in the battery. When he reached the last gun, he climbed up and straddled number six's long, tapering muzzle. He slid forward on his stomach until he was well over the apron of the gun. Gingerly he put a hand inside and felt the priming.

Thank God, the interior of the muzzle was dry or at least dry enough. He inched back down the gun and whispered for the gun crew. They were waiting for his command, their bare feet dug into the sand sprinkled on the bricks. As he'd taught them over the past twenty-four hours, the gun crew was ready with handspikes to turn the gun, if necessary.

That flicker of light on the river. He peered over the brick wall. How far ahead could enemy barges have moved in the minutes it had taken to return to the battery?

Webster thrust a rolling handspike under the gun's carriage and whispered to the crew, "To the right…heave now, a half a foot."

The strongest of the young men stumbled to the tackles on either side of the cannon, and at his command threw themselves fiercely against the carriage. Webster heaved with them, and the gun let out a squeal as it scraped over the bricks. Now, the challenge. There'd been no way to mount the guns properly with chains and ropes in the battery. When fired, the recoil of the cannons would be dangerous for the gun crews. It worried Webster, but he had no options.

"Cartridge ready?" he asked.

Close at his side, Jason pulled the serge bag from under his shirt. The boy handed the bag of gunpowder up to Jesse Stewart, who had taken on the job of gunner's mate without question. With an awkward but sure thrust of the hand ladle, Jesse pushed the cartridge of powder deep into the cannon's muzzle.

Webster watched the vague dark shadows of his crewmen moving around him. He'd never commanded a gun battery, but the command came natural to him—a certainty, a flow of energy he'd not expected. He barked out questions.

"Are the wet wads in? Aye. Are you certain? Carry on."

First the wads, and then the heavy cannonball was coaxed into the muzzle by Will Adams, who could be heard breathing hard, maybe from fear or maybe from excitement. "I packed her in. She's in."

"Run out," Webster commanded. The crew heaved the big gun forward. "Stand clear, men."

✶ ✶ ✶

Jesse Stewart flipped up the iron apron over the touchhole and took the linstock from Mingo's hand. He sheltered the faint flame with his palm.

"Almighty God, be with us," Dan Frazier muttered behind him.

Jesse closed his eyes and thrust the flame into the touchhole.

The roar of the cannon was deafening. A shudder ran through the gun. Webster leaped back from the recoil. From the river came shouts of shock and the splash of men jumping and falling overboard.

"What if they come ashore?" Jake Edwards whispered.

There wasn't time for Webster to answer the question. The British barges were returning fire. "Take cover," he shouted, and the men huddled around the cannons in the Babcock battery.

"You think they be coming after us, sir?" Edwards whispered again.

Webster grabbed the midshipman by the arm. "You must go for reinforcements. Take Andrews with you. Bring some men to Babcock from the fort. We need swords and knives and pikes. Go!"

The young man slipped away from Webster's hand as if grateful for the chance to leave the battery.

Mingo shook his head. "He ain't worth a bucket of spit. I told you that."

Webster moved down the line of guns. "To cannons now, my fellows. Move smart." He watched as the men scrambled to their feet and returned to their stations. They were struggling in the darkness, but with a certain jauntiness, as if his confidence in them gave them courage.

"Where's the rammer?" someone shouted from the second gun.

All the Babcock cannons were firing now, earsplitting, mind-blasting slams of sound. The return fire from the river was fast and rapid. In the light of the explosions, the enemy boats could be clearly seen. A schooner and a line of open barges. There were cries now from the river, the cries of wounded men.

✧ ✧ ✧

A half hour passed, and Edwards and Andrews did not return.

"I never trusted them boys, no way," Mingo muttered. "I'm taking a musket and going down on the beach. Ain't nobody come ashore alive but what I catch 'em."

He was only a dark shadow standing beside Webster.

"I'm going with you," said Caleb. "I'm going down to the beach, too." He had a smoothbore musket in his hand that clinked as he moved.

"Me, too." Jason stumbled into the battery.

"Not you," Webster ordered and wiped the rain from his eyes. "We need you here." He turned to tell Mingo and Caleb to take care. No one could predict what might happen on the beach. But they were gone.

The clatter and shouts and starbursts of explosives went on. Webster was thinking of the black man and the drummer boy making their way down the slope, which was mostly rock and sand and dangerous open space. He should have told them not to go.

All eyes in the Babcock battery were turned toward the river. But for sure, someone was moving behind them, moving through the briars.

Quietly, Webster left his gun crew, stepped to the back of the battery, and peered into the darkness. In the flash of cannon fire, he recognized the shoulders and the round bullet head of the cook. For a moment, he was relieved and almost on the point of calling out to him. But, in the brilliance of an exploding enemy bomb, Webster saw an open sack and the snakelike trail of powder toward the magazine in the hill.

"Hold there!" he shouted and grabbed up a handspike. In a great thrust of energy and anger, he sent the metal spike flying. It struck Soames full in the face. The man groaned, and his shadow pitched forward. Webster bent down and found the man lying still in the sand and briars, facedown.

"Dirty, stinking traitor," Webster muttered. "I should have known your intentions. Your biscuits were proof enough." He was trembling now, his senses alert. Where the devil were Andrews and Edwards? It was obvious the young men had taken off to find safety. There would be no reinforcements. No matter, he calmed himself. He and the crew would do what they had to do.

"A spark...there's a spark in the muzzle. I seen it!" a gunner on the number two cannon cried out. "The gun's a'fire."

If the cannon exploded...no, it couldn't happen, not on his watch, by God! Gritting his teeth, Webster turned from Soames's prone body and scrambled onto the battery wall. He grabbed up a wet sponge and braced himself against the hot iron of cannon number two's muzzle. He leaned out and plunged the long stick with its fuzzy head deep into the smoking maw of the eighteen-pound cannon.

"The capt'n's gonna get his head blown off," Will Adams shouted.

Webster rotated the sponge to the left, and then hard to the right. Again and again, he turned the stick until his hands were shaking. He'd never done this maneuver, but once he'd watched Tom Warner put out the fire in a smoking cannon. The memory brought him confidence and new strength to his hands.

"She's quiet," Adams shouted. "The capt'n's done it."

Leaping from the wall, Webster peered into the breech end of the muzzle. Only darkness. "Aye, the fire's out," he said quietly. "Let her rest a few minutes, then reload. Step handsomely now, lads."

With caution, a cartridge of gunpowder was ladled down the muzzle of cannon number two and the wet wads pushed in. A seaman struggled up with the cannonball, and the shot was clapped into the muzzle.

"Roll her out," Webster cried.

When fired, the gun recoiled so fiercely, the very ground seemed to shake. The seaman grinned, his dirty face and bloodshot eyes visible in the brilliance of the explosion. It was Charles Ball.

He announced, "A good job, if I say so, sir."

✧ ✧ ✧

Jason was serving as the powder monkey for cannon number six. He called out in a high, thin voice as Webster approached, "Where's Mingo, sir? Where's Caleb gone to?"

The bombing was loud and thundering in their ears. Webster meant to answer. He was distracted by a glimmer of dancing light on the shoreline.

"A fire on the beach!" he screamed and grabbed up his musket, ramming in the bayonet. He raced down the incline with Jason hard on his heels.

A British barge had drifted ashore. She'd been hit by one of the Babcock Battery cannons, and a fire blazed in her stern. The flames lit the night sky, and men in black garb were struggling to leave the boat. They were only vague dark shapes leaping into the water and crawling in the sand to shore. A shot rang out, and the men ducked back into the shallow water. Flames from the burning barge on the river illuminated a British sailor kneeling in the sand. He raised a musket and fired into the darkness.

Webster drew in a breath. Someone from his crew was moving forward, creeping toward the enemy soldier. The slight figure, with the barrel of his musket pointed toward the man at the shoreline, was Caleb. The boy fired, and the man tumbled backward. Caleb gave a shout and turned to run. A dozen British seamen were on the shore now, and they raced after him.

The boy stumbled into the darkness, and the men followed after him.

Webster heard a high-pitched shout and then a splash. He knew that Caleb had gone into the river. He ran toward the water and found himself in a tangle of shadows and shouts. The intruders had run headlong into the crew of flotilla men who'd followed Webster down to the beach.

The fighting had turned desperate, hand to hand, steel to steel in the gritting sand. Webster used his bayonet to fend off two dark figures that came from nowhere. Musket fire sounded down the beach, and he heard the cries of his own men. Mostly the cries were battle shouts, and he took heart from that and plunged forward, falling on rocks and standing again.

"Foolish American," someone muttered behind him, and he was leaped on by a bulky fellow who plunged a knife or a handspike hard into his shoulder.

Webster thrust up with his elbow, met the man's chin, and twisted and stabbed out with the bayonet. The man groaned and fell.

✵ ✵ ✵

If only he could see, but the fire in the barge had gone out. The darkness was so great that it felt like fighting in the hold of a ship. Webster felt someone beside him at the shoreline and turned with his bayonet up. Mingo's voice came to him, and he lowered the musket.

"They're going," Mingo reported. "They got their barge righted, and they pushing off. Hear 'em now."

Jack Webster could only hear the pounding of his own cannons. He could only see the explosions that illuminated the enemy barges when they took a hit from the Babcock guns. His shoulder was burning. He moved his right arm gingerly and wondered if his shoulder was broken.

"Back to the battery," he croaked out to Mingo. "Tell the men we'll regroup behind the guns."

He felt Mingo stiffen beside him.

"Where's Caleb? Listen…"

Somewhere in the noise and shouts, there sounded a boy's voice. "Help me." The voice was reedy and far off. It came from the dark water.

"I'll go get him," said Webster and tried to lift his right arm, but he couldn't. A muscle was severed in his shoulder.

In the flare of a new explosion, Mingo saw this. "No, you ain't." He hesitated. "I'm going."

"Can you swim?" Webster's question was instinctive, some kind of quick understanding, a memory of that day at the inlet of St. Leonard's Creek. "That's it, isn't it? You can't swim."

✫ ✫ ✫

Mingo Jones had never learned to swim. But if he had a choice in dying, it would damn well be by water and not in the burning of a fire. Mingo thought this as he stumbled into the river. The sand caught at his feet, and he steadied himself and called out, "Where you be, Caleb?"

Mingo moved gingerly forward toward a gasping sound and some splashing until the water lapped about him waist high. Then another explosion on the river showed him the boy only a few feet ahead. Caleb wasn't so far out, only encumbered by his clothes and black boots. He was struggling to reach shallow water, now on his back, now under water.

When Mingo was chest high, he caught hold of the boy. "I got you, boy. Stop your struggling. Hold on to my arm."

He pulled Caleb to him and turned back to shore. The boy spit and coughed and clung to Mingo's arm.

Between gasps, he asked, "How come you came to get me, Mingo? How you know'd where I was? I lost my musket. I lost it in the water when the johnnies were chasing after me."

"Hush now. They still be Britishers about."

A few yards down the shore, he could see that not all the black-garbed sailors had been chased back to their vessels. Rockets from the enemy barges in the river were streaming in the sky above-head, flaring out in red and gold against the darkness.

"We got to make it up to the battery 'afore they catch us."

"I knew you'd come get me," the boy breathed out as they made their way up through the sand toward the battery. "I knew it'd be you that would save —"

It was the last thing he said, for a shot rang out and took the boy down.

Mingo saw in the light of a burning flare that a man in black was only some feet away. A second Britisher was behind him, with his musket at his chin. Mingo heard Caleb groan, and he pulled the boy behind him, taking the second shot in his own chest.

✫ ✫ ✫

Webster lay prone for a long while on the brick floor of the battery. He let the pain in his shoulder fill him and remind him that he was still alive. This was a night of war. The battle on the beach had been more vivid and real to him than the fighting on that sun-bright day at Bladensburg. That was playing war, at least at the beginning. Maybe it was why he'd faltered so when the British were on the ridge. It was at that point the fighting became real. But, on this night everything was at stake.

He groaned and turned his head so he could see the sky above the fort. A night bombardment of Fort McHenry had commenced a short time after they'd heard the enemy boats on the Ferry Branch. The thunder of the enemy's cannons was steady now, like a drumbeat, and the rain-swept sky was bright with flares and signal rockets and the fireworks of exploding Congreve rockets. Above it all thundered the occasional bursting of the two-hundred-pound bombshells sent out from the British bomb vessels. So brilliant this sky, it was almost beautiful.

He struggled to his feet and peered over the battery at the dark stretch of the Ferry Branch. The enemy vessels had moved farther upstream and were receiving fire from Fort Covington. He could hear the clatter of their guns. He turned to Dan Frazier, who was at his side. "Have we any wounded? Are all the men accounted for?"

"Most is all right. Soames is nowhere around."

"Well, damn." So he hadn't killed the cook after all. Webster allowed himself a small regret. Soames must have crawled off in the night to save his miserable hide.

"We've two gunners down, and Edwards and Andrews are still not back." Dan Frazier's voice was ragged. "Me, I killed a man with my bare hands. It was terrible, sir. I wish…"

Webster closed his eyes for a moment and then said what he himself knew was true. "I understand, Mr. Frazier. We do what we have to do."

The big man's voice broke as he said, "Mingo Jones is missing. He was last seen on the beach. And the boy, Caleb."

Webster let out a breath as if he had been struck hard on the back. Vomit rose in his throat as it had when he'd looked down on Warner's body. The bile was worse than the pain in his shoulder. He felt the truth in his bones. He heard again Caleb's cry,

"Help me," and remembered Mingo striding out into the inky blackness of the river.

A shoulder brushed against Webster as a man stumbled into the dark battery. "They're coming again, Cap'n," Charles Ball said. "See them lights? They're coming back downriver, and we got a good shot at 'em. What say you, sir?"

✷ ✷ ✷

The enemy schooner and the barges were fighting to escape and return to the British command ships out on the Patapsco. Their sweeps plowed into the water, and their guns fired at random and in desperation. Rockets swept the sky above the Babcock Battery. Patches of the woods along the shoreline were on fire.

"Men to cannons! Move lively!" Webster ordered.

He sent Will Adams and some of the flotilla men to stomp out the burning brush, especially the flames near the magazine. He took personal command of the number six cannon once again. To command a cannon took his mind from thinking of anything but the gun and its purpose.

"Double slotted," he ordered curtly—knowing well the risk that the gun's barrel would explode.

"Where's Mr. Jones? Where's Caleb?" the powder monkey whispered as he handed up the charge.

Webster shook his head. He couldn't answer Jason's question. To steady himself, he held to the thought of Barney and how it was on the *Rossie* when he was young and war seemed glorious. It was still glorious and terrible and warmed your heart and broke your heart all at the same time.

"Load, you buggers," he called down the line.

Again and again, the six cannons rang out. The gun crews were holding nothing of themselves back. The six cannons fired in a rhythm within seconds of each other.

"Are the linstocks smoldering?" Webster called out hoarsely. "Have we enough cannonballs? Move handsomely, lads...stand clear when you fire!" By God, they'd got the hang of it now. This crew, these watermen, these ragamuffins, to command them, to fight with them, was an honor. To die with them would be an honor.

"Once again, double slotted," Webster ordered. A second ball was lifted on the wad hook and rammed into the muzzle of number six.

"Stand clear. Fire!" The recoil was terrible and threw Webster back against the brick floor. This time his shoulder was broken, for sure. There was a certain mercy in it. He fainted from the pain.

✡ ✡ ✡

Dawn, September 14

The morning was slow in coming. The sun didn't show, and a gray mist covered the water. The night had proved to be a horror that Vice Admiral Sir Alexander Cochrane had no wish to relive.

Everything possible had gone wrong. The advance on land was strangely halted—so the most recent note from Admiral Cockburn read. Colonel Brooke, having reached the outskirts of Baltimore, surveyed the campfires on the hills above the city and reconsidered the advance. His spies reported that ten thousand Americans were on Hampstead Hill behind the barricades with French cannons. To risk his troops against this fortified port was not in the best interest of Great Britain. That was Brooke's decision. The army turned in its tracks. In the dark of night, they headed back on the road toward North Point and the waiting transports.

The news of this retreat was vastly disappointing. Cochrane's last hope lay in the divisionary force he'd sent out at midnight at Cockburn's urging. But that too had been a failure. The darkness was absolute, and the vessels became separated. Eleven barges rowed straight into the Northwest Branch, where they met the iron chain and the barrier of sunken vessels. They'd turned their bows and sheepishly made their way back to the fleet.

Until the last, he'd held out hope for the rest of the squadron. But those vessels had limped back from the Ferry Branch in the early hours of the morning. Their mission was a disaster. To their surprise, they'd faced a staunch defense from men and cannons on the shoreline. It was reported the defenders were the flotilla men who'd served under Commodore Joshua Barney.

Napier was anguished, crying out, "Blood devils, those flotilla men. We could have been successful if it weren't for them."

Admiral Cochrane had contained his anger at the men of the divisionary force. He remembered George Cockburn's report after Bladensburg: Barney's flotilla men held the hilltop until the last. Damnable scrappy fellows. Napier also reported there'd been hand-to-hand fighting on the beach.

✫ ✫ ✫

And so, it was over: this Chesapeake campaign.

Sir Alexander Cochrane turned wearily to his second in command and called for a retreat. Cockburn and Brooke and the army would be waiting at the North Point. The British admiral consoled himself with the thought that this was only a small battle in a small war. There would be other wars of greater importance—against enemies of greater importance.

But just for a moment, he lifted his head to gaze at the American fort on Whetstone Point. The sky had brightened just enough that he could make out the red-brick walls and the parapets.

And there, flying above Fort McHenry, was that blasted flag from yesterday. An odd flag, obscenely large, all those stars. He counted them, fifteen stars and fifteen stripes. They'd hoisted it again on its long pole. The flag had caught the easterly breeze and was billowing out like a great banner of victory. No doubt the three Americans aboard the *Minden* would be beside themselves with triumph when they realized the fort had withstood the attack. He turned his face away.

✫ ✫ ✫

Jason saw the flag. He'd slept a few hours on Mingo's blanket. Now he was awake and looking at the dull gray sky that was burned with streaks of red to the east. He couldn't go down on the beach. Captain Webster had forbidden him to do so. But he knew that Will Adams and a party of flotilla men were down there, burying the dead from the night's battle. Caleb wasn't coming back. And Mr. Mingo Jones wasn't coming back. That's what Captain Webster said.

It was a hard thing to know. Like his pa, Mr. Mingo Jones was gone. Jason moved closer to the low battery, where Captain Webster was stretched out on the wall, moaning in some kind of pain. Mr. Frazier had folded his blanket and put it under the captain's head.

Captain Webster was feeling powerful bad because of his shoulder, Jason reasoned. It might be he was fever'd, as his face looked sickly under the dirt. The captain's eyes were watery, like he was close to tears. The boy put his head close to Mr. Webster's head and whispered, "I'm here, too, sir. I'm here if you're needing me."

Jack Webster stirred just slightly. The sky was low, pressing down. It was as if he was coming out of dark water, unsure of the day or where he was. Or if he was even alive. His voice was thick as he asked, "Is it morning? Can you hear the gulls?"

"I hear 'em, sir. There's a flock of ring-bills down on the river."

"Can you see the stars?"

"No, sir. Ain't no stars. Sky's clear but gray-like, some streaks of red to the east."

"Can you make out the fort?" Webster groaned and made room for Jason to climb up on the battery wall. The boy looked downstream at the pinkish brick walls, still indistinct in the mist. He could make out a flag, not the small battalion flag that was flying all through the night, but that big one that was high on the pole two days ago.

"I see that there's a flag flying over the fort."

"A white flag?"

"Oh, no." Dan Frazier broke in and answered for him. "It's a fine-looking flag. Ours, sir."

A mighty fine-looking flag, for sure. It had a meaning behind it, but Jason was not quite sure what it was.

"Are the British ships still there?" The captain's voice was stronger now.

"Gone," Frazier answered. "They're gone downriver. Ain't none in sight." There was something like pride in his voice.

Jason fought down the lump that was like a stone in his throat. So, it was over, all this fighting, with Mr. Mingo Jones gone and Caleb gone with him.

"Come down here, boy," Webster whispered. "Come close."

✡ ✡ ✡

The captain held out his hand, and Jason slid down from the wall and knelt close to the captain. He saw the blood on Webster's jacket and the poor face with a bad scar on his forehead that wasn't yet healed. The captain was looking at him, and his eyes were sad like he knew about Mr. Mingo Jones and Caleb being dead and how bad it all was.

"Hold on to me now. Take my hand. I'm powerful dizzy." Webster's fingers closed around Jason's hand. It hurt him to speak, but he breathed out the words, "They'd be proud to know we sent those Britishers away in shame, Caleb and Mr. Jones."

"The commodore, he be proud, too," Jason whispered.

"Aye, Jackaroe. He will. Listen…the gulls! Can you hear them?"

The petty officer was leaning over Webster with a strip of wet cloth to wipe his brow. For a big man, Dan Frazier could be gentle with his hands. "I sent Jesse Stewart to the dock to go out to the Lazaretto and find Mr. Sellers and bring him to you."

"I don't know whether I can…"

Frazier said in an anguished voice, "Hold on, sir. Hold on if you can."

Jack Webster felt pain surge hot in his shoulder and chest. It was as if a heavy body was lying on his chest, choking him. It took all his will to press back against the pain. He felt Jason Hayes's fingers tighten in his hand, and he was comforted.

It will be all right somehow, he told himself, it will be all right. He shut his eyes and listened to calling of the gulls.

Morning had come.

EPILOGUE

The Battle for Baltimore was a turning point in the War of 1812. Three months after the successful defense of Baltimore and Fort McHenry, U.S. commissioners signed a "Treaty of Peace and Amity between His Britannic Majesty and the United States" on Christmas Eve, 1814, in Ghent, Belgium. Buoyed by the success at Fort McHenry, Baltimore, and other battles in this war—in particular, Andrew Jackson's December 1814 New Orleans' triumph—the United States of America took on a new stature, both internally and to the world, the image of a young and dynamic nation that could take care of itself.

Commodore Joshua Barney would never again go to war or to sea. The city of Washington—as it underwent a spirited rebuilding and renaissance in the Madison and Monroe administrations—presented Barney with a sword of honor for the defense of the capital city by the flotilla men under his command in the Battle of Bladensburg. He was appointed the Naval Officer at Baltimore, a position he held for a short time. He died on December 1, 1818.

Rear Admiral George Cockburn returned to Great Britain in 1815. He commanded the *Northumberland* when she transported Napoleon Bonaparte into exile on the island of St. Helena. He died in 1853.

Sailing Master John Adams Webster was especially noted in Commander John Rodgers' report to the Secretary of the Navy, following the battle at Fort McHenry. He was presented with gold swords by the citizens of Baltimore and by the State of Maryland. The U.S. Congress paid him for the loss of Shoe Tail. Webster invested some of the money in a silver coffee set with the figure of the gallant horse on the larger pieces, appropriate for his marriage to Rachel Biays in 1817. His recovery from the wounds he received at Babcock Battery was difficult. In November 1819, he was well enough to accept a commission as captain in the Revenue Service, the precursor of the American Coast Guard Service. During the Mexican War, he commanded a fleet of eight cutters as part of the campaign on the Rio Grande and in the battle for Vera Cruz. Over the years his birthplace, The Mount, was renamed Mount Adams and was home to fourteen children born to John and Rachel Webster. In 1865, John Webster retired from duty and died at home at Mount Adams, in Harford County, Maryland. He was then the senior officer in the service.

The body of **Major General Robert Ross** was transferred to the HMS *Royal Oak* when the British left the Chesapeake, and he was buried with full military honors at St. Paul's Church, Halifax, Nova Scotia, on September 29, 1814. Two years later, a two-hundred-foot granite monument was erected on the shores of Carlingford Bay, Ross-Trevor, Ireland. The monument to honor Robert Ross was funded and erected by the officers and men who served with him.

AUTHOR'S NOTE

Shelby Foote, that great Mississippi-born author of *The Civil War: A Narrative*, is one of my literary heroes and his work has helped foster my love of historical fiction. I love the way he could make you see clearly the happening of the battle and also into the hearts of the warriors.

When, some twenty years ago, I first came upon a small historical note about the Chesapeake watermen and their vital if little known role in the War of 1812, it struck fire with me. I wanted to know more about this small but important American war and the role played by the bay watermen, white and black – these sons of the Chesapeake.

In seeking to tell this story with authenticity, I've studied all the historical information I could find on the war as it was fought in the bay and in Washington and Baltimore. Of greatest interest to me were the documents and maps and accounts pertaining to the *Chesapeake Flotilla*. Research was a passion and labor of love. I've walked the bay shoreline near St. Michael's, Maryland, and followed the flotilla men's journey along St. Leonard's Creek. I've studied the blackened tree-stumps in the marshes at Pig's Point on the Patuxent River and stood on the ridge where 'the third line' held position as long as possible in the Battle of Bladensburg.

It was on this ridge that the star-splendored sailors tried so desperately to hold back the advancing British soldiers. Commodore Barney was said to have been asked if his black seamen would falter as the enemy approached. He responded that they were fearless and would hold their ground. Not only did the watermen, black and white, stand with Barney, it was said that some of the flotilla crew ran down the slope of hill toward the approaching solders shouting out, 'Board 'em."

I once had the pleasure of attending a White House reception and stood in awe in the beautiful Oval Room remembering the poignancy, the heart-break and the tragedy of 'the night of the burning' in August, 1814.

At Fort McHenry, I studied that stretch of shore-line where Sailing Master John Webster commanded the small post called Fort Babcock. It was there on a dark September night in 1814 that the bay watermen, despite their losses, turned back a stealthy attack by British Seamen intending to storm Fort McHenry by land. It was an hour that might have profoundly changed the outcome of this war. Unsure of the outcome of their defensive action, the watermen waited at Fort Babcock fearful to learn if the British had taken Baltimore. In the dawn's early light, the American flag was still flying over Fort McHenry. Their sacrifices had not been in vain.

.

Made in the USA
Charleston, SC
30 October 2011